PEACE, WAR AND [illegible]NG-IN

PEACE, WAR AND WIGGING-IN

Charles Cane

Published by Courtney Publishers

A CIP catalogue record for this book is available from the British Library.

ISBN 978-0-9567201-3-9

Book layout and cover design by Clare Brayshaw

Prepared and printed by:

York Publishing Services Ltd
64 Hallfield Road
Layerthorpe
York YO31 7ZQ

Tel: 01904 431213

Website: www.yps-publishing.co.uk

CONTENTS

ACKNOWLEDGEMENTS

Although my memory of Courtney Street and district in the 1930s and 40s is fairly comprehensive it would, for the purposes of this book, have been inadequate without input from The Hull History Centre. Their facilities and dedicated staff made my initial research so much easier. In parallel were valuable contributions from my wife Sandra in the form of ideas and suggestions, good criticism, patience and love.

Also my gratitude goes out to my late parents, and all those long departed tenants of Courtney Street and district, whose determination carried them through the depressed 1930s followed by their exposure to a kaleidoscope of horrors, which they bore bravely, as World War Two made its disastrous passage into the darker pages of world history.

These experiences both inspired and motivated me to continue with post school education from which I achieved professional qualifications, and a successful scientific career, within a major world company.

INTRODUCTION

What would be achieved if a fictitious orator stood up and opened his public address with the statement, "It began in Courtney Street," and then, without further comment, immediately sat down? At the very least his opening proclamation would lose its desired effect and, without doubt, he would create bewilderment and dismay within his audience. Those with a kind-hearted disposition would assume that he had forgotten his lines and had paused to collect his thoughts; whereas others would fire at him, with all the ferocity of a verbal bullet, the terse demand, "What the hell did begin in Courtney Street?" Let us remember this question because it is my cue to leap from the realms of fiction and into these pages of reality, from which I am honoured to proclaim, "I began in Courtney Street and, in the autumn of my life, I hope to record my pride, in written form, before the celestial *flitting van* arrives to take me away!"

Having attained my 80th birthday was sufficient incentive for me to reflect, in greater depth, on my birth and early life in Courtney Street which, in parallel with similar working class areas, contained a wealth of local and social history that will fade away with those whose formative years began in this street. Such a tragic loss of urban anecdotes, and life styles, was driven home to me when I recently walked along Courtney Street and noted that it no longer has direct access to its historic companions Dansom Lane and Holderness Road and, in general, its daily life is now restricted to the working hours of many commercial units whose foundations rest within what was a teeming residential area consisting of shops, schools, sawmill, wood yard, terraces and many houses. All that now remains of that lost age is, as I begin my writing, a commercial showroom that began life as a Baptist Mission at Courtney Street's junction with Dansom Lane; and a former bank cum social club at the Holderness Road end.

As I walked along I literally felt, despite myself, that I was experiencing a latter day *Brigadoon* time warp as, with no effort on my part, I was once more a young boy happily limping along with one foot on the kerb and the other in the street gutter. Surely that lad waving to me from the distance was none other than Dennis who, every Friday, swapped his Beano comic in exchange for my Dandy version? Suddenly I was aware of many people around me and heard again the familiar screeching sounds of an operating sawmill, the rattle of horse drawn cart wheels being drawn along the street together with inaudible shouts from street vendors, the mouth-watering aroma of a fish and chip shop and a little old lady at the passage end surveying all from the depths of her shawl. Then I saw a decorative party being held at the top of one of the terraces and laughing children running along with their *boolers* (hoops) and sticks. In parallel I was aware of a chorus of voices from the 1930s seemingly urging me, above the sound of an air raid siren, to do something about telling their story before it was too late.

When I reached Dansom Lane I turned and looked back along Courtney Street, drank in its galaxy of memories, and vowed that I would do my very best to tell others about my experiences. Thus at the 'Danny lane' end of the street this book was born and within its pages I hope to chronicle, and thus preserve, my personal experiences of life in an area now gone but still treasured within my memory. I also owe my East Hull background a great debt of gratitude for lessons taught, and examples given, which have gone far to help me achieve much in this life which, as an active octogenarian is far from over.

My first written draft was a series of isolated events that, in my view, fell more into the realms of a text book which, as important as they are, was not my intent for this work. My vision was to create a factual local and social history book capable of being read with the same ease as most novels. Resulting from several inspirational walks, up and down present day Courtney Street, I eventually decided to begin my narrative in the marshland terrain from which my story was born and follow this with a chronological summary of the growth of Courtney Street in terms of industrial and housing development.

I was then faced with introducing social history into this work which I addressed by presenting a very brief outline of my life, from birth in 1931 to the end of World War Two in 1945. The purpose of this was to create a literary platform from which I was able to introduce many aspects of social and local history, which are consistent with the sole objective of this book. It is also necessary for me to stress that my many scenarios, anecdotes and written comments are, in essence, an amalgam of information provided, often unknowingly, by my parents, street neighbours and playmates alike.

In those days my world was Courtney Street in which I lived, played and went to school. Hence I cannot comment upon what happened in adjoining streets other than to suggest, without fear of correction, that life therein would follow a similar pattern. I found that much I overheard had later to be deciphered because, with full respect to the many orators involved, they were hindered by age or experience in effective speaking. If I had expressed their words verbatim it would have made for difficult reading and, in consequence, hindered the flow of this book. Thus in the interests of readability I have converted all I heard into non-localised terms of expression; having taken great care to retain every aspect of original meaning.

I have always had a strong sense of curiosity through which I painstakingly collected information using any means that came my way. In this respect it must not be forgotten that several children, including myself, obtained a lot of our knowledge from listening in (***wigging-in***) to adult conversations!

A lot of information thus gained, and mentally stored, was disjointed and acquired over a finite period of time which, like a mental jigsaw puzzle, I later pieced together to give many of the accounts you will read. Such a wealth of information readily found a place within the 'deep interest archives' of my memory and, when of adult age, it was added to by judicial questioning of my parents. I felt it necessary to share with you just how I came about all the data that, in due course, became the bricks and mortar from which this narrative was built.

At all times I have been careful to remain alert to my initial objective of not allowing my drift of words to develop into a 'Cane family history study' which, in my view, would seriously be at odds with the targets I have set for this work. In fact I have deliberately minimised references to my immediate family except when they form part of some social or local history account that is central to the flow of this book.

My sole desire is to give readers a comprehensive picture of life in Courtney Street and surrounding regions in the socially depressed 1930s and how it, and adjacent areas, suffered during the horrors of World War Two air raids admixed with austere living conditions. I am aware there are several excellent publications dedicated to WW2, both locally and nationally, hence my war references are generalised and only become specific when describing feelings and responses, be they laughter or tears, shown by the people who this book is all about.

If this work achieves my objectives then my level of delight will be secondary to the joy of keeping alive important memories of Courtney Street, which have effectively guided me through childhood and continue to give me on-going inspiration.

PART ONE

UP TO 1930

COURTNEY STREET DIRECTIONAL AID

IN THE BEGINNING..........

A cold and searching wind from the River Humber brushed aside a multitude of marsh reeds and gave brief rippling life to the surface of stagnant pools, as if giving a passing caress to land that had yet to fully escape from the relentless tide. Yet nature's breeze was not without purpose because it dried the soil and slowly awoke a natural habitat for land and sea birds within this haven of newly formed land.

As many centuries passed by its role would dramatically change when the time came for it to host the foundations of Courtney Street, and its many urban counterparts, who drew their livelihood from a jungle of surrounding factories. Developments of this nature had no regard for smoke and pollution that damaged health, withered away remaining grassland, and converted once clear streams into verminous drains. But for the moment nature in its glorious isolation ruled supreme and human presence was restricted to the stalwart hunter or traveller who dared to venture across this waterlogged waste. However the spread of mankind cannot be contained and the spearhead of development was eventually launched by monastic pioneers who sought to develop trade creating work for the struggling peasants of that time.

Thus it all began with the founding of Wyke on Hull in the late 12th century when the monks of Meaux Abbey needed a port in order to export wool from their estates. They chose a place at the junction of the rivers Hull and Humber to build a quay from which development began. In 1293 King Edward I purchased the land from the monks and Kingston (Kings Town) upon Hull was born.

Since Hull owes its beginnings to the good friars of Meaux it is right, before we part company with them that I should record a broad outline of whom they were. Meaux Abbey was founded in 1151 by William le Gros, first Earl of Albemarle, Earl of York and fourth Earl of Beverley, for a group of Cistercian Brothers. With permission I have visited the site of this abbey which is situated to the west of the village of Meaux. Sadly only scattered stones and earthworks now remain but it is worth a visit if only to experience a feeling of peace that still resides at the site of the once influential Meaux Abbey that, in turn, gave us what is now east Hull. Perhaps we should also record that the monks of Meaux Abbey were involved indirectly with the naming of a certain lane that is both central to my theme, and the lives of many who may read this book. These dedicated, hardworking friars also kept cattle which they moved along a track that was first known as Clow Lane. When windmills were built along the lane its name changed to Mill Lane, and later to Cowhouse Mill Lane. Eventually a farm sprang up alongside the former cattle track which was owned by one Robert Dansom, bringing about a further name change to the more familiar Dansom Lane. Thus Dansom Lane and indeed the entire eastern side of Hull took its first faltering steps towards industrialisation that, in 1838, was described as not being very extensive but steadily persistent in its growth. Perhaps the recorder of the day had taken heart from a slow growing number of wind and steam mills that refined and produced linseed oil and by-product seed residue that was used for cattle food. There were cotton mills, soap and white lead works and, on the nautical side, ship building yards and sail-cloth manufacturers. Several breweries and extensive ropewalks were added to the industrial scene.

THE BIRTH OF COURTNEY STREET

As I seek to launch the advent and subsequent development of Courtney Street it is, perhaps, fitting that I do so through the neighbourly presence of an extensive manufacturing company as illustrated in the 1891 Ordnance Survey Map. This organisation was called the Hull Rope Works that stretched (excuse the unintentional pun) from what would be the bottom of neighbouring Burleigh Street, and after running in parallel with the fledgling Courtney Street, it came to a halt at what was destined to be the cul-de-sac end of Upton Street. From all accounts it was a flourishing Company that was mentioned in the 1892 Directory of Trades and Professions under the heading of Hull Rope Works Company Ltd of Burleigh Street, Hull. The Company Secretary was Mr A. Jarman (Ref.1).

I have no record of the actual opening date of the Hull Rope Works but it is fair to surmise that it would have been around the late 1840s. This premise is based upon the fact that a pronounced increase in the Hull fishing fleet occurred in 1840 creating an immediate requirement for rope that was essential in the manufacture of fishing nets, rigging stays and mooring lines to name but three outlets. In the wake of this demand several rope manufacturers grew rapidly on both banks of the Humber. Rope works by their very nature required plenty of space, not least to lay out lengths of rope-in-process in what was, essentially, a long alleyway better known as a *ropewalk*. We are fortunate to have on our doorstep a preserved example of a rope works situated on Maltkin Road, Barton upon Humber (DN18 5JT) which is both a museum and regional centre for arts and crafts. As part of my research I paid a visit to the site and

The restored Hall's Barton Ropewalk where long strands of material were laid before being twisted into rope (downloaded from the Barton Ropewalk web page.)

was totally amazed at the size of the restored Hall's Barton Ropery, which is the longest Grade 2 listed building in the country in that it stretches a quarter of a mile along the length of Barton Haven. Also it gave me some insight as to the design of the long defunct Hull Rope Works alongside which Courtney Street was to take shape.

Thus let us return to our 1891 stage set consisting of the Hull Rope Works and adjacent Rope Walk that was, in broad terms, loosely sandwiched between the high rail embankment of the Hull, Barnsley and West Riding railway on its northern flank and the N.E.R Victoria Dock line on its southern side. Thus expressed it would have painted a truly depressing picture. Surely if nature had bathed this dismal scene in the gentle shadows of summer or, by contrast, a dusting of fresh winter's snow, then its efforts would have failed to catch the eye of a single passer-by.

If given the ability then long lengths of rope betwixt straight sets of railway lines would, in vain, knock hard upon the door of artistry only to find every bolt set hard against them. What was needed was the presence of a live and vibrant street, awash with houses and humans, to breathe life into commerce which, as if by divine response, came to pass in the late 1850s when Courtney Street made its slow and almost apologetic appearance; as yet another new street off the well-established Holderness Road (ref. 2). Why was it given the name Courtney? Detailed research failed to unearth anything other than a prominent Courtney family from Beverley were owners of many acres of land in Hull. On this basis alone it is reasonable to assume that they may be the source of the name (ref. 3). I was surprised to note that, according to the 1891

Ordnance Survey Map, Courtney Street had grown between the Hull Rope Works and the N.E.R Victoria Dock railway to around only half of the length that it would ultimately occupy. Considering that it had taken around 30 years to reach as far as it did may reflect a scarcity of investors, or potential tenants, or perhaps it was building competition from nearby Burleigh, Nornabell and Garbutt (later Barnsley) Streets that were fast taking shape. I know not but, for the record, I have detailed below how the partly developed Courtney Street appeared following its commencement in circa 1860 up to our survey year of 1891, which are the first steps of our historical walk together.

East side of Courtney Street beginning at its junction with Holderness Road.

Sarah's Terrace	(no gardens – open plan – washing lines across the terrace).
Welton Terrace	(no gardens – open plan – washing lines across the terrace).
Charlie's Terrace	(no gardens – open plan – washing lines across the terrace).
Gertrude's Terrace	(no gardens – open plan – washing lines across the terrace).
Gladstone Terrace	(no gardens – open plan – washing lines across the terrace).
Filey Terrace	(no gardens – open plan – washing lines across the terrace).
Portland Terrace	(no gardens – open plan – washing lines across the terrace).
Grove Terrace	(with front gardens accessed by a central walkway).
Garden Terrace	(with front gardens accessed by a central walkway).
Freehold Terrace	(no gardens – open plan – washing lines across the terrace).

Crystal Terrace	(no gardens – open plan – washing lines across the terrace).
Spring Terrace	(no gardens – open plan – washing lines across the terrace).

In general there were four street facing houses and shops between each terrace and, in 1891, Courtney Street ended at Spring Terrace; beyond which was undeveloped grass land.

West side of Courtney Street beginning at its junction with Holderness Road.

As a growing boy I was always interested in this section of Courtney Street because it began with a line of eight ordinary looking street facing houses. To me a surprising feature was that behind numbers one and three there was an urban oasis in the form of a walled garden, containing many bushes and wild roses, which seemed very much out of place amidst tile, brick and concrete. It quickly became my secret and treasured garden that was brought to life at school story time when our teacher read, in serialised form, Frances Hodgson Burnett's novel "The Secret Garden". My mind ran riot over my discovery until, some time later, I found that my covert garden had originally been three separate plots of land that were rear gardens for houses that fronted Holderness Road. When these were converted into shops their redundant gardens became the walled-in plot that so captured my imagination. Nevertheless it was an interesting little group of properties with an intriguing side alley, close to the school wall, that led to an inner development known as Mawer's Terrace which, in my thoughts, was a little kingdom tucked away within its secure borders!

However the time has arrived for us to leave behind all thoughts of secret gardens, and isolated kingdoms, and continue our northerly walk along Courtney Street as it appeared to visitors in the year 1891. After but a few steps we would immediately become aware that we were standing within the shadow of that great and much loved edifice known as Courtney Street Board School for Boys and Girls. Below, and looking at it from Courtney Street, is the 1891 plan of how the school buildings were arranged:

COURTNEY STREET BOARD SCHOOL

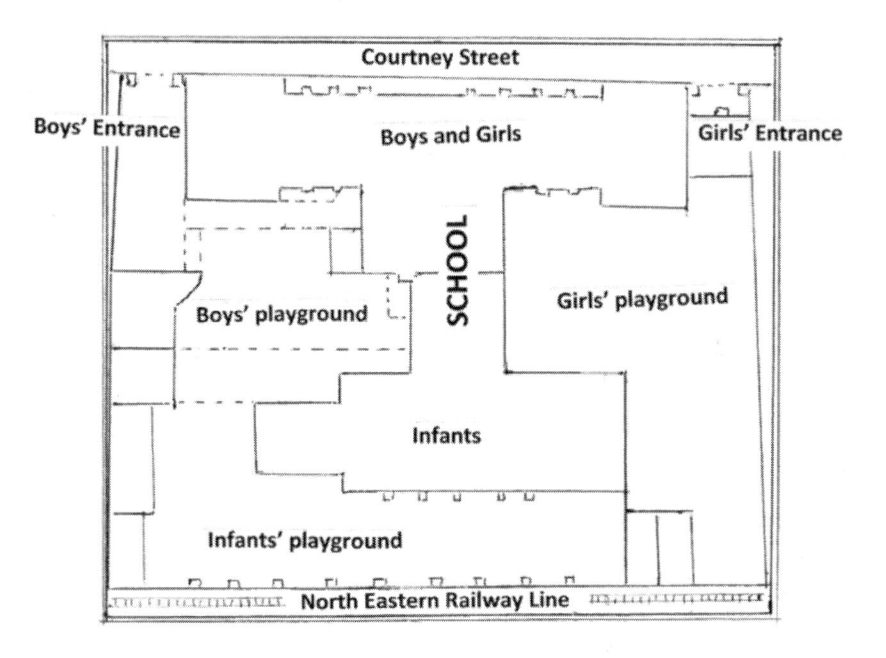

Often in later years I would look up at the two storey building and admire the three crowns of Hull beneath which was the inscription 'Board School' that meant so much to so many, including those of us who have made it to the 21st century. As an aside I will add that, as a young boy having first read the title 'Courtney Street Board School,' I thought that its pupils once lodged (or boarded) there as they did at Greyfriars, of Billy Bunter fame, which my older brother Jim was always talking about.

In homage to this great school that features later in my book I will pause and share with you just a little of the history behind the launch of rate-aided schools under the patronage of the Hull School Board. In reality it all stemmed from the 1870 Education Act that led to a large expansion in elementary education. Problems were encountered by the authorities in the wake of compulsory education in 1880 followed by free schooling in 1891 which led to a scarcity of school buildings. Fortunately these problems were, largely, foreseen and addressed by the formation of a forward looking rate aided Hull School Board, which began by hiring teaching rooms mainly in churches and chapels with space to spare. Then, in 1874, the first three Board Schools became available and, in the following order, they were opened in Daltry Street, *Courtney Street,* and Lincoln Street thus providing a total of 2,580 school places. Shortly afterwards a further six were opened in other parts of Hull (ref. 4).

Without doubt this was a progressive and highly commendable initiative that provided a good standard of basic education for many youngsters who, otherwise, would have been penalised by working class family poverty that was ever present; and was no stranger to street life even in the early 20th century. Fortunately I am in possession of a photograph of my 13 year old uncle in a group photograph of children with their teachers taken in Courtney Street School yard in 1920. *The picture is displayed below and it will be noted that two of the lads, seated on the front row, have turned up for school in their bare feet.* It may be that their only pair of boots, which was not uncommon, was being repaired or that they simply did not own any footwear. When I began my school life in 1936 I never saw anyone in their bare feet although many wore battered boots, wellies (wellington boots) or sandshoes (plimsolls) – even the occasional pair of clogs!

In order to highlight my point I have, in the picture below, cut out and enlarged the area including the two boys referred to. This photograph may well contain other children in their bare feet since it was a common feature in the depressed years of the 1920s and 30s.

For the moment let us leave the school behind and continue our survey of the west side of Courtney Street as we continue to walk away from the Holderness Road end. A rear access passage separated the school wall from a continuation of the previously described terrace system as detailed below:

Wycliffe Terrace	(no gardens – open plan – washing lines across the terrace).
Primrose Row	(with front gardens accessed by a central walkway).

Next is a space without title or commentary. From its position it appears to be land set aside for the future Courtney Street Junior School which, because of an increasing district population, was quickly built and in operation by the year 1895. Beyond this reserved piece of land we continue with:

Villa Row	(with front gardens accessed by a central walkway).
Wesley Terrace	(no gardens – open plan – washing lines across the terrace).

It was apparent that, in 1891, little effort was made to separate domestic and school buildings from full scale commercial units. Or, perhaps, they argued that it was necessary for the work force to live close to places of employment due to commuting problems in an age when motorised vehicles, and even bicycles, were outside the reach of most working class budgets. Nevertheless local factories had their employees at heart when, usually around 5.00am, the factory 'buzzer' would tell the neighbourhood that the new working day had begun! That little addition to our street walk was not without reason because it adds weight to my observation that an access passage was all that separated Wesley Terrace from a Sawing and Moulding Mill that was in operation in 1891 and, unabated, noisily carried out its trade through to the 1950s. The agonising screech of circular saws and the sliding clatter of horses hooves, as they objected to reversing a timber loaded cart into the sawmill yard, were as much part of street life as were the songs of Gracie Fields that, through open windows and doors, generously reminded us of 'the biggest aspidistra in the world!'

Finally, and buttressed to the sawmill boundary wall, were five street facing houses that, in the 1930s and onwards, were never occupied and remained boarded up. There is the possibility that they were acquired for sawmill use or some other purpose that is not immediately obvious. Conversely, what is evident is the fact that we can go no further because ahead of us are fields of grassland and, facing us across the road is Spring Terrace and the Hull Rope Works, which tells us that we have fully explored Courtney Street as it was in the year 1891.

COURTNEY STREET IN 1904

Through the resources of the Hull History Centre I came across an Ordnance Survey map for the year 1904 which confirmed that Courtney Street had continued its gradual, yet determined, rate of progress towards completion; albeit all activity was restricted to the western, or school side, of the street. The Junior School was established and further housing developments were completed during the 13 years following our last visit to the area. Thus let us position ourselves alongside the still flourishing sawmill and it's adjoining five unoccupied houses, which are now numbered 67 to 75 Courtney Street, and are separated from further new developments by a side access passage. The property additions are:

West side of Courtney Street continuing to Dansom Lane

Arthur's Terrace	(with front gardens accessed by a central walkway).
Rose View	(with front gardens accessed by a central walkway).
Gladys's Grove	(with front gardens accessed by a central walkway).
Blanche Grove	(with front gardens accessed by a central walkway).
Florance Avenue	(with front gardens accessed by a central walkway).

Let us pause in our walk and read again the name of the above avenue. From my viewpoint it created havoc for my computer spell check because it could not understand why I repeatedly instructed it to accept *Florance* Avenue. As is the habit of computers it eventually made allowance for human behaviour which, sadly, was not the case for two Courtney Street pupils who were residents of the said *Florance* Avenue. I well remember the hard time they had, with their class teacher, when they were berated over an alleged inability to spell their home address. In vain their plea of, "Please Sir, that is how it appears on the Avenue name plate," was dismissed with scorn as they were ordered as a punishment to record, in their best writing, several copies of "I live in Florence Avenue." Sadly their teacher did not bother to walk the few yards down Courtney Street and check for himself; or perhaps he did and decided to sacrifice the flower of gentle apology on the cold slab of professional embarrassment?

Thus said let us continue our walk to the junction with Dansom Lane which involves passing:

Burleigh Grove	(with front gardens accessed by a central walkway).
Marion's Crescent	(with front gardens accessed by a central walkway).

Marion's Crescent was set upon a sharp bend in Courtney Street as it moved towards its junction with Dansom Lane. The Crescent was composed of eight houses with front gardens, and a central walkway dividing the Crescent from the rear yards of three houses and a shop that fronted Dansom Lane. The shop was the corner building between Courtney Street and Dansom Lane and, in the 1930s was a cycle repair shop. The opposite side of Courtney Street was waste land because, for reasons unknown, Spring Terrace still remained, in 1904, as the official end of the eastern side of the Street. Further study of the 1904 Ordnance Survey map revealed that Dansom Lane gave way to grass land, at its junction with Endymion Street, and that Upton Street had yet to be built.

It has been an interesting exercise for me to trace the development of Courtney Street, together with its houses, factory and schools which, at times, has resembled a jigsaw puzzle wherein the pieces interlock and confirm my memory of this street. One major difficulty for me was to come to terms with a building time scale of around 45 years and still the street was not fully completed. Perhaps I am, unfairly, comparing 19th century/early 20th century building methods with present-day procedures in which the hand operated spade has been replaced by JCBs and other mechanical aids. However there does appear to have been a sudden injection of urgency into the Courtney Street project because the 1910 Ordnance Survey map presents the street in its completed form. Obviously I cannot be certain what brought about this acceleration, but results from the following parallel study I made may provide a viable reason.

From a variety of sources I learned that in the late 19th century the number of Hull timber merchants more than doubled, and a plethora of sawmills quickly appeared upon the industrial scene. This was due to a decline in the supply of home grown larch and fir trees thus creating a demand for foreign grown timber. The main source of imports to Hull was timber from Norway and Sweden which served our mining requirements (pit props) together with building and manufacturing outlets. As a further incentive the growing popularity of steam powered machinery greatly improved rates of productivity in the latter industries. Naturally there was a parallel increase in the working population looking for somewhere to live that was close to these new industrial outlets and, as if to confirm this claim, my grandparents 'emigrated' from west Hull and finally settled in Burleigh Grove, Courtney Street. The family was composed of George Dennis (who was a sawyer), his wife Annie Elizabeth and their children Ellen Doris (my future mother) and her younger brother George. My grandfather George Dennis spent his entire working life as a sawyer employed by W. North in Sitwell Street, Hull. So, without further delay let us look at how Courtney Street continued to expand since our last visit six years ago.

COURTNEY STREET IN 1910

My first *news flash*, consistent with the expansion of the timber industries, is that the Hull Rope Works is no longer with us and has been replaced by Humber Saw Mills and a large timber storage yard. This new complex extended from the bottom of Burleigh Street, along Courtney Street and to its exit gate at the cul-de-sac end of the now completed Upton Street. Throughout my life in Courtney Street and district I was always aware of this massive timber works that literally dominated the skyline in the form of high stacks of wooden deals, mobile cranes and goods wagons in abundance. A link line with the nearby Hull to Barnsley railway had been installed for rapid despatch of inland orders, and a rail goods yard with shunting facilities was, much to my boyhood delight, set in place with full viewing rights from my bedroom window! Little more can be said about the wood yard until later so it will be as well if we take out final northward walk, along Courtney Street, following our previous method of recording terraces.

East side of Courtney Street continuing to Dansom Lane

For this final survey we begin to walk from the existing Spring Terrace in a northerly direction:

Granville Avenue	(with front gardens accessed by a central walkway)
Derwent Avenue	(with front gardens accessed by a central walkway)
Claremont Avenue	(with front gardens accessed by a central walkway)

Leonards Avenue	(with front gardens accessed by a central walkway)
Albion Avenue	(with front gardens accessed by a central walkway)

Beyond Albion Avenue the street followed a sharp bend to its left as it proceeded to its junction with Dansom Lane. An access passageway ran the entire length of the exposed side of Albion Avenue, which also served to separate the houses from yet another sawmill that stood back from the street, and was wall joined with the end house in Ferndale Avenue, Upton Street.

I must add that as sawmills go it was much smaller than others in the area. In fact its very presence intrigued me; so much so that, in my school years, I wrote a short fantasy story about an infant sawmill that ran away from home, got lost, and decided to live behind Albion Avenue! In reality it followed the ways of its larger cousins, and generously contributed much noise and dust to the houses around it; but for active and adventurous boys it had its uses. It was less secure than larger sawmills meaning that its dilapidated front gate was defenceless against the onslaught of scavenging boys who, as bonfire night approached, were desperate for wood for their forthcoming blaze. According to neighbours of that area the sawmill owner would, as the 5th November grew nearer, appease foraging groups by freely giving them old pieces of timber in his quest to thwart a full scale commando-style raid.

The Birth of Tin Mission

So let us now complete the task before us which is to examine the last building remaining between us and the completion of our walk along both sides of the fully built Courtney Street; and that structure is the former Courtney Street Baptist Mission Hall. In many ways it is a very special building more so because it is the only structure in the Street that has survived into the 21st century. For posterity, I have included, with the permission of the present business occupier, the following photograph taken in October 2011:

In 1897 the Yorkshire Association of the Baptist Church launched its presence in East Hull by building a Mission hall on Courtney Street's last remaining building plot at its junction with Dansom Lane. The original building was smaller than the present one and its walls were constructed from corrugated iron painted an attractive dark red colour. I well remember this building, and its surrounding iron railings, as a local landmark that was fondly referred to as 'Tin Mission'. When I was involved with this chapel it was managed by Pastor and Mrs Percival Finch and, at the age of five years, I attended its Sunday school which is the subject of a later report. In the 1940s the building was extended and became the brick and pebble dash building that remains to this day.

Thus by 1910 the Courtney Street I was to be born into was historically complete in terms of buildings, and was moving on to don its clothing of character which time, through many changing fashions of laughter and sadness, was slowly tailoring to its needs.

COURTNEY STREET LIVING CONDITIONS IN THE 1930S

Having reached the junction with Dansom Lane it is as well that we pause and reflect on the 40+ years between the first and last domestic building erected in Courtney Street. I have no evidence to contradict my belief that Courtney Street was composed of houses of uniform design in that they were all *sham four* properties (two rooms upstairs and two rooms downstairs) with a small rear yard that contained the toilet and coal house. It was not unusual for the occupants to refer to the downstairs rear room as their 'back kitchen' because, in a sense, both downstairs rooms could be used for cooking purposes. The front room contained a traditional coal fired Yorkist range with a side oven and open grate. The fire grate heated the room, kettle and cooking pans if required. Several houses extended their cooking options by installing a gas oven in the back kitchen. However this arrangement, depending upon the size of the family, may have caused congestion due to the presence of a coal fired brick enclosed copper, in the corner of the room, which was the main source of hot water for the household. Rear access to and from the house was via a communal passageway that served the tenants and gave right of way for coal deliveries and the all-important dustmen.

It is also a fact that the majority of these houses were erected in a series of terraces; but there our pattern of uniformity ends. In my circa 1860 to 1891 survey I reported the existence of sixteen terraces in Courtney Street, of which twelve were of the open or shared plan, thus allowing for washing lines to be stretched across the terrace – weather permitting. This communal style of living had its advantages in that younger children could safely play, as a group, in close proximity to their home. Additionally the open plan terrace gave extra working space for the residents and I often saw men sitting in the terrace happily cobbling their boots, repairing bikes or chopping firewood whilst enjoying banter with their mates. A bonus for the women was that they had the space, outside the front door, in which to scrub their washing, rinse and mangle it prior to pegging it out across the terrace. An open-plan terrace also allowed a busy housewife to simply open her front door and '*shek*' her carpets into the prevailing wind; but this option had its problems unless simple yet vital precautions were taken. For example consider any terrace housewife who, since 5am, had diligently completed all stages of her weekly wash and, with a sigh of relief, had just completed hanging it out on a line across the terrace. How would she react when a neighbour's door suddenly opened and a hearth rug, firmly held in a pair of hands that meant business, was furiously shaken without reference to what was in its vicinity? Those rugs were mainly home-made from rag clippings which, so I was told, had the capacity to retain copious amounts of dust, soot, grit, crumbs and even stubbed cigarette ends. It had also been noted that a line of clean wet washing readily attracted and held onto whatever was blowing in the wind, including the said contents of shaken fireside rugs! I have witnessed, from a safe distance, several Courtney Street rows between women when a neighbour's inattention meant that her victim had to repeat the weekly wash. Hence this style of shared living did have its problems and the modern expression of "invading one's space" may well summarise its major disadvantages.

Exceptions to this were the remaining four housing developments known as Primrose Row and Villa Row, situated on the school side of the street, and Grove Terrace and Garden Terrace situated on the opposite side of the street. Each of these houses had the benefit of small yet private front gardens that were fenced off from their neighbours and the central access pathway. Additionally a downstairs bay window replaced the traditional line of flat fronted houses thus allowing more light into the room together with a little extra living space. Although the gardens were small they provided an area of privacy and the opportunity for tenants to experiment with the basics of gardening, rather than renting a plot of land on nearby allotments which, particularly in wartime, was very popular.

Regardless of terrace design I can confirm that Courtney Street houses could not be described as spacious; and any attempt to do so would hint at arguing that black was white. From first-hand experience I can confirm that such houses did have several space related limitations that could be eased, depending upon the ingenuity of the tenants; although their resourcefulness was severely tested when faced with drying wet washing in the absence of outside drying facilities – which is where open plan community terraces in the older part of Courtney Street could boast an advantage.

In life we are faced with several facts which, for our welfare, cannot be changed. Prime examples of these are that the earth rotates around the sun whilst moving on its own axis; thus giving us our seasons and days. These are unshakable facts that are above argument *as is the parallel reality that sham four houses were just not designed for drying wash day clothes!* The only option available was a labyrinth of lines set up in the kitchen and living room from which wet washing evolved steam, which became condensate on every window in the house and, by way of an encore, it left the house feeling like a primitive sauna unit. On such days a routine journey from the front to back door demanded a level of ducking, weaving and footwork that would have graced a professional boxing ring; only on this occasion your opponent was an assortment of wet clothing that, given the opportunity, would seriously dampen your progress!

The art of 'Wigging-In'

There are few lifestyle claims that can exist without challenge; yet I would wager the national debt that the tendency for children to '*wig in*' on the conversation of adults was above dispute, and that this time honoured action was just as active in stately homes as it was at a terrace end in Courtney Street. A group of women engaged in a serious gossiping session would pay little attention to a couple of children, ostensibly intent on playing marbles in the nearby street gutter, but never moving out of *wigging-in* range. Or that ginger headed lad leaning against the wall studiously reading his Radio Fun comic that, in reality, defied his intent simply because it was upside down. The truth is they were engaged in the age old tradition of '*wigging- in*' through which much knowledge could surreptitiously be gained although never fully understood. For my part I both relied heavily upon, and in the process developed into an art, the need to *wig in.* After all I lived in an age when 'children should be seen and not heard' and convention made no allowances for my need to know what was going on.

Thus much of what I will record is the result of eavesdropping which, in later years, I have been able to analyse and understand what was originally meant. Yet as children addicted to this information-gaining-process we became aware of an undertone, from certain adults, that there were rough families living in 'those terraces' at the Holderness Road end of the street and that contact with them should be avoided. The same 'grape vine' also entertained a theory that Waller Street, which was on the opposite side of Holderness Road facing Courtney Street, was populated with people who thoroughly disliked those who lived at the Dansom Lane end of Courtney Street; for reasons that were never defined. These adult views meant nothing to Courtney Street children who, in total harmony, freely roamed the length of the street but they never entered Waller Street. In truth their reluctance was fear related but only of their parents who, in no uncertain terms, had threatened them with the '*braying of their lives*' if ever they were caught trying to cross busy Holderness Road.

Points for and against terrace gardens

Within this topic there is an interesting item of social history that I cannot allow to pass by without comment. Its origin is in the fact that the completed street had terraces at one end that were open plan, whereas at the other end each house had a front garden and, to complete the picture, there was an imaginary boundary line half way along the street; or so I was often led to believe. To growing children this made not a scrap of difference. We all went to the same school, fish and chip shop or frequented which ever Goody Shop was selling our favourite sweets at the lowest price; and if we became aware of street bargains we would pass on the good news regardless of where our mates lived. Perhaps street adults had much to learn from their young daughters, who happily shared their front gardens, with girls from open terraces at *t'other end* of the street. Looking back at houses with front gardens I do not recall evidence for competitive gardening. Some were wild and neglected whereas others displayed a colourful simplicity of purpose. Many years ago I read a quote that went along the lines, "Almost any garden, if you see it at the right moment, can be confused with paradise." That was true of Courtney gardens particularly through the eyes of young girls. For example the humble dandelion flower offered two unique opportunities to inquisitive youngsters. The first was a test made by young damsels to determine if a handsome prince was in love with them. This required a dandelion globe that had gone to seed. If with one dedicated blow you blew away all the seeds then everyone was in love with you. If some seeds remained then partial love was the reward whereas if they all remained ...well need I say anymore! Alternatively if the same girls, playing in the same garden, wanted to know the time, in terms of the hour number, then all they did was count the number of blows taken to remove all the dandelion seeds from the plant.

Then it became the turn for girls from the Danny Lane end to visit the open plan terraces and thoroughly enjoy skipping, and chanting rhymes, over a rope that stretched the width of the terrace without hindrance from front gardens. Looking back through mature eyes it would appear that young girls, from both ends of the street, had hit upon a cultural exchange policy that remained popular even through the war years. As I grew older I often reflected on those strange and unjustified beliefs held by some local adults and wondered if they were, perhaps unknowingly, claiming a social distinction gained from sitting in their bay window and viewing a front garden rather than an open plan terrace? If so it was a minority view that was soon to be swept away with enhanced street unity that followed the declaration of war in 1939, which I will share with you as my narrative progresses.

PART TWO

(1931 TO 1936)

MY BIRTH AND EARLY LIFE IN COURTNEY STREET

There is no doubt that my father, James William Cane, worked hard for his wife and family. Should anyone of that era have chosen to challenge that fact then my mother, without hesitation, would have directed their eyes to his wearied face and hands stained by tanning agents which, through the years, had replaced natural skin lubricants in favour of open cracks. These wounds were the trademark of a tannery labourer toiling under the hardship of piece work. It is a fact that I never saw my dad with ordinary skin coloured hands and when he died a widower in 1967 my last sight of him, as the coffin lid was lowered, were those tannery stains upon his crossed hands. He was from a tradition when the 'man of the house' was responsible for the financial upkeep of the family and, after his funeral, men who had worked with him drew me to one side and, with emotion shining in their moist eyes, proudly told me, "Your dad was a great workmate and a bloody good grafter. We will miss him."

Few would argue that dad and his mates worked very hard because, from his accounts, hardship was an integral part of a system known as 'piece work.' I must add that the word hardship was used as a compromise because it is more acceptable than expressions reportedly used amidst the discordant noise of assorted machinery, and the acrid smell of steaming animal hides bubbling away within the cauldron of a tanning pit. Such were the working conditions of the early 1930s that led many tannery workers to express their feelings in a tirade of oaths and blasphemies when under pressure – which was a common feature of their long working day. Piece work led to higher than average wages hence it was liked by many of the fitter men, although it could have health threatening consequences for those less able to meet its physical demands; yet they clung onto it because their need for money was so desperate in the depressed 1920s and 30s. In broad terms it meant that each work gang was paid a rate for every piece of work completed, rather than on time actually employed on the site; hence the more pieces of work done the heavier the weekly pay packet.

Literally time was money and working comfort and personal safety, regardless of Company notices to the contrary, were consistently ignored. Gangs of six men, in shirt sleeves, leather aprons, ragged trousers and clogs laboured on regardless of the weather, and they relied on hessian sacks around their shoulders to protect them from direct rain, or condensed steam dripping from the peak of their caps. I recall my father telling me about the occasion when their difficult working conditions were not understood by a fresh faced visitor, from a local church, who was being conducted around the work area. His guide was describing to him the nature of the work being done during the course of which he heard, for the first time in his life, the expression 'Piece Work.' He was clearly moved by this and he was heard to say, "I think peace work is a lovely name for their tasks and it must help the men to work in peace." Clearly his spelling, if not his patronizing attitude, was seriously at fault. From then on he was known through a range of whispered titles from which the most complimentary, and thus suitable for publication in this book was, "That stupid young sod!"

Obviously all I have discovered about tannery work I learned at my father's knee because he seemed keen to talk about his work and, as if to confirm his account, he would often show me the bad state of his hands and sections of cracked skin than never seemed to heal. In later years I had reason to think back upon those conversations and now believe that it was his way of taking the burden away from his mind through what, to him, was a verbal safety valve. In abridged terms I have related to you extracts from a typical working day in the life of my father that, without doubt, would not have been greatly different on Friday 17th April 1931 when I was born. Dad often referred to his Tan Yard workmates, captured in the photograph below, yet never in critical terms and always by their nickname, which never varied through the years.

The gang of six are sitting upon bales of animal hides and, looking at the photograph, my father is seated on the right of the centre row (with his hands on each leg).

In later years I did learn of a strong sense of camaraderie that carried them through the rigours of each working day during which they shared their problems, and looked after each other's interests, particularly when the foreman was around. It was hard labouring work and if one of the gang was feeling off colour then his mates would work even harder to carry him through the day. Sick pay (Ref 5) was said to be derisory and, literally, most working men of that era could not afford to be off work which, in itself, was a powerful driving force and a prime example of mind over matter.

Perhaps those who suffered the most were men who were not up to the work either in physical or emotional terms, and such a person was my Uncle Albert Coopland who for a short period of time worked at the same Tan Yard, but not in the same gang as my dad. Albert was a meek and friendly man with a speech impediment and was, from all accounts, treated badly both at home and by certain bullies at work.

Often he would turn up without a packed lunch because 'their lass' had turned awkward; which was the signal for dad to share his packing up with him. Then there was the time when a 'loud mouth' threw Uncle Albert's meagre clothing out of the changing hut because he claimed, "they were full of fleas." In his dinner break dad cornered Albert's tormentor and – well he never described the outcome but I can imagine the way it went. It was an indisputable fact that my father was a fit and strong man who delighted in bending iron bars, either across his knee or behind his neck which was a carryover from weight training practised in his earlier years. It would be nice to say that his youthful work-outs were for the sole purpose of keeping his body in trim; but this was not so. Dad's motivation, from a young age, was to gain sufficient strength through which he would be able to thrash his father who, sadly, was a street fighter and drunken bully. Dad vowed to avenge the many attacks he had made upon his mother, who he loved dearly, but all came to nought when his errant father was kicked to death by a cart horse; but that is another story. Sufficient to say that Albert Coopland was never again troubled by Tan Yard bullies.

Yet despite their difficult working conditions dad and his mates enjoyed rare moments of humour and raucous banter. From what I know I would not have been surprised if, on Friday the 17th April 1931, their conversation had gone along the lines of, "Today's the day Jim. After a gap of eight years it will be like your first baby all over again!" "Eight years between his two kids," gasped another, "Why George the Piker over there managed to knock out four kids in that space of time!" "Only cos him and his lass are piece rate workers when in bed," added the dry humour of Bolshie the yard union man.

A chorus of factory 'buzzers,' and a nod from the foreman, was the signal to stop work for the day and make for the changing room cum canteen in which they ate their midday 'packing up.' As they got changed the manager brought in their sealed weekly wage packets, with the amount it contained written on the side. The reverse side of the packet consisted of a series of holes through which, by judicial shaking of the sealed packet, its contents could be checked and confirmed. In no time they were queuing to clock out and each of them left the site to the 'ding' of the clocking out machine that was said to resemble a cracked bicycle bell. I would like to wager that his mates paused to shake dad's hand and, with hearty cries of, "See ya tomorrow morning Jim and we'll prop you up if you get no sleep," they made their various ways home.

17th April 1931. The birth of a baby

Dad was a man who enjoyed walking which, perhaps, is as well because public transport did not span the route from Holmes Tannery in Wincolmlee to our then family home at number 2, Blanche Grove, Courtney Street. His preferred route was a short walk over the Wilmington Swing Bridge, which is still a landmark in that part of industrial Hull. With the River Hull now behind him he would continue along Foster Street and onto Cleveland Street, which ran through a conglomeration of factories and engineering works, and was noted for its unpredictable cobble stones; particularly where the road dipped and rose beneath an overhead railway bridge. The uneven cobbles were a great help to cart horses but were lethal to cyclists when the stones became wet and slippery. A sharp turn to the left would take him by "Chappy Street School" and into Chapman Street. On the corner, and facing the school, was the surgery of the local dentist named Mr Eales, who was well used by many in Courtney Street and surrounding areas. In those days dental surgeries were not often visited on a regular check-up basis and many patients, desperate with toothache, would rush to Mr Eales with the plea, "I may never have enuff nerve to come again – so gimme a shot of gas and tek the bloody lot out!"

Although Chapman Street was of no great length it contained several houses along its frontage that were interspaced with four cul-de-sacs known as Poplar Parade, Poplar Crescent, Poplar Street and having rather over-worked the title "Poplar" the final off-shoot was named Gordon Avenue. Almost as an afterthought, or so it appeared to me, a rather sad line of houses, known as Howard's Row were, for some inexplicable reason, wedged in between Gordon Avenue and the Foredyke Stream (locally known as Sutton Drain). Only a gap of around thirty feet separated their front doors from the unfenced drain embankment.

However, housing development was restricted to the school side of Chapman Street because the opposite side, up to Sutton Drain Bridge, was dominated by the local authority Corporation Yard and refuse destructor. A regular stream of horse drawn carts, filled with the contents of household dustbins, would deposit their loads and then depart for the next street in their schedule. In the 1930s global warming and carbon footprints were unheard of and, on a 24 hour basis, household and industrial waste was burned in a large incinerator. Frequent change to the colour of smoke billowing from the incinerator chimney was a regular feature. To some it appeared quite attractive and possible health disadvantages were never, within my hearing, offered as a point for concern. In fact experienced neighbours, who had developed an interest in waste incineration, would predict or even argue over the origin of waste that was currently burning; based entirely upon the colour of the smoke. But regardless of its ancestry the incinerator chimney outflow would eagerly unite with sooty by-products, from neighbouring factories, to become a malevolent carrier of respiratory ailments to many in the area who were prone to such attacks.

By now dad, who passed these sights year in and year out, would be on 'Drain Bridge' and there would be much for him to think about despite the fatigue of a hard day's work. So let us pretend that he stopped for a few moments and gazed down at his reflection in the slow moving water as he thought about what awaited him at home, where his wife Ellen Doris was due to deliver her second child. He knew that he ought to feel happy, as indeed in a fatherly way he was, were it not for nagging concerns over the difficult time his wife had with the birth of their son eight years ago. In 1923 their first child, James George Cane, was born after a very difficult and painful delivery, despite help from an experienced neighbour and my grandmother Dennis. He thought that his wife would not survive and, when normality finally returned, they both declared they would have no more children. Largely that held true except that my mother always held the vision of both a son and daughter as her ideal family dream; and then the time came for the dream to be put into action. Hence eight years later they were both convinced that the day had arrived for the birth of their longed for daughter, who they agreed would be called Joyce Cane.

This thought may well have put a spring in his step as he continued along Chapman Street and through the aroma of last night's now stale beer that hung around the Victoria Tavern, situated across the road, and next door to Reckitt and Colman. This pub was locally known as 'Vicky Vaults' and was very popular in the area. Yet its fame did not end there because it also held a record it was duly proud of, in that it contained the longest bar counter in Hull. Should a visitor to Vicky Vaults care to dispute its popularity then the residents would quickly draw their attention to the stone entry step which, due to the constant erosion of a myriad of feet, had adopted the shape of an executioner's chopping block. But, for the moment, dad had far greater matters weighing heavily upon his mind. His pace increased as he turned left into Dansom Lane, and over the Hull to Withernsea line level crossing, followed by a sharp right turn into Courtney Street, with its entrance guarded by 'tin mission' and a second hand bike shop on respective corners. With his mind focussed upon Blanche Grove he would have been oblivious to other workers returning home or the ringing of cycle bells and general street noises. By now his mind would be awash with worrying about his wife yet his concern, in part, may have been neutralised by the thought of baby Joyce who even now may be waiting for her dad! He quickly turned into the rear passage that led to his house and was soon at the yard door marked with number two, from which a rivulet of excess paint had frozen in its downward flow. With his heart pounding he took a deep breath and in four strides was across the yard and into the back kitchen of his sham-four house. In front of him stood the local midwife, who the family doctor had insisted must be present in the event of any birth related problems.

From what I was to later learn the conversation went along the lines, "Is my wife alright?" dad asked with his heart almost in his mouth. "She is very tired but she will be fine in a few days. Her mother is looking after her upstairs," smiled the midwife. "And was it a girl?" he added as his body tensed for the answer. Briefly the smile faded on her face then, with renewed tenderness, she said, "I am sorry Mr Cane that you didn't get the daughter you both wanted, but be assured that your new son is fine and healthy, and I know that you will be proud of him, and he of you." As if in a trance dad expressed his thanks and he hardly noticed the doctor's account, for fifteen shillings, as it was placed in his shaking hands.

My welcome into the depressed thirties

Hence it is a fact that I was born in Blanche Grove, Courtney Street. My entire family together with the immediate neighbours were aware of this as was the local Registrar whose signature upon my birth certificate bore legal testimony to my arrival in this life. Additionally aware was the Reverend Clarke, the vicar of St. Marks-in-the-Groves in nearby St. Marks Street, who christened me. This was not a quickly forgotten incident for the Reverend Clarke because, for the next three years, he marked the event with an ornate Baptismal anniversary card, which he hand delivered to our house in between routine pastoral visits. It was also a fact that my name was not Joyce Cane but it did not seem to matter. Through the years I have thought hard about that once important issue but, it has to be said, even my earliest recollections failed to detect the slightest resentment that I was not the girl they had so much longed for. At all times I was aware of a great bond of love and protection, and that was enough for me.

As I grew older I became aware that my parents had far more on their minds than I, at my then tender years, could have even begun to appreciate. There can be no doubt that their hard working lives and the state of the nation, following the great depression that began in 1929 with the fall of the American stock market, and its global economic shock wave, gave them more pressing matters to worry about. British exports had plummeted to a record low and unemployment rose to three million and, in my year of birth, the then Prime Minister Ramsay McDonald cut workers' insurance benefits and introduced a more stringent, if not draconian, system for establishing an applicant's level of poverty before benefit payments would be granted. The title for this new system, which by name alone struck dire fear into many Courtney Street homes, was the Means Test.

In terms bereft of political spin of the day it simply meant that applicants had to prove just how poor they were. This process involved form filling based upon impertinent questions and a detailed examination of the applicants house. The rule was one chair per household member and any over must be sold along with spare blankets and other items deemed to be household luxuries. Since I am stressing the terrible pressures that many of the Courtney Street families had to endure, I felt it necessary to spend just a little time outlining one of the social problems that 'welcomed' me into this life. Fortunately dad retained his work at Tan Yard although many, including those who were employed on the docks, or within the ship building industry, were not so fortunate. Nevertheless my parents did take precautionary measures like hiding nominal household trinkets that might catch the eye of a Means Test inspector, should the time arrive for them to fall victim to his clutches. Believe me when I stress that Courtney Street adults, and no doubt many others, were not noted for knuckling their foreheads and kowtowing to Means Test requirements. In a short space of time systems were put into place whereas those who had applied for benefits, and were awaiting a visit from the Means Test Inspector, would store targetable items, like furniture, jewellery and other 'luxuries' in a neighbour's house. Even the coalman would loan out his empty bags so that coal could be shovelled out of a vulnerable coalhouse and hidden next door. I heard of some classical dramatic performances when a person who was being Means Tested would, with shaking finger, point to a meagre heap of coal dust and, between her best Dickensian consumptive coughs, would ask the inspector for his help. By way of support her neighbour in the next yard would add, for the benefit of the inspector, "Don't worry love. I may be able to lend you a shovel of coal tomorrow."

Looking back on this war of wits I can only marvel at the ingenuity of the women of the street, for it was through their guile that benefits were won. Had it been left to the majority of the menfolk then tempers would have quickly risen and fists would have replaced words, meaning that the objective would have been lost. However men did play their part in 1936 when the Jarrow Crusade was launched with the objective of drawing attention to deep poverty and lack of work in the north-east of England. Two hundred men, chosen from hundreds of volunteers, staged a 300 mile hunger march to London. Wherever the marchers stopped overnight, local people would give them shelter and food, and even provide them with boots to enable them to continue. Along the way they were applauded and encouraged yet, when they arrived in London and tried to present their 11,000 name petition to Prime Minister Stanley Baldwin, he refused to see them, or their representatives, because he said he was "too busy." The marchers achieved nothing but publicity and, as a token, they were each given one pound for their train fare home.

In my developing years I enjoyed asking questions about what people were doing and why they were doing it, although by no stretch of imagination could I claim that I fully understood why many things happened as they did. There were times when I felt that my mother was also unsure because, in reply to many of my questions, she would say, "I'm busy now so go and play." I suppose that for my then age, which would be around three years, I was more that usually curious about what was going on around me. It could be that isolation was a factor because, from an age viewpoint, I was an only child as my brother was eight years my senior and, to my mind, he was a member of the grown-up strata. But persistence paid off because I clearly remember the time when mother, probably in desperation, gave in and said, "If you must know we are flitting to another house next week." With that I retired to my little den, in a corner of the room that was boxed in by the couch, in order to try and understand the meaning of 'flitting' which was a new word in my developing life. I even involved 'Jelly Legs' in the discussion but sadly to no avail. JL, who was my dear and friendly teddy bear, had his own problems as he could not stand up on his two legs – as his name suggests.

The noble art of house flitting

It was some years later before I fully understood what 'flitting to another house meant' in Courtney Street terms. It was a ritual and with all such time honoured activities it had to have its rules that meant, nay demanded, that the flit must be completed before 'Mister' came home from work. The process involved moving from your current rented house and into another which, invariably, was no great distance away and could be a matter of just moving across the road. The thought process behind this was the necessity to remain within convenient walking distance of the site where the 'wage earner' worked. The mechanics of the movement were simple in that you carried your furniture and belongings over to the new property or simply borrowed a handcart through someone who owed you a favour. A flit had its attraction for neighbours and family in that, after their help had been freely given, there was the celebratory jug of beer that made the day worth its efforts. In later years I clearly remember a flit that Jim and I helped with, in the depths of winter, when the pavements were thick with frozen snow which we used to our advantage. All large items including a sideboard, couch and beds easily slid along the ice, with judicial nudges to prevent them following the camber of the pavement and sliding into the middle of the road. With regard to flitting there had to be a reason and, before we move on, perhaps we should consider what motivated Courtney residents to move as frequently as they seemingly did.

There were occasions when financial anxiety led to extreme measures known as 'moonlight flitting' wherein severe rent arrears led tenants, by the light of the moon, to pile their belongings onto a handcart and never be seen again. In desperation the landlord would ask surrounding tenants for help in locating the runaways but had to suffice with a shrug of the shoulders and an unwavering "I never heard nowt" to add to his frustration; having overlooked the high level of street camaraderie born from fear they might be the next to go! The majority of house moves stemmed from living conditions that varied by the house. A leading contender was rising damp – "cos it's bad for mister's cough and my rheumatics" or being over-run with ' black clocks' (cockroaches) that were sufficiently agile to gain squatters' rights even on the highest pantry shelf. Hence the decision to flit was, at times, a better option than arguing with the landlord. I mention this because for reasons, not declared to me, my mum and dad chose to flit from Blanche Grove into number 13, Leonards Avenue; which was diagonally opposite on the tin mission side of Courtney Street. One clue for this move was that my mother often repeated neighbourhood praise for a Mr Baker, the landlord of Leonards Avenue, for his quick attention to house repairs. But regardless of the reason it was a good move because she always maintained those years in Leonards Avenue were the happiest of her life. It is conceivable that there could have been other reasons for the flit, not least was the fact that Blanche Grove was separated from the North Eastern Railway line by a wall at the bottom of the terrace. This was a busy rail system that ran a passenger service from Hull to Hornsea and Withernsea together with a wide range of freight traffic. Its drawback was the noise and vibration that, from regular street complaints, was capable of 'sheking' house doors and windows and had been known to 'bring the plaster down.' Alternatively they could have decided to move because they had lived there long enough. Ten years or so would have elapsed since they moved from their first matrimonial home, in Lily's Terrace, Parrott Street which ran off Selby Street. My brother Jim was born in that house hence, by default, he never fully qualified to be 'Courtney born and bred' thus leaving me with sole bragging-rights!

Shopping on Holderness Road

Obviously I was blissfully unaware of these and other mini dramas that were being played out around me as I began the process of growing up. My earliest retained memory was being pushed in my tan-sad up Courtney Street and along Holderness Road to the Maypole shop, which was one of a line of shops between Courtney and Burleigh Streets. Obviously I enjoyed looking in shop windows because I can recall furiously stamping my feet, on the tan-sad foot rest, as a signal that I wanted my mother to stop at certain shops. Throughout my pre-school days I enjoyed the almost daily shopping expedition; which was as well because there was little scope for keeping food fresh in the days before refrigerators and domestic freezers. Perhaps the coolest place in the house was on the stone tiled pantry floor which, for that purpose, had to be used with the greatest care. As ever there were the marauding 'black clocks' aided and abetted by house mice and, in hot summer months, the ill-fitting pantry door invited wave after wave of attacks from flies and bluebottles, with back-up from mysterious flying creatures that appeared to have exclusively evolved in Courtney Street. But I survived and, indeed, thrived upon it. I was discovering an exciting new world and would stand open mouthed with amazement at the sight of the counter assistants, in Home and Colonial, furiously and skilfully 'butter patting' which I silently concluded must have been one of life's hardest challenges. This feat was closely followed in Lipton's by a lady with a length of wire who could, with consummate ease, remove from a mighty block of cheese a small section to exactly meet customer requirements. Then there was the biscuit counter in Maypole – and what a sight that was to a small boy with a sweet tooth. Open and tilted biscuit tins were strategically arranged to display a mouth-watering sight of practically every brand of biscuit that human imagination could create and, without exception, each one of them seemed to plead with me to eat them. I wondered how grown-ups could expect one so young to resist such temptations but, as ever, mother had read my mind and solved my dilemma with, "Touch those biscuits and I'll clatter you," in her sotto voce delivery that was not heard around the shop but was loud and meaningful to my ears. Then I was led next door into Collie's butchers shop and it was not long before the glorious spread of sawdust, on his floor, drew me to my knees and, seemingly, invited me to draw faces in it. That was until my mother suddenly hauled me to my feet by my coat collar, dusted me down and muttered that I was showing her up, as she led me from the shop. "Why can't you behave yourself like your brother does – I can never tell what you're going to do next!" she said almost in desperation as, holding on to her shopping bag, we began our homeward journey. I remember this particular day because after a period of silence she reached down, rubbed my hair, and asked if I was alright? Looking up at her, with what I was later told were big innocent blue eyes, I nodded my head at which, with a wry grin, she slipped a biscuit into my hand.

Black Manna from Heaven

That was just one of many enjoyable outings I had with mother in my pre-school days and very few went by without some sort of incident; perhaps that is why I remember them so well. Like the time a goods train, travelling at speed and pulling a load of full coal wagons, had to apply its brakes urgently before clearing the overhead bridge at the corner of Burleigh Street. The result was spectacular in that dislodged coal, from the violently disturbed wagons, shot up in the air and showered down the embankment and, from the bridge, onto an area of Holderness Road pavement that fortunately was free from pedestrians. However in direct line of the deluge were two dogs intent upon getting to know each other through their time honoured procedures, only to have their ardour dramatically curtailed by what was, to them, a broadside of well-aimed stones that sent them yelping down Holderness Road. Perhaps it was an exaggeration but, according to my mother, later reports had it that they were still running as they passed East Park! But the sequel was without parallel when, seemingly from nowhere, a host of women materialised and lost no time in filling their shopping bags with this valuable commodity. Still open mouthed I caught sight of the railway embankment which, in record time, became inundated with Burleigh and Craven Streets residents who either bucketed the coal away or simply threw it into their respective backyards. In later years when I looked back on this desperate gathering of much needed coal, so scarce in an age of recession-led low incomes yet so vital to the survival of all ages, I found myself sharing the joy they must have felt at what, to them, was black manna from heaven. They did have their dreams that one day the poor would be given realistic help but, perhaps as well, they were unaware that first they would have to endure the terrors of a World War to bring this about.

A quick look at Waller Street

Occasionally we would go to the other side of Holderness Road and I was able to view, first hand, the mysterious Waller Street that, for reasons unknown, had struck such unfounded fear into the minds of some residents of the Danny Lane end of Courtney Street. As I peered down the street nightmarish visions of bilious looking monsters with an appetite for eating young boys were nowhere to be seen and, perhaps with a tinge of regret, I had to admit that it appeared to be a perfectly ordinary street. I was intrigued by the name of the pub on its corner known as the 'Nags Head' yet my comments were cut short by my mother's rejoinder that I should keep out of that place when I was grown up. The fact of why I should keep out of the 'Nags Head' was left unsaid hence my strong sense of curiosity took over which, on this occasion, was well matched by mother's determination to get on with her shopping. My opening words of, "Mam, does my dad go in there and if he does then why can't I......" came to an abrupt end with her, "Will you shut up for a minute, I'm trying to remember why I came over here."

On the opposite corner of Waller Street there was a butchers shop and on the business display sign above its window, through which mother was looking, was the name of the butcher. My mother often read the shop name for me until one day I noticed some smaller words further down that I could not understand. "Mam, look!" I urged whilst pulling on her coat sleeve. "What's the matter with you now?" she sighed with growing exasperation. "What do those little words say?" Mother looked up and had to admit that she had never noticed them before. My interest barometer reached record levels when mother read that the sign was made out of glass and, in fact, the entire shop sign was painted on a sheet of glass. "Didn't know you could paint on glass," I murmured. "Shall we paint our windows ...." Suddenly I was whisked away by my collar which was a sure sign that my mother was losing her patience. Nevertheless I will leave with you the fact that for many years afterwards, when passing Waller Street prior to its demolition, I paused to read and remind myself that the corner shop sign was still set upon glass and, as an act of defiance, it had remained unscathed in the face of all that the Luftwaffe could throw upon the area in WW2. C'est la vie!

The joy of standing on a railway bridge

Let us remain on the Waller Street side of Holderness Road and walk towards the level crossing footbridge which, for many boys and girls, within a wide age range, would be the signal for their hearts to race with excitement. Quickly they would scamper up the stair treads, albeit one or two at a time depending upon competing agility, until they gained the all-important centre point of the overhead bridge. After all there could be no denying the fact that the train was on its way. Loud and clear they heard three distinct ding-a-dings within the signal box, meaning that the train was in its area. This was confirmed by the slow grating fall of a semaphore signal arm in favour of an approaching train. Already the furious waving of the gate keeper's red flag had brought traffic to a standstill as the gates began to open to allow the passage of the train. The gates either opened or closed in response to a large control wheel that was manually operated by the signal box man. Oh, how I envied that man who, by the strength of his arms, controlled the flow of road and rail traffic with nonchalant ease and, before my 'Tarzan phase', I had set my sights on taking over his job when 'I was grown up.' But let us return to the centre of that overhead bridge and become infected by an atmosphere of undisputed exhilaration, which had many jumping up and down in wild excitement, as the now visible train could be seen passing over the Dansom Lane crossing and chugging along in parallel to Courtney Street. Already experts were commenting on powerful bursts of preferred dense white smoke that were coming our way, as opposed to darker shades that meant coughing bouts which, I hastily add, did not detract from the overall enjoyment. Nearer and nearer the steam engine came as it pulled its line of passenger coaches towards Withernsea via Southcoates station until suddenly the engine was beneath our feet, and instantly we were suspended in a world of swirling vapours created to delight young children. In response to a powerful whooshing sound a bright sunny day would instantly become a sinister deep veil of white mystery within which your companions, or indeed your own hand, would disappear into distant realms of the unseen. Then, as if by divine intervention, the mist would slowly fade to reveal the full glory of life, together with several cyclists puffing and panting, with their bikes hooked over a shoulder, as they rushed across the bridge trying to justify not waiting for the gates to open.

And then it was wash day

My most vivid pre-school memory of Courtney Street has to be the weekly wash day. This is because it was a regular event that left its mark upon my developing memory and, as a bonus, gave impetus to my evolving sense of adventure and an eye for a story. For example – would that scurrying 'black clock', caught between the yard sink and a fast advancing rivulet of water from the mangle, manage to avoid a watery death? My shouts of encouragement and the ultimate escape of the beleaguered beetle would be met by my rousing cheer which, as ever, brought from mother little more than a resigned shake of her head as she continued turning the handle. Consequently, I think it most fitting that I end my pre-school memories of Courtney Street by sharing with you my recollections of a typical wash day, which was a common denominator throughout the street, and would be a familiar scene in most back yards or open plan terraces.

Monday was wash day and that was that! Other household activities were not so rigid and mother, at her discretion, may choose to reschedule them to suit weather conditions, visits from relatives, shopping to be done or an overwhelming urge to tap her feet to the piano playing of

Charlie Kunz, courtesy of Rediffusion radio. But never on a Monday would such distractions be tolerated because wash day and Monday were inseparable, and any attempt to dissolve this union would shake the very foundations upon which Courtney Street life was built. It was, without doubt, a domestic commitment as binding to many households as strict rulings are to extreme religious organisations.

Don't forget the firewood

The ritual began after tea, on the Sunday before the event, when sufficient firewood to light both the brick copper in the back kitchen and the front room Yorkist grate had to be made available. Any excess firewood was then stored in the warmth of a lid accessed hot water tank that was an integral part of most Yorkist units; albeit in our house it was only ever used for drying damp firewood. Our main source of kindling was Tan Yard where the men were allowed to take home lengths of well-used wood that was of no further commercial use. Another lucrative source were off cuts and sometimes longer pieces of wood that bounced from many horse drawn carts that lumbered up and down Courtney Street, carrying timber to and from several sawmills in the area. Approaching timber bearing carts could be clearly heard by eager children, or desperate adults, who feigned disinterest until a timber cart met with a larger than normal pothole. The victim of this conflict was the timber load wherefrom insecure pieces became detached and fell upon the road. Before the rulleyman could shout "Whoa" a horde, not unlike a pack of prairie wolves, descended upon the kindling and were away. By the time he managed to stand up in his cart the scavengers had disappeared down whatever passage or terrace bore their house number and, as I remember, the philosophy of the foragers was that timber on the cart was company property whereas timber lying on the public highway belonged to the first person to grab it and run. Occasionally there were times when pickings were lean and mother had to resort to the grocer's shop, at the corner of Gladys's Grove, who sold firewood by the bundle and, as a customer service, eagerly updated street gossip free of charge.

Wash day begins

Dad was in charge of filling the back kitchen copper with water and preparing the fire box for mother to light at around 4 o'clock on the Monday morning. This water heating unit, set in the corner of the kitchen, was the only source of bulk hot water available in Courtney Street houses in the 1930s; hence it was treated with great respect. Its design was simple in that it was a deep metal bowl set above a coal fire, and the whole was enclosed in a chimney vented brick structure complete with a lid. Without its contribution there would be insufficient hot water for washing clothes on a Monday, or bodies on a Friday, which was our traditional family bath night. The prime reason for dad's involvement with it was mother's fear of birds at close range, more so the ones that often fell down the house chimney and ended their lives in the copper grate. In parallel, mother would prepare dad's packing up for Monday and ensure that his tea caddy unit, comprised of individual containers for tea, sugar and milk were in his Tan Yard bag together with his pipe and tobacco. Thus completed the household would retire for an early night in preparation for the demands of the weekly Monday wash day. Needless to add that I would have been dispatched 'up the dancers', which was the usual expression for the house staircase, long before the rest of the family retired.

Before the onset of dawn I would be aware of the local knocker up with his long stick tapping on certain bedroom windows with, what sounded to be, a hard rubber ball with strings of buttons hanging from it. Then, not to be outdone, local factory buzzers would add their contribution to the birth of a new day or, to be precise, they simply stirred up the worries and concerns within the waking minds of most families in Courtney Street of that era. On wash day both mum and dad got up together around 4am when the back kitchen copper and the front room fire were quickly lit. Then he would help drag the scrubbing table, dolly tub and wringer (mangle) from a recess in the yard situated between the toilet and house, with the neighbouring boundary wall completing the enclosure. A previous tenant had concocted an unusual covering for this small storage area in the form of a roof composed of assorted pieces of asbestos sheeting supported by a hotchpotch of part decaying timber which, when times were particularly hard, would be 'borrowed' to augment firewood supplies. Some time after our arrival in Leonards Avenue dad demolished this hazardous unit and replaced it with a tarpaulin sheet. If mum and dad had breakfast, which I was never entirely sure about, then it would not be more than cups of tea with a slice of bread and dripping for my dad which was the prelude to the sound of his boots, clumping up the back passage, and heading off towards Tan Yard.

The next person to be summoned downstairs was Jim who, perhaps understandably, was quick to wash in the kitchen sink, eat his breakfast, and depart for school much earlier than the arrival time demanded probably to kick a ball around the playground with his mates. In pre-school days my descent downstairs was invariably greeted with, "Keep out of here. Your breakfast's on the table and there's a flannel to wipe your face and hands when you have done. Don't touch the fireguard!" For my part I was happy enough to comply because in front of me were two slices of bread and jam and a bowl of the only cereal I would eat. Its name was 'Force' and it was popular on many Courtney Street tables because of its pleasant taste and low price. My attraction was not its economic advantages but its logo which was a caricature of a socialite, named 'Sunny Jim,' from the Georgian – Regency period (1714 to 1830). Often I would just sit and stare at Sunny Jim, whose place in history meant nothing to me until mother, on one occasion only, asked what I was looking at? I can clearly recall each word of my reply which was, "My hair used to look like that." She paused then began to say something, only to stop and walk away shaking her head.

Meanwhile mother was using to the full her wash day skills, based upon lessons taught by her mother and grandmother, and fittingly improved upon by self-developed expertise. Conveniently placed in the yard were the tools and additives of her trade in the form of a dolly stick (later replaced by a posher), family metal bath and dolly tub both containing hot water, scrubbing table, bucket and mangle. Within easy reach were her packets of Oxydol, Rinso, scrubbing brush and a thick block of soap. Also at hand was a supply of Reckitt's blue and dolly dyes which may have been used for washing curtains but, to continue further down this road, would confirm that I was irretrievably out of my depth! Regardless of the season she wore a long waterproof apron, not unlike the type used by Hessle Road fish workers. Mother, without the shadow of a doubt, had never heard of time and motion study programmes that are often developed at great expense to the user. In fact she would have no use for them because with an inherent skill, born from necessity, mother's system worked well and remained unchanged through her family support years. In broad terms this was her adopted procedure:

1. Selected soiled washing was boiled in the copper, in the presence of Oxydol or Rinso, for a varying time period after which it was transferred, via the bucket, on to the scrubbing table in the yard – regardless of the prevailing weather.

2. Without hesitation the block of soap was liberally applied to the hot and steaming mass of wet washing and its presence was stressed by spirited action from the scrubbing brush, which mother handled with great gusto and determination. Perhaps she was working out her aggression upon the reported actions of Means Test Inspectors which, if it were the case, would not surprise me in the slightest.

3. If the weekly wash could experience basic human feelings, through which it 'thought' its ordeals were now over, then it was catastrophically wrong. In the blink of an eye the contents of the scrubbing table were hurled into the dolly tub in which, regardless of size, they were thoroughly pummelled and thrown about by the merciless actions of the dolly stick, wielded by the hands of one who knew her business which, to the more judicial mind, was to punish her churned up 'victims' for becoming dirty!

4. Sometime later the limp and lifeless laundry was transferred from the dolly tub to the bath, which had been filled with warm water. Thus left to soak in this pond of bliss, without being boiled,

scrubbed or generally beaten about, may have led the mass of wet shirts, towels and allies to believe that the 'battle of the back yard' was really over; but not quite ....

5. For without warning the now clean wet washing was carefully fed into the large wooden rollers of a bulky metal framed hand operated wringer (or mangle), that was intent upon squeezing the last drop of water from each item of laundry. The final act was to carefully lay the wrung items, within a clothes basket, ready for hanging out to dry.

It may be interesting to know that at the onset of stage (5) my regular pre-school wash day offer of, "Mam, can I turn the mangle wheel?" was graciously declined by the one who had placed me under strict orders to keep away from it. To me it was a truly a marvellous machine that had the capacity to serve many of the needs of a fertile mind. Was it not a fact that the ancient Steam Roller, that regularly clanked its way along Courtney Street, had its direction controlled by a wheel identical to the one on mam's mangle and, to gain even the smallest movement from the lead roller, the driver had to furiously turn the steering cum mangle wheel much to my enjoyment. It was a pity that mother never knew of the joy I derived from my clandestine moments with her mangle. In support of my imagination I, with both hands rapidly turning the mangle wheel, drove my imaginary Steam Roller through every conceivable danger that a vehicle such as this would encounter when deep in an African jungle. To my mind there was far more for this machine to do than squeeze water out of soggy clothing every Monday morning. For example it was ideal for converting my ball of plasticine into a sad looking pancake or cracking nuts occasionally given to me by the lady proprietor of the Sunkist fruit stores, which fronted Dansom Lane close to Tin Mission. Then there was the time I was caught 'red handed' when mother appeared in the yard when I was slowly turning the mangle wheel and singing, at the top of my voice, "Sweet Rosie O'Grady, my sweet little rose," which was my imitation of a Hurdy-Gurdy player who regularly entertained the full length of Courtney Street, come rain or shine, in exchange for donations towards the upkeep of his wife and twelve kids. Essentially that was the end of wash day save for the drying stage which relied upon a criss-cross of lines set across the ceiling, of both downstairs rooms, augmented by a large clothes horse placed around the front room fire.

Traditional wash day food

Through the years I was able to collate much evidence, through expressions of joy or downright disgust, that many houses in Courtney Street had the same traditional evening meal at the end of Monday wash days; and our house was no exception. Obviously mother was very tired and so was dad after a day on piece work in Tan Yard; hence a filling yet quickly prepared meal, known in Courtney Street as 'Pan-Hag', found pride of place upon the oil cloth covered table. I must quickly add that its only table companion was a plate of dry sliced bread that awaited its turn to be dipped into the steaming main course, whose aroma had quickly dispelled the smell of hot muggy washing that pervaded every corner of the house and clouded each window in the process. Those Courtney Street gastronomes who dared object to this regular Monday menu were advised to mull over the alternative which was, "It's Pan-Hag or nowt, so mek ya bloody mind up!" I did a little research into the origin of Pan-Hag and found it began life in Northumberland and quickly spread throughout the north east, and down into Yorkshire, where its original name of Pan Haggerty became abbreviated. The basic Pan Haggerty recipe was a quickly prepared meal, in a three pan steamer on the Yorkist range, and was composed of potatoes and onions. If the budget could run to it the addition of a little meat and cabbage would successfully quench the most voracious appetite, at an acceptable cost.

Mam – please let me spit on the iron

The period Monday afternoon to Tuesday lunch was the time taken to dry the washing to mother's satisfaction and, with instinctive body movement, we four could move around the clothes horse, for access to, and viewing rights of, the household fire. After all this fire had to be kept ash and clinker free and stoked up, with fresh coal, in order for it to maintain its multi-tasking role of providing heat to warm us, dry the washing and keep the kettle in 'singing mode.' Before the washing got too dry it had, if applicable to its end use, to be ironed on the back kitchen table after its oil cloth had been removed and replaced with several old and frayed blankets, whose many scorch marks stood out like wash day campaign medals. Two flat irons were necessary for this process using a system of one in use and one heating up in close contact to the fire. The need to occasionally put the hot iron down was met by a heavy duty metal support ring, judiciously placed on the table at a point where it was, according to mother, out of reach of my ' inquisitive fingers that were everywhere' (unquote). Forgive the unintended pun but it is ironic that many of these heavy old flat irons have survived the decades in the form of objet d'art companions to designer fireplaces, or a door stop cum trip hazard as the case may be.

Although I cannot speak from experience I would venture to suggest that modern electric irons, fitted with thermostatic controls and the option of steam emissions when required, are more user friendly than their pre Second World War ancestors. But we must not forget that even in the 1930s it was most important that the operator had some control of the temperature of the basic flat iron, before it made contact with the washing. Perhaps it was the latent chemist within me that activated my attention each time a new technical operation came into my life and, what is to follow, raised my scientific pulse to new heights when I met the technique for confirming when the flat iron had reached the level of heat required. I cannot credit my mother with developing this innovation because, through childhood years, I visited other Courtney Street houses when the lady ironing used the same procedure. In short the iron was lifted away from the fire and, after a brief visual inspection of its working surface, the operator would pucker her lips and spit smartly upon it. The flat iron was declared to be at optimum working temperature when, on impact, the spittle broke up into small globules that briefly did a hectic jig on the hot metal surface, until steam pressure betwixt the metal and spittle expelled the latter into some distant corner of the room. I was fascinated by the technical implications of this process and with a desire, above definition, I would cry out, "Mam – mam please let me spit on the iron – go on, please!" When mother said, 'No' she always meant it and my involvement in the spittle process never became an exception to her rule. Ruefully I would watch mother briefly rub the flat iron surface, over a large block of soap to enhance its slide- ability, and then with a smile of job satisfaction continue with the ironing; whilst the partner flat iron took its turn in the fire.

In fairness I cannot leave this account of interim stages that made up the weekly wash day, in many of the Courtney Street houses, without touching upon a rather obvious point. The ironing process was a long and tiring business that must have been close to the relegation zone in a league of 1930s household chores. I have in my possession one of the two original flat irons that was used by my mother which I have weighed and found, much to my surprise, that she spent several hours pushing a flat iron that weighed just over 5¼ pounds! Accordingly, few would argue against the fact that it must have been very thirsty work and, I dare say, the majority would applaud the way that many Courtney Street mothers addressed this problem. Throughout the ironing stage mother kept at hand a cup of beer that, at intervals, was sipped and occasionally topped up from a jug that was kept covered on the pantry floor. The supplier of this thirst conqueror was a thriving off- licence, known locally as the 'Beer Off,' that was situated at the corner of one of the terraces facing the sawmill. I was familiar with this establishment because the Saturday afternoon task of keeping the jug topped up fell upon Jim and, in later years, it became my duty. A glance at the worn entrance step to the shop was a reliable clue to the frequency of its visitors, as was the tired and unenthusiastic response from an ancient doorbell which, to say the least, had lost a lot of its original 'jingle-jangle.' I suppose like many other Beer Offs the first impression, on entering, was a smell of warm stale beer only in this shop it had to compete with smoke from a Woodbine cigarette, that permanently hung from the lower lip of the proprietor, and seemingly beat time to his spoken word. He was a jolly man whose growth had favoured his waist line rather than his height, consequently when his arms were getting tired he would stand upon a stool in order to operate the ornate hand lever that drew beer from the barrel below straight into mum's jug. Paying for it was via a pre-arranged system of handing him some coins that were wrapped in a piece of paper, into which the change was duly re-wrapped. Arrival home was always greeted with, "Put it on the pantry floor and don't forget to put the saucer over it – then you can go and see if your Grandmother Dennis (across the road in Burleigh Grove) wants any errands doing."

Street events

My final recollection of street life, before I began my school career, was the May 1935 Silver Jubilee of King George the fifth and Queen Mary. This national event was celebrated throughout the entire length of Courtney Street in the form of street and terrace parties with impromptu entertainment provided by local men draped in the Union Flag and staggering along on home-made stilts; having first been filled with liquid courage in Vicky Vaults. In parallel there was an assortment of wandering minstrels who moved from street to street entertaining group parties with a varied range of acts. I particularly remember a George Formby impersonator twanging his ukulele to the words of "When I'm cleaning windows" and a male duo impersonating Flanagan and Allen singing about life beneath the arches. To me the highlight of the entertainment was a husband and wife act that consisted of the man solemnly handing his false teeth to his wife after which he fitted a Jaws Harp (sometimes called a Jews Harp) into his mouth from which he generated meaningless sounds whilst his wife, still clutching his teeth, smiled benevolently at anyone who looked her way. Then, of course, we had our regular Hurdy-Gurdy player who for the umpteenth time regaled us with "Sweet Rosie O'Grady," followed by an 'uncertain' rendering of the "Rose of Tralee." In honour of the occasion tips were not asked for with the exception of a plea for alms, coming from our Jaws Harp player, who concluded his act by shaking an empty Fry's cocoa tin, cum cash box, in the hope of a reward for his efforts; in anticipation of which he poured down upon us God's blessings because, to quote, we all "had kind faces." His wife, who seemingly had at her command a storehouse of relevant smiles, beamed radiantly at us as she followed closely in his wake lovingly clasping his false teeth to her generous bosom. On this special day the street was free from traffic so we children had space to play whatever games took our fancy and, from memory, there were many skinned knees from the more boisterous events. It was a memorable day that left many children drunk with delight and their parents in a similar state induced by jugged ale from the over worked beer off. On a sober note it was good that Courtney Street could, albeit for one day, put aside thoughts of low incomes and shortage of work plus the growing menace of approaching war as the German Fascist party gained momentum. In the face of all this I am very fortunate to have inherited a family photograph of one of the Courtney Street Silver Jubilee events, in the form of our very own Leonards Avenue party held at the terrace end and shown below:

PART THREE

(1936 TO 1939)

SCHOOL LIFE AND STREET EVENTS

As an author faced with writing a historically true account, in the course of which I play a small part among a cast of hundreds I must, by nature of my intent, fall victim to the product of my own pen. Although I enjoy walking again with family and neighbours from a past age, and reliving their laughter and sighs, I alone have the sole disadvantage of knowing what the future held for many of them; whereas they are free to blissfully re-enact their lives on my stage of memories until my advancing narrative brings all this to an end. Perhaps many of us, including myself, have on occasion held close a desire to remain in a cherished moment of life and trust that time, in deference to our feelings, will obligingly move on and leave us in peace. Yet deep within we know this can never be.

I first became aware that my life was not a constant recycle of treasured joys when, clutching my mother's hand, I began my first walk towards the gates of Courtney Street Infants School. My mind was in panic mode and a surfeit of memories jostled for immediate attention. What about my shopping trips with mother which I always enjoyed? How would the Home and Colonial butter patters manage without my adoring support for their creative handiwork? What about those trams rumbling along double line tracks in the middle of Holderness Road who relied upon me to wave to them, as did the steam engine driver as he slowly went through the level crossing towards Southcoates railway station? My grip upon mother's hand became even tighter as we turned into the playground so much so that she quickly looked down at me. It was then I became really alarmed because I saw tears running down my mother's face. "Mam, are you alright?" was my anxious cry, as mother sniffed and wiped her face with the back of her hand. "Don't worry about me – it's only dust that blew in my eyes as we passed that damned sawmill," she replied as we joined a group of other mothers on the same errand. I accepted her answer without question and it was only in adult years, when I was in similar situations, that I realised the genuine reason for her tears. Then matters began to move very quickly as, via my mother's replies, I was officially enrolled on the school register and, after a cuddle and kiss, together with the reminder that she would be waiting for me at the school gate, I was led away into the beginners' classroom to meet my peers.

Initially I was unnerved by the large number of boys and girls that made up the reception class more so because several of them were, with no small amount of inter-rivalry, feverishly bewailing the absence of their mother or person who had brought them. Several had entered the realms of near hysteria whereas others preferred to sob alone and brush away the hand of support with a guttural, "*Ger off.*" The sight of such concentrated tear-shedding did very little to boost the morale of those whose feelings bordered upon uncertainty. Yet throughout this turmoil two teachers were patiently moving around trying to console and cheer up those in distress whilst the more philosophical, including myself, sat in silence and contemplated all that we thought lay ahead. Slowly raising my head I gazed at the figures around me and realised that I knew only a few of them, having seen them out in the street, but the others were strangers; most probably from adjoining streets that were within the School catchment area. Most of the boys were dressed like me in home knitted clothing consisting of a navy blue jersey and socks complete with a knitted navy blue tie. It was a fact that Courtney Street mothers and grandmothers spent most of their sitting down time knitting for their family; in fact it was only yesterday I heard a neighbour shout to my mother, "Our Nora's having another *bane* (bairn) so I'm getting my needles clacking again!"

A trip to the seaside

"Please Miss, was that an earthquake?" asked an alert boy with a light Irish accent. "No Timothy," replied a teacher seemingly pleased to enter into something approaching normal conversation. "It was just the Withernsea train going by and our classroom is very close to the railway lines." The same teacher, seemingly inspired by the passing of the seaside train, suddenly asked the children, "Would any of you like to go to the seaside?" In itself it was a perfectly ordinary question yet, within the environment in which it was asked its effect was awesome. A succession of loud sniffs followed by jersey cuffs being drawn across leaking nostrils was sufficient to transform once sad faces into images of attentive joy, whilst those of sullen and perverse attitudes instantly became pillars of unswerving commitment. Hands shot up into the air and a verbal avalanche of reasons favouring a trip to the coast were carefully collected by the teacher and written on the blackboard. Some five minutes later the entire class was dedicated to her leadership, more so when the seaside was high on her agenda.

Having got their undivided attention, and in a voice that promised adventure to come, she slowly announced, "Then we will play going to the seaside right now!" With the help of a colleague she turned around her high style teacher's desk and chair unit so that it faced the wall. "Now," she said proudly to the sea of wide eyes around her, "Here is our steam engine." With that she slowly climbed onto the seat and, looking most important, began to adjust imaginary controls. Soon a credible "toot – toot indicated that the engine was going to move and with her bent arms moving forward and backwards, thus imitating the drive motion of engine con rods, her "chuff – chuff –chuff" was soon picked up by the children and assistant teacher alike! "Now who will help me add the passenger coaches?" was her next question. A forest of raised arms responded and soon a column of paired chairs were positioned immediately behind the 'engine.' "Now which clever boy or girl will be the first to tell me what you need to do before you get on a train?" asked teacher. The sudden silence was broken by an Irish accent from the back of the room which declared, "Buy a ticket miss." "That's right Timothy

– well done!" Soon an assistant teacher cum ticket clerk was seated at a table and, in exchange for pretend money, began handing out hastily cut squares of paper whilst adding, in a pretend basso profondo voice, "Thank you."

After a call for "All Aboard" the children quickly filled their two-seater coaches and, in her new role of guard, the former ticket clerk blew her teacher's whistle. Propelled by the piston style arms of their teacher the mighty train slowly chuffed off to a range of sound effects provided by children and teachers alike. As for the passengers their former tears were long forgotten as they enjoyed their pretend trip to Withernsea, whilst acting out all happy memories of previous journeys that had been recorded on the black board.

I chose to share with you the memory of my first day at Courtney Street Infants School because, 75 years later, it is still crystal clear in my mind. From an adult viewpoint I firmly believe that the class teacher was a loss to the professional stage in terms of improvisation acting and spontaneous stage direction. As for the children, when home time came, it was hard to get them to leave the classroom and parents had to be called in to assist with the exodus process. I can recall happily holding mother's hand and skipping alongside her as we walked home, whilst breathlessly trying to tell her about all that had happened. My declaration that I liked school and could I go again tomorrow was met with a knowing grin because, in essence, mother knew that I had outgrown the sight of butter patting and cheese cutting in favour of my new social life at Courtney Street School. In many ways this was true because as the weeks passed by I became aware that close contact with children of my own age, both in the classroom and school playground, was beginning to widen my understanding of companionship; which was in direct contrast to playing alone in our small backyard in which an occasional sparrow on the wall was my only friend.

Promotion from slate to pencil and paper

It was getting close to Christmas 1936 when our teacher called us to attention and read out a small list of names, including my own, after which she praised us for our hard work and good behaviour. "Was this the moment I have been waiting for?" I hopefully muttered to myself. My hopes were based upon the fact that the classroom was split down the middle with new reception children on one side, and those who had served a term longer on the other. There was no visible demarcation line to be seen but, to the more studious class members, it was a wall that had to be scaled as a matter of personal fulfilment. All this stemmed from the fact that new arrivals were issued with a graphite pencil and a wooden framed slate upon which to record their work; whereas the more senior group had access to paper and a pencil together with much coveted wax colouring crayons. Joy upon joy only partly described my feelings when those named on teacher's list were invited to cross that great divide, betwixt slate and wax crayon, which must rate as the first rung on my ladder of academic progression. My new desk partner was a girl of friendly disposition who whispered to me that her name was Annie and that she lived in Crystal Terrace (opposite Courtney Street Junior School). Overcome with shyness I looked over at my former desk colleague who, for reasons I was unsure about, scowled back at me and put his tongue out. Our teacher, who rarely missed anything, was quick to tell him that it was rude to do what he did and there was a good chance that his tongue would drop off if he did it again. I have a vague memory of him spending the rest of the morning surreptitiously fingering his tongue – as if seeking reassurance it was still in place!

The Basket Chair Pianist

I suppose few of us are strangers to quiet moments of daydreaming when our unrestrained thoughts wander at will and, perhaps, light upon household objects that were part of our lives, yet totally beyond our comprehension as to where they came from. The presence of a piano in our Leonards Avenue house is well suited to that description. We did not own it and, if a Means Test inspector had reason to call, then the glint in his eyes would fade through the fact that my grandmother Dennis, in Burleigh Grove, was the legal owner. If this was challenged she would then have produced documentary evidence to show that she was paying the vendor a weekly sum of money by joint agreement.

Without doubt the singular and incredibly involved tale of the Cane piano is, to me, a fascinating story which, if further developed, would be in direct violation of my promise, in the introductory section, to avoid detailed reference to lengthy family history topics. Therefore it is sufficient to say that Jim and I went to piano lessons and to this day I still enjoy my sessions at the keyboard. My reason for referring to the piano was by way of introducing my act in the 1936 Courtney Street Infants' Christmas concert but, before I type another word I must stress that, unlike the great musician Mozart, I could not play the piano at the age of five. Nevertheless I loved the piano despite being told by my mother, in no uncertain terms, that it was not a toy and I could go to lessons when I was older and, based upon her experience of my insatiable level of curiosity, she kept the piano lid closed and locked except when it was time for Jim to practice. Nonetheless I soon discovered, in common with a number of other boys in the street, that piano keys had an exposed underside which, when pushed *upwards* from beneath the keyboard, responded as a piano should. Jim was livid when he found out about my clandestine piano sessions and, following his appeal to mother, my argument that I had not directly touched the keyboard was quickly dismissed as irrelevant. In later years she often referred to this incident and how furious Jim was and, whilst giving me a good talking to, she admitted that it had been hard to keep a straight face! She also liked to refer to the compromise that was reached when my plea to practise along with Jim was, much to his chagrin, accepted because it kept alive my interest in the piano. So when Jim sat down to play I followed suit; only my piano was a small basket chair before which I knelt and moved my hands in unison with what I saw in action on the real keyboard. Also as he turned a page of his music book I followed suit with page turning of whatever comic was at hand to act as my musical score. Despite himself Jim came to both accept and recognise my interest, such that, with mother's permission, he taught me how to play simple scales from the Roland's Pianoforte Tutor book. A hidden bonus from being a basket chair pianist was that I developed an ear and memory for retaining classical melodies that Jim practised on a daily basis; which brings me back to the Courtney Street Infant's Christmas concert.

The Caliph of Baghdad visits Courtney Street School

Our teacher had a great flair for inspiring her class through which she could feed her ideas to us in such a way that we immediately believed, without doubt, that we were the authors of her intent. Our 1936 Christmas class party was a prime example of her leadership powers when it was unanimously decided that we would stage a concert, composed of individual acts, which were not particularly related to anything other than a desire to do our bit. There was no shortage of volunteers as measured by a forest of arms stretched upwards, as if in their zeal they sought to touch the distant ceiling as a mark of their commitment. Confidence was high and a lack of pre-show rehearsals was shrugged off as totally unnecessary. However on the day of the concert when the Headmistress had taken her place as guest of honour, and His Master's Voice gramophone had screeched out the closing lines of "Away in a Manger," several performers began to have second thoughts. After teacher had welcomed the guests the opening act was promptly sick and had to be helped out of the room. The momentum picked up a little but some of the performances were, at the last moment, called off when sudden mind blowing attacks of nerves either froze the artiste to the desk seat or, in one spectacular case, rapidly propelled him out of the classroom hotly pursued by a staff member. I missed some of the acts because I was mentally rehearsing my turn but I can remember Annie singing an abridged version of the Gracie Field hit, "I took my Harp to a Party ...," and a lad named George, whose dad was a stand-up comedian in the Nags Head pub, shared with us two or three laboriously delivered jokes. One that remained with me was:

Mother: Arthur, put some more water in the Goldfish bowl please.
Arthur: I put some in yesterday and it hasn't finished drinking that yet!

A good sense of humour is a valuable if not essential attribute within most adult life styles; more so if you happened to live in Courtney Street in the 1930s. However it does not happen overnight and it has to develop along with all other features that are part of growing up. Accordingly in my 1936 infants' class there were some children who struggled hard to understand the mechanics of humour whereas their level of derision was far in advance of their years. Therefore with more than a hint of mockery they were quick to remind comedian George that water was for fish to swim in rather than drink! In defence of his act he immediately launched a verbal attack upon their intelligence, followed by physical threats upon their person that led teacher to quickly diffuse the situation with well-chosen words of arbitration. She then quickly announced the next act, which was the one before mine, having struggled to salvage her compere's smile and composure from the tightening grasp of anxiety. Originally I did not intend to comment upon the act she introduced, but that was until I realised that its theme centred upon a strange character from the era of our parents and, consequently, he could claim a part of Courtney social history. Following his introduction the boy, whose name I cannot remember, quickly slid over his head an elastic garter to which was attached a false red nose. Thus attired he took his place on stage, bowed, adjusted his nose and declared that he was *Ally Sloper*. The character then swayed around the stage on alternately raised and lowered stiff legs, maintained apart like a pair of open scissors, whilst uttering guttural sounds from a mouth that was permanently open! The actor remained in character despite howls of laughter from teachers and pupils alike and even those, previously referred to as without humour, saw and reacted accordingly to the bizarre performance before them. To us infants the character of Ally Sloper had filtered down through our parents; and even my own father, when in a jocular frame of mind, would entertain the household with his Sloper impersonation. Not to be outdone many Courtney Street fathers, particularly after a Saturday afternoon in the pub, would walk home in the Ally Sloper style much to the humiliation of their wives – if they happened to be gossiping at the terrace end!

A brief literature search revealed that Alexander (Ally) Sloper was an early fictional comic strip character described as a red nosed blustery beer-swilling and lazy schemer. He spent much of his time 'sloping' through back-alleys to avoid his landlord and other creditors. He first appeared in the British Magazine *Judy* which, through the pen and ink of artist and writer Charles H. Ross, was premiered in the year 1867. His popularity rose and in 1884 he featured in his own comic, 'Ally Sloper's Half Holiday,' and was thought to be the influence behind Charlie Chaplin's 'little tramp' character. The arrival of the First World War in 1914 saw massive paper rationing that quickly led to the demise of Ally Sloper and other publications.

A full two minutes went by before laughter and hand clapping finally died down and the performer returned to his seat – only to be badgered by several friends who wanted to try on his false nose. Eventually teacher restored a sense of composure and, after a few complimentary words, handed the performance spot over to me. After a short burst of restrained hand clapping I began, in faltering terms, to explain that my brother and I were learning to play the piano; the distinction being that only he used the keyboard whereas I joined with him on my basket chair. From the moment I mentioned the concept of a basket chair piano I held my viewers in spellbound mode, and even a superficial glance at their facial expressions would have confirmed that I had their full attention. However, even at my 5⅔ years of age, I could detect that their responsiveness arose from them not understanding what on earth I was talking about whilst, in hope, they awaited a punch line that would make everything clear. I felt my confidence beginning to slip, and an unscheduled dash for the classroom door was an attractive option, until I caught sight of Annie smiling and waving encouragement to me from the back of the classroom. Thus inspired I presented a mishmash of words which, much to my surprise, appeared to convey to my audience what I intended to do. Many decades later I looked back, through mature eyes, at my five year old self with full knowledge of what he was trying to say and, as a belated act of completion, I will now record his thoughts in the same adult terms he strove so hard to deliver:

"As I kneel at my basket chair my fingers move in unison to my brother playing his practice piece. Each wicker strut of the chair seat is, to me, a piano key and the imagined sound it liberates is stored in my mind and reserved for a day such as this. Therefore from my mental music book I will now hum to you the opening bars of the overture to the opera *"The Caliph of Baghdad."* With that, and in a series of in-tune la-la-las, I delivered the first seventeen bars of the said work having paid attention to matters of timing and volume variation. As my last 'la' died away I glanced at teacher whose opening applause was quickly followed by the others. I began to walk away when the headmistress called me back and thanked me for reminding her of a much loved piece of music, and went on to explain that it was from a popular comic opera frequently performed in the early 1800s. Whilst I did not understand what she was saying I managed to recognise a very significant point – that I had been openly praised by the head teacher herself! As an aside I will add a 75 year old epitaph of tribute to the 5⅔ year old basket chair pianist whose humming inspired the head mistress, whereas all the wiles of *Ally Sloper*, in the previous act, achieved nothing more than a gentle clap of her hands!"

Rumours of War

In my mind I was now an accomplished public performer and, according to my fertile imagination, had entered the domain of experienced entertainers. As part of my newly found worldliness I paid more attention to our rented slim line Rediffusion radio which had been screwed across adjacent walls, to thus form a room corner triangle. Gone were the days when I would peer up at the rear of the set in the hope I would see little men and women acting out all that could be heard! Initially my favourite radio song was 'Whose Afraid of the Big, Bad Wolf' but I was now beginning to understand and derive enjoyment from such popular Courtney Street radio broadcasts as 'Henry Hall's Guest Night' and the comical exploits of Rob Wilton who, in three years hence, would further boost his popularity when he opened his monologues with, "The day war broke out, my missus said to me, "It's up to you...You've got to stop it." I said, "Stop what?" She said, "The War......."

However there were serious radio moments, which meant nothing to me, but I tried to understand more because I could see that my mother was getting upset and dad was trying to comfort her. "Just because Mussolini has signed a joint action pact with Hitler does not mean that we will go to war," dad stressed as he strode over to the radio and switched it off. "All this government is trying to do is convince us that we should butter-up to Germany so that they will attack Russia and end communism. They are already having a go at the Reds by fighting alongside Franco in the Spanish Civil War." Mother wiped her eyes and stared into the fire and, as if drawing inspiration from the burning coals she half whispered, "It's just that things are going well for us and I don't want anything to split us up." "Nothing ever will," dad replied as he lit up his pipe. "Don't you see, Jim, it will do if the country goes to war? You're 35 years old and you'll almost certainly have to go into the army."

I could feel a distinct atmosphere of uncertainty hanging over our house and, indeed, the entire street; and talk of a possible war with Germany topped most terrace end gossiping schedules. Several of my mates where similarly aware that something was wrong and one in particular grumbled that it was making his mum and dad very bad tempered at his expense. Eventually an older lad came up with a good idea which was to ask the daily newspaper delivery man if we were going to go to war with Germany; for after all he must know because he sold papers that were full of what was going to happen. It was unanimously agreed that something had to be done so we decided to wait at the terrace end and ask him when he came round with the evening papers.

It is not unusual for street residents to take daily happenings for granted and, in later years, to look back and appreciate the tenacity of one who was determined to work regardless of his disabilities. Such was the case of our one legged newspaper delivery man who served the entire length of Courtney Street, astride his fast moving bike, regardless of the state of the weather. Rumour had it that he was a disabled soldier from WW1, but no one was ever sure about that because he was a man who had little to say and he mainly relied upon a nod and a smile as he sped by. In general his occasionally used expressions were restricted to, "Hi-ya mate," or "Is your family alright, missus?" Nevertheless he had great power in his single leg which, seemingly, propelled his bicycle with effortless ease. In open plan terraces his task was simplified because he could stay on his bike and simply push the newspaper through the designated house letter box. When the terrace was composed of houses with front gardens it meant he could ride down the centre access way but, at each garden gate, he had to get off his bike and hop to the letter box that awaited his delivery which, I suppose, is an argument in favour of garden free terraces. However, seemingly unmoved by his physical efforts, he would continue with his deliveries until he had visited every house on his list. I am not aware that 1930s sporting events included disabled people but, where it the case, our newspaper delivery man would have been a potential record breaker and medallist in hopping or cycling events. As he pedalled his bicycle along Courtney Street he would advertise his presence by shouting what sounded to my young ears to be, "Lost his shoe, lost his shoe." He made no attempt to name the victim of this misfortune and left me baffled as to what I could or should do about it. Even at that age I was not one to dismiss and forget, so I secretly decided to be more observant in the event that a solitary shoe may appear in the gutter or someone's front garden. As it turned out I had to wait until I was a few years older when, to my embarrassment, I realised that he was really telling the public, in a voice rich in carrying power at the expense of word clarity, that he was the bearer of the, "Last Issue, Last Issue" of the daily newspaper he sold. Yet another forward step had been taken in my CV of life! But on this particular day when we saw him bearing down on Leonards Avenue, with his one leg pumping away like the connecting rod of a two stroke piston engine, we gathered together as a group and, as he sped by, we shouted the agreed question, "Hey mister – is there going to be a war?" Without breaking his pedal rhythm his loud reply was, "Yes, a bloody big one – if I don't get these papers out on time!"

The Family Structure, Quest for Work and Household Economies

In an earlier draft of my book I began this paragraph with the expression, "Looking back at those tense times in the 1930s ......" which I immediately discarded because it was not a true representation of how I felt. Had I continued with my original wording then I would have reached the impasse of having to explain how I managed to look back upon something that was always with me? These matters are still engraved upon my mind because, as a young boy, I was fortunate to retain all that I heard, particularly when it brought worry and distress to my parents and other people I knew in the street. Obviously I understood only a small part of what, to grown-ups, were serious troubles but these matters were filed away in my mind until the advent of adulthood gave me the answers I longed for.

Even at an early age it was blatantly obvious to me that my father, like many other men in Courtney Street, tried very hard to hide the fact that they were angry and worried men. Their mental turmoil reflected the poor state of the labour market, particularly in the dock and mining industries, which undeniably was filtering down to most other sources of work income. For the welfare of their household most men tried to keep a positive attitude, although their quiet moments were filled with dark spectres of unemployment, short term dole payments and the horror of the Means Test system. This situation was blamed, by many, upon the aftermath of the First World War when, due to the domestic war effort, many of our international trading markets were taken over by other exporting nations. Others have argued that the abysmal failure of the 1926 General Strike, which was blamed upon insipid action by the TUC, led to the 'bosses' stamping even harder upon the working class of this nation. However, it must be understood that this is a massive and contentious topic upon which many authors have advanced diverse theories, of cause and effect, which can have no part in the aims of this book.

Hence I believe it to be important, even at the risk of being repetitive, that I again stress that my objective is to widen my childhood memories to the level where they fully reflect social conditions that affected the lives of many *Courtney Street residents* in the lead up to World War Two. But how did these people live and behave compared with life today?

Role of the father figure

In stark contrast to present day life styles there was a well-defined border separating the duties of father and mother in a typical Courtney Street family home. It was 'misters' job to go out to work and provide financial support for his wife and family. What he earned was his business and the majority of housewives, including my own mother, never knew the content of his weekly pay packet. She relied entirely upon the housekeeping allowance he passed over to her every Friday from a wage packet she never saw. A further example of this curious act of secrecy happened when I was a young teenager and dad had to go into hospital for a few days. From his hospital bed he asked me to go to Tan Yard and collect his Friday pay packet whilst stressing that I must not let mother see it, because its cash content was written beneath his name. I was instructed to take it to him in the afternoon so that he could give mum her housekeeping during the evening visiting period.

Many twenty-first century parents may be aghast at this apparent master to servant relationship, which was the norm in the 1930s, but it must be remembered they were simply following a tradition that had passed down through many generations before them. From my treasure chest of retained memories, mostly gained by 'wigging in' to adult conversations, I was aware that some Courtney Street men retained the lion's share of their earnings whilst their household lived as best it could. In such circumstances it was not uncommon for their wives, in desperation, to fit in early morning and late evening office cleaning duties in order to help feed and clothe their children.

Nevertheless I gained the impression that the majority of wage earners faced up to their domestic responsibilities. I would have imagined that my father's strength enabled him to bring home a goodly wage, earned through the previously described hard grind of the piece work system, and the fact that we could dress according to the weather and regularly eat good basic food supported my belief that he generously subscribed to the weekly budget. My sawyer grandfather who lived in Burleigh Grove was, perhaps, more open than most men and his declared policy was to hold back just enough to buy some Friday pay day goodies (sweets) for me, and a little beer for himself on a Saturday afternoon, and the rest went to 'mother.' Additionally the average 'man of the house' was expected to understand wider national issues and, to the best of his ability, act as guide and mentor to the household within his care.

Mother's role in the house

Courtney Street women, in the 1930s, had a very flexible job description – to say the very least. As they grew up from youngsters they were trained by their mothers in the art of dealing with a broad range of household tasks which, in the absence of modern appliances, were very labour intensive. In parallel they had to bear and raise children and still retain enough energy to do the washing, shopping, cooking, cleaning, knitting and be ready to greet 'mister' home after his hard day at work. An additional requirement was to be inventive in order to balance the weekly allowance and ensure money was put aside for the rent, insurance man and club man among others. Most Courtney Street households took out a 'club' which involved a weekly payment towards an agreed savings target which, when reached, meant that the payer was given written authority (club check) to purchase whatever from a shop within the system; as indeed most were in return for a discount payment to the club agency. Along the length of Courtney Street there were many examples of how the majority of women worked very diligently to make 'both ends meet', and one in particular had all the elements of a cottage industry. It was the much relied upon technique for making 'clip rugs' which was sometimes referred to as 'prodded carpets'. In simple terms a square of hessian became the backing into which short lengths of rags were prodded (or looped) so that the ends of each rag or the loops formed a hardwearing, warm carpet surface. A combination of artistic ability, and an abundance of coloured rags, often produced carpets that were stunning works of art alive with unique and original pattern formations; all at minimum cost to the household. A shortage of rags often meant that some households had to make do with rugs that appeared to have dog mange but, nevertheless, it was better than walking on cracked and flaking canvas or bare floor boards. It also promoted social gatherings as judged by the number of women I saw sitting out in open plan terraces busy with their rug making, whilst their children chanted skipping rhymes over a rope that spanned the width of the terrace. As in similar activities there was the downside to be faced, and the person who suffered most from clip rug making was the local rag and bone man, who having asked, "Have you any old rags, missus?" and receiving the standard street reply, "Sorry mate. We're either wearing 'em or they're under our feet," would turn on his heels and mutter his way back to his horse and cart tethered to a nearby lamp post.

Let us pause for a moment and fully appreciate the strong and positive attitude that united most families within Courtney Street, despite a never ending list of worries from areas outside their control. They were happy for the day and as for tomorrow – well that was left to look after itself and for many, particularly those households wherein the father figure was unemployed, the next and indeed every other day was beset with problems without a lasting solution.

Health and social issues

On the whole adults in Courtney Street were, in my view, reasonably healthy albeit in a robust and determined style. Their tenacity and resolve to keep family and household fed and happy, whilst ignoring the many pitfalls, took priority over all else including health issues; which they summed through their much used expression, "I haven't got the time to be badly!"

In my boyhood days increased attention was being paid, via the school clinic, to the care of eyesight and teeth. Many adults of my parent's age would visit the Co-op optician or, if funds were very low, they would rummage through a pile of second-hand spectacles on a stall in Hull's open market, until they found a pair that suited their needs. With regard to dental care most of them would, as I mentioned previously, wait until the pain was unbearable then appeal to local dentist Mr Eales to pull the lot out. Exceptions to this were many from my grandmother's generation who had bad memories of street dentistry in the 1800s. In a word they were *terrified* at the thought of sitting in a dentist's chair which led them to make their own arrangements. They were quite prepared to slowly remove the offending tooth using household appliances, not least a dirty pair of pliers, whilst enduring pain beyond imagination. To me this had all the ingredients of a Hammer Horror Movie which, without further ado, I will bring to a close!

However from a positive side street grandmothers introduced a wealth of community derived remedies that were claimed to be cheap, and highly effective, and were used by many Courtney Street families. For example if one of their children began to cough, lose their appetite or develop a temperature then what would they do? Thinking back to those days, both in my home and many others, if a family member was 'badly' then calling the doctor was the last resort because they could not afford to pay his professional fee. Passed down trusted family remedies were very much to the fore and, in our house, a mustard bath was the considered panacea of all ills. The patient, huddled in front of the fire, would sit with their feet in a bowl of hot water in which was dissolved an unspecified amount of mustard; depending upon its availability. Alternatively the simple onion, if eaten raw, was said to cure head colds and reduce high temperatures which did not impress my dad who, in his down to earth way declared, "I'd rather be 'badly' than eat a sodding raw onion!" As a product of 'wigging in' sessions I learned of a woman in Arthur's Terrace who supposedly had been ordered by her doctor to drink a glass of whisky every day – to which my mother declared, "What a good complaint, I wish she would *smit* me with it!" As an aside it is worth mentioning that I often heard the expression 'smit' in the context of passing an illness on to someone else; perhaps it was a colloquialism derived from the word 'smite?'

Again in Arthur's Terrace there lived, allegedly, a man who was warned that he must never get out of his bed and if he disobeyed the doctor's orders, and allowed his feet to touch the floor, then he would immediately drop dead. Apparently his wife believed him and betwixt looking after the house and two kids she managed, with the help of her mother, to fit in three part-time jobs in order to swell their income a little. I mention these 'tongue in cheek' disorders because they were a light hearted cover, adopted by many I listened to, which shielded their constant fear of how they would cope if family illness destroyed their earning capacity; at a time when national trading was in the historic depths of a deep depression.

This was particularly cruel because it made victims out of the most vulnerable of society. Their plight was relatively improved by the abolition of the former poor law, and the terrors of the Union Workhouse, by a fully government funded unemployment benefit scheme which was designed to address cases of real need. The downside was that unemployment benefits were controlled by the previously mentioned strict system of the Means Test, through which inspectors were empowered to ensure that households had no hidden savings or 'unnecessary' items that could be sold. This was deeply resented in Courtney Street and passions remained at critically high levels thus allowing the odious Means Test, like the proverbial bad penny, to randomly creep back into my narrative; as if returning to torment the memory of those who hated it so much.

When my mind returns to Courtney Street in the 1930s I not only recall a host of anecdotes and life styles but, almost uncannily, I feel able to absorb and empathise with their laughter, worries, fears and living nightmares. The latter was always the spectre of Means Test Inspectors ordering them to sell their homes or starve by default. Please be assured that this was their greatest dread because it threatened the welfare of their children, and elderly parents, in their family orientated life style. As my writing progressed I felt more and more the emotional burden they suffered, which would be minimised if I allowed reference to the Means Test to hide within a few words in some isolated paragraph. Surely its presence must be felt throughout my entire narrative much like it was in their lives; as it awaited its demise in the wake of World War Two.

Although they put on a brave face I cannot disguise the fact that poor health was also a problem and, from a young age, I can recall seeing bent and hollow cheeked men and women struggling along the street battling with severe bouts of coughing that, from sheer exhaustion, caused them to lean against anything suitable to recover a little of their strength. Yet many of them, despite their pain, would still try to laugh it off with such expressions as, “My lungs will be on the flags (pavement) in a minute” or “It would save my family a lot of trouble if I sat in the cemetery and, after my last cough, quietly fell into my grave.”

Enter the Grim Reaper and Co-op ‘Divi’ payments

News of someone ‘passing away’ was a regular item on my wig-in network, and condolences followed certain traditions that included closing all front window curtains in the terrace where the death occurred; and they remained closed until the funeral cortege had left the terrace end. Also a close friend of the deceased would go door to door collecting for an inscribed flower vase to stand on the grave as a symbol of neighbourly love for the person who, to use a regular expression, had gone to join their family in heaven. Unless death occurred in hospital the first non-household person to visit the corpse, if it were that of a male person, would be the street barber who would shave his face and tidy up his hair if applicable. The Courtney barber was a man of great character who always reminded me of the then popular film actor Wallace Beery in voice, manner and appearance. He always took a pride in his calling and, from various reports, his cue that he had finished work on the deceased was when he stood back, rubbed his hands, and announced to all present, “There now, doesn’t he look nice. It’s as if he’s smiling in his sleep!”

Funerals were prepared for well in advance of the event and, throughout the street, the life insurance branch of the Hull Co-operative Society was to the fore; mainly because its customers were also shareholders of this organisation. Many brides-to-be were taken to the Co-op (always pronounced as **Corp**) by their mothers and formally enrolled, given their Dividend (**Divi**) number, after which they agreed to pay a refundable £1 membership fee deductible from their first Divi payment. With each purchase from a Corp shop their receipt contained the amount spent, and also their allocated share number, which was known as a '**Corp Slip**' which they would stick on their Divi sheet. When the sheet was full they would add up the Corp Slips, record the total and take the Divi Sheet to a Corp shop. The Divi accrued was then paid in the form of a credit note which could be used in any Corp shop. Hopefully this much abridged description, including local phonetic expressions, is of general interest to those new to the then popular Corp Divi scheme, although absence of the word 'but' may, to some, have suggested that it was without its problems. I would fail you if I did not instantly correct this delusion.

The epicentre of a colossal problem was within my above words, "When the sheet was full they would add up the Corp Slips ....." I would be very aware that our Divi Sheet was full when mother turned off the Rediffusion radio and sat down at the kitchen table; having firmly instructed me, in a voice that meant business, not to make a noise. An eerie sort of stillness fell upon the house wherein the gentle sound of a cinder, falling onto the enamel hearth, was a momentary yet grateful break in our cotton wool existence. Then reality would return when a pencil was slammed down on the table followed by a very loud, "Damn it! I've added it up three times and got three different answers." Dad would then volunteer his services with much the same outcome; only his comment was restricted to a brief, "Sod it," as he stormed back to his chair and buried his head in the Hull Daily Mail. The matter was then left until Jim came home when, without further ado, he would quickly give a confirmed answer after which the Divi Sheet was duly signed. Fortunately I was too young to become involved in this strain upon household tempers but, in all fairness, this was not a problem restricted to our house alone. I am of the opinion that every household in the street dreaded the moment when the Divi Sheet required to be added up; and from a wigged- in terrace end conversation I heard a woman, with an unusual dialect, exclaim that Divi Sheets, "Were enuff to mek a Passon sweea and bon his books" (Were enough to make a Parson swear and burn his books). I can certainly sympathise with them and, in mitigation for my forebears and neighbours, I would argue that it is much easier to add up a column of money using the current decimal system, than to be faced with the same challenge expressed in terms of pounds, shillings, pence, half pence and farthings! (As an aside the farthing went out of circulation in the early 1950s).

It would appear to be the case that Co-op funeral accounts also qualified for a discount, rather than dividend, payment according to this now historic 1938 funeral account for my grandfather, which I have shown overleaf.

It was interesting to note that the account made provisions for a cremation charge which, according to several references, were beginning to become fashionable around that time. However I am not aware of any Courtney Street cremations within my period of comment, although from a young age I heard many adults express their fear of being buried alive. Even my own grandmother tried to make me promise to stick pins into her corpse to make certain that she was well and truly dead.

Perhaps that was in my mind when, at the age of seven, I crouched down and peered over the edge of my grandfather's open coffin so that I had a lateral view of his shrouded chest. After a little while I became convinced that his chest was moving and, as my excitement grew, I blurted out, "He's breathing – Grandad isn't dead!" There was no response because my words were lost within a tumult of voices and wailing from many relatives and friends, who were packed into the Burleigh Grove sham-four as the time for the funeral grew nearer. Eventually I convinced myself that his chest was not moving so I stood up and noticed that his missing left hand ring finger, the hallmark of most sawyers of that era, was more noticeable in death than it ever was when he was alive. As I pondered on that phenomenon I was unceremoniously pulled to one side to make way for the undertaker who had arrived to put the coffin lid in place.

1056

Telephone :
Central 31724
or any Branch number.
After ordinary hours :
Manager's Residence,
436 Anlaby Road, Hull,
Telephone : 32939.

Funeral Undertaking Department.

MEMBER BIE BRITISH INSTITUTE OF EMBALMERS

Registered Office :
26 JARRATT ST.,
HULL,

F. W. Wright, M.B.I.E., Manager.

Mrs. A. E. Dennis,
2, Burleigh Grove,
Courtney St., HULL. 1st April 1938

Dr. to

HULL CO-OPERATIVE SOCIETY LTD.

Re the late George Dennis

1938		£	s.	d.
Mch.25	To Elm Coffin, complete with upholstery, fittings and robes, also special services	9	12	6
	Vehicles	5	-	-
	1 Floral Gates of Heaven		12	6
		15	5	-
	~~Less special Co-operative Discount~~			
		15	5	-
	~~Cremation~~ Interment charges, as per attached official receipt	3	-	-
	Bearers Private			
	Sundry Fees			
	Share No. 14071 If paid by 8th April £1/0/6d. Discount will be allowed			
	This Account is payable at the General Office, Jarratt Street. Business Hours : 10 a.m. to 1 p.m. and 2-30 to 4 p.m., except Thursday close 12 noon and Saturday open until 5 p.m. 2000/H.P.L./MC5616.	£18	5	-
		1	-	1
		17	4	6

I suppose that funeral undertaking departments of the 1930s would have contained a chapel of repose wherein the recently departed could rest amidst sentinel lilies, and pictures of well-fed cherubs showering roses down upon no one in particular, but I was unaware of such being used by the Courtney deceased. Although they were dead they were still 'family' and would remain in the family circle until that final moment when they were lowered into the grave. As a lad I visited many of my mates' sham-four houses, by the back door, because the front room was a shut off sanctuary for someone who, for the first time in his/her life, had the room exclusively to themselves. As soon as his mother was out of sight there would be the familiar whisper, "Do you want to have a look at the dead body?" This was an opportunity not to be missed because many of us had a deep interest in viewing the dead which was almost matched, in later years, by our attachment to collecting cigarette cards.

I do not know to this day why we entered the room on our tip-toes, but I can clearly remember the solemn tick of a clock whilst closed curtains moved gracefully in response to draught from poorly fitting windows. Within the coffin the body lay in its eternal sleep with its hands crossed over its chest, and to complete the viewing my host would carefully turn-back the traditional face veil which, he explained, was there to keep the flies off. Some Courtney bodies lay in their coffin clutching a photograph of someone they hoped to be reunited with but, by far, there was one viewing that will never leave my memory regardless of the passing of time. On the first glance it appeared to be yet another body lying at peace within its coffin, until you caught sight of his right hand, into which had been wedged a pair of spectacles. If such a sight caused a degree of bewilderment then a glance at his left hand would immediately resolve the matter for there, carefully folded, was a copy of the Hull Daily Mail destined to spend eternity with someone with poor eyesight who loved to read it!

When I reflect upon our apparent lack of juvenile compassion I immediately realised that we, when in single years of age, looked upon dying as something that happened to someone much older than us. We didn't understand what it was all about so we simply focussed our attention on the day before us. We did stand in respectful silence when a funeral procession made its slow way along Courtney Street led by the chief undertaker, with his inscrutable expression enriched by his shiny black top hat, duly complimented with flamboyant twirls of his walking cane. Additionally any passing men would remove their caps as a sign of respect and the local beat bobby would come to attention and salute the passing cortege. I only once forgot the solemnity of the occasion when, as a reflex action, I waved to the family funeral car from which my one of my school friends beamed happily at me!

Give us a job please

Despite the shadows of death, illness, poverty and the Means Test daily life still went on which meant that most unemployed Courtney Street men set off on a daily round of seeking work from every conceivable place of employment. Many desperate job seekers would join the early morning throng at the dock gates, furiously waving their caps to attract attention whilst avoiding being pushed to one side by more belligerent applicants. The centre of their attention was a dock foreman standing on a lorry trailer from which he carefully scrutinised the sea of eager faces before him and, from time to time, he would select someone by pointing at him whilst shouting, "You there, that fella with his tie round his bare neck," or "That tall bloke over there with both arms in the air," to be followed by the longed for words, "You're hired!" The fact was that each foreman knew most of the men and their capabilities, and he was also aware of the ships that were in dock and the type of cargoes that had to be unloaded that day. When successive foremen had completed their selection campaigns, and the daily labour market came to an end, the rejected hopefuls would shuffle away either in emotion filled silence or muttering, "I must have gone invisible because the buggers never even looked my way." Clutching their work attendance ticket they would walk the familiar route to the Dole Office, queue their weary way to the clerk and despondently sign on once more. After this the day was theirs. Some would huddle with their mates at street corners with hands deep in their pockets and chin upon chest, gazing endlessly at the uncompromising pavement at their feet. Others would drift to open air meetings led by local Communist party officials who, as if demonstrating their care for the workers, would hand around shreds of tobacco for a much welcomed free 'roll.' It is worth noting that the emergence of an active and rooted Communist Party was one of the features of the crisis decade of the 1930s. The party was overwhelmingly working class. At its head was a talented group of worker- intellectuals led by the Party's general secretary, Harry Pollitt, whose name, perhaps as a product of the Hull accent, came over to me as Harry Pullet reminding me of the chickens my uncle George kept in his back yard!

The quest for income – legal or otherwise

In later years I was told of some frustrated workers whose natural acting ability led them to push back the borders of legality in their quest for family income. One speciality act was to dress in 'home designed' ragged clothing and then carefully rehearse their well-used script; after which they were ready to set out on what was known as a 'Kind Lady' door to door appeal in more affluent areas of Hull. Imagine the scene of pathos that met the gaze of whoever responded to a gentle late evening knocking on the side door of the house. A flickering gaslight above the door would add a yellow pallor to a face tormented with practised concern as, with all the skill of a 1930s Uriah Heap he would, between stifled sobs, relate why he was desperate for help from one whose face displayed such charitable concern. He cared not for himself but for the welfare of his ten dear children and his consumptive wife who had not eaten for two days. Frantically twisting his cap in his hands he would explain that this was the first time he had been reduced to begging and he felt that God had led him to this house and, as a gift for not shutting the door in his face, he would produce from his pocket a simple flower which, with shaking hand, he handed over to the person within the threshold. Fortunately in the poor light it would not be recognised as a flower from their own garden!

Another and perhaps more daring enterprise was to purchase, for a few coppers, fish 'on the turn' from a special stall on the Fish Dock and without further ado offer it for sale as "Cheap fresh fish straight from the North Sea!" For obvious reasons he hawked his basket of dodgy fish far away from Courtney Street and, the moment it was empty, he made a quick exit never to return again!

Then there were the more conventional street operatives who in all types of weather provided a variety of services in return for a small addition to their income. My mother regularly dealt with 'Button Man' whose wide assortment of buttons were carefully set out on a large tray fastened to a belt round his waist, and supported by a strap around his neck; with an umbrella hanging from his belt if needed. He was to all accounts a very popular door to door trader in an area where buttons were always needed to sew onto hand knitted garments.

This brings me to the furtive looking 'Wool Man' with his many skeins of wool packed into two or three hessian bags. No one ever questioned why his wool stocks, that were mainly navy blue in colour, were so very cheap; or why he always knocked upon doors when it was dark, as if he didn't want to over- advertise his presence. Dad had a theory that he was related to Dracula and only came out at night! But no one cared because he asked little for his good quality wool which was a help for strained household budgets. The downside for the children of Courtney Street was that mother had to roll the wool into a ball, and children of all ages were compelled to hold the skein, looped over the backs of both hands, whilst under strict instructions to hold it tight to avoid getting it into a tangle. Believe me in my claim that hell hath no fury like an enraged mother, faced with untangling great lengths of wool, caused by the skein holder losing concentration! Despite such setbacks we children, myself included, would eventually appear in the street wearing our newly knitted navy blue socks, jersey and tie.

Another street agent was Sam the knife sharpener whose grinding wheel was mounted on his bike handlebar and powered by a chain connected to the bike pedal in place of the one that normally drove the rear wheel. Much to his irritation the sight of him pedalling furiously, with a cascade of shimmering sparks issuing from a knife held onto his grindstone, attracted many children who were fascinated by the sight of an 'extraordinary bonfire night display'. But we kept our distance because his temper was as sharp as the products of his grindstone.

Then, as ever, we had our street hardy perennials in the form of firewood hawkers, Old Moore's Almanac sellers, Lucky Joan the Wad vendors, street singers and gypsy peg sellers whilst not forgetting the Hurdy-Gurdy player who regaled us, and in particular the pub leavers, with his traditional "Sweet Rosie O'Grady" followed by his still uncertain rendering of the "Rose of Tralee."

Poverty and family stability

Sadly there were times when, for a list of reasons led by severe cash flow problems, despair finally destroyed the stability of what seemed to be a minority of Courtney Street homes. I learned of one such case from my little play den in the corner of the room securely boxed in by the couch where, to all intents and purposes, I was quietly playing with a lump of plasticine. In actual fact I was 'wigging in' as a visitor related to my mother the tragic account of a family breakdown, in Wesley Terrace, near to the school. Apparently her husband witnessed all that went on and gave his help and support to the family. The original story was delivered piecemeal, with several digressions, and was later expanded with data from other sources thus enabling me to present the following revised account: -

Most of the Courtney Street men were hard workers, good husbands and fathers, in return for the occasional night out in the pub or enjoying a house 'do' that I will touch upon later. When such men reluctantly swelled the ranks of an estimated country-wide figure of four million unemployed they would, in the fullness of hope, patiently submit to a daily ritual of pleading for work; only to be turned away from dock, sawmill or other work entrances as, in the words of some of them, "Like yapping stray dogs at the door." I do remember the name of the man at the centre of this overheard account but, out of respect, I will defend his privacy and simply refer to him as 'Jack.'

On this day Jack, together with his mates, gazed in despair at a factory gate that had been unceremoniously slammed shut in their faces. His day had started badly when his wife, who had little money, fuel and food in the house raged at him to stop being a mouse and stand up for his family's needs ...... and the exhortation to, "Wake up and get a damned job," echoed in his ears as he trudged along the terrace, with an empty stomach and a sad heart, at 5 o'clock on a cold late Autumn morning. Jack was by nature a quiet man who was well liked by his mates and, in common with most other men, was known by a nickname. His was 'Professor' because of his deep love for reading and learning from whatever came his way. Not surprisingly his studies widened his vocabulary to include many non-Courtney Street expressions such as "we must make haste" and "can you spare me a moment please?" rather than "'urry-up" and "cum ere will ya" respectively – to quote but two examples. He owed his broader than normal vocabulary to a friend who worked on Chapman Street tip and salvaged anything readable for him. Additionally, when he could afford one old penny, he would buy a copy of the Hull Daily Mail which added to his local knowledge and gave credibility to his 'Professor' title.

Throughout successive job seeking ventures the same group of men had stuck together, and had been rejected together, for reasons that were all variations of the expression, "Sorry mate – there's nowt going ere." As the last vibrations of the slammed factory gate faded away Jack would quickly defuse rising passions, with a range of calming expressions, that rarely failed to restore normality; but on this particular day, and for the first time, he offered no words of advice. Jack had been tested to his absolute limit both at home and in his quests to find work and had finally cracked. Even his friends sensed a difference in his self-control as a real life Jekyll and Hyde scenario was, seemingly, played out before them. His once placid face became a crimson facade of twisted hatred, through which a demonic snarl was matched by his bulging eyes. His mates were stunned into total silence as Jack screamed at those behind the closed gate, "You Bastards!" after which he picked up a large stone and hurled it through the gatehouse window! Immediately the spell was broken and the now demented Jack was swept off his feet and carried away along a series of side streets and alleys, as if the proverbial 'hounds of hell' were close on their heels. Eventually they found hiding places in the backyard of a derelict house and restored their breath amidst a pile of bricks, discarded furniture and rotting timber, whilst convincing each other that no one had followed them. "When the bosses pick up on this one they will say we are Communists trying to start a revolution. Someone once said that a brick though a window is all that it needs," opined a voice seemingly from a rotting couch. "Which means we could all hang for this," muttered another from the roofless shell of a coal house. "And we all know that this government lives in fear of a Russian revolution over here," added a figure whilst rising to his feet and brushing dust from his person. Most of them agreed the best solution was to go home and swear that they had been nowhere near this district and, as they stumbled over the rubble to firmer ground they notice that Jack was heading in the opposite direction. "Where are you off to Jack," was the obvious question which was quickly answered with, "I'm off to the pub." "But you don't drink," replied a disbelieving voice. "I do now!" was the unexpected reply from a fast disappearing Jack who, according to another report, was followed by a close mate whose name I never knew.

Jack was new to beer and simply had no head for it; so much so that his friend rounded up the rest of the gang to help get him home. Predictably he was, in a short space of time, totally legless and had to be carried back to Courtney Street and, quite surprisingly, his wife was very concerned about him – more so when she heard the full account from his mates about the now notorious broken window incident. "I never knew he had it in him!" she smilingly replied with no small amount of admiration. Household incidents involving a man being carried home, by a vocal group of men, never failed to attract the attention of many neighbours both local and nearby who, with arms folded, would gather around in silent awe. On this occasion they would not be hushed because they had quickly picked up the story and without hesitation they welcomed a hero in their midst! "Good for you Jack! We all ought to follow you and be out there smashing their windows" and "Stand for Parliament Jack you'll have my vote!" were two of many loud cries of support that filtered through the alcohol bemused mind of the now famous Jack, the Champion of the Poor!

By contrast the factory manager was furious and, according to witnesses, almost did a jig of rage at the sight of his broken gatehouse window. Quickly he summoned the police and gave them a list of names of all those who had applied for employment on that day. Officers of the law painstakingly interviewed every name on the list and, according to our friendly Courtney Street beat bobby, those interviewed consistently replied with "What window?" or "I didn't hear or see owt." To this day the case remains unsolved!

In an age when Job Seekers were not given a State Allowance they either had to find work or watch their families suffer both in health and living standards. From first-hand experience I know that the majority of Courtney Street men did take their responsibilities seriously and, as I have previously mentioned, my career achievements were a continuation of the tenacity and dedication I learned from such men.

With hindsight I can assure everyone that life in Courtney Street was varied and frequently lively but never, within my experience, could it be described as boring. Whilst much effort was put into generating household income there were other street 'happenings' that were varied yet highly original to my then young mind. So let us begin with ....

Showdown at Courtney Corral

Like almost any other street Courtney was not without its terrace or street rows – mostly between women and mainly over children. I believe conflicts stemmed from weather conditions because most flare-ups occurred on hot summer days, during the mid-point of school holidays, when time seemed to move very slowly. Street rows followed a standard pattern in that they were fiery, noisy and of short duration; and ended up with the antagonists not talking to each other for a few weeks. However I can remember a colossal row that erupted one hot day over a boy who got very wet during a street water fight – but I would argue that it was more the shock of the weapon used to discharge the water that reduced him to tears.

Before I begin allow me to stress that the principle warhead in a traditional street water fight was a water pistol; and there can be no doubt about that. I concede that warfare, for whatever reason, encourages experimentalists to design alternative weapons but, when it comes to water based confrontations, a well handled water pistol reigns supreme – or it did before this day was over. For example a bucket of water was difficult to hide and attempts to throw its contents at an advancing enemy required stronger arms than those available – as confirmed by a front line of self-drenched defenders as they fled the battle field. Another very ingenious idea was to fill a balloon with water, tie the end, and then pressurise it by holding it in a bear hug. A pre-briefed colleague would then produce a pin and prick a hole in the part of the balloon facing the enemy. Had it gone according to plan a relentless stream of water would, under controlled conditions, have left the balloon and driven off the opposition in total disarray. As it happened the pin hole immediately became a deep split and its holder went home wearing a pair of soaked trousers.

However I must leave you with what was a *piece de resistance* of water warfare that I was honoured to witness; in fact it has remained with me to this day. The defending 'army' was, in this instance, led by one who employed subterfuge in the form of 'borrowing' his older brother's bike pump which, in suction mode, he filled with water. He then cunningly concealed the pump beneath his coat. For outward appearances he even held, in a pretend shaking hand, a battered water gun that he was ready to drop when his moment came. We must remember that he faced water pistols requiring strong fingers for maximum effect. Also those same fingers must be capable of resisting the pain of rapidly pumping a trigger that punished inferior effort with a weakening jet of water, thus promoting derision rather than fear. Whereas one mighty blast of water from his bike pump, suddenly produced from beneath his coat, was sufficient to put his drenched opponents into panic stricken flight! The victor was left verbally drunk with bragging rights whilst the victim, who received the initial impact as the torrent scythed through the crowd, ran home '*ruoring*' (a popular local word for crying).

The inevitable confrontation between the two mothers hinged on a claim that the pump-action cowboy was a bully whereas the counter-claimant maintained they were only banes (bairns) larking about, so she should shut her big gob!

Highlights from the yard toilet

I must admit that in the mid-1940s I placed my first and last bet on a horse race; after all I was then a wage earner and I looked upon this as an investment opportunity! Trying not to look guilty I nonchalantly slid into a side passage and furtively tapped on the back door of the Courtney Street bookie, who I knew because his son had been at school with me. I slowly delivered my rehearsed lines and committed two shillings (ten pence) in the form of one shilling each way on the famous racehorse 'Prince Regent.' Later that day this horse romped home an easy winner having left the field standing. Elated with the result and clutching my winnings tightly in my pocket I resolved, there and then, to hold on to my good fortune by never gambling again.

My inward promise was never broken and is unlikely to be ... unless ...unless someone asks me about life in Courtney Street in the 30s, when I would willingly wager that, within five minutes, I would be asked about our backyard toilet. Like the Prince Regent Horse episode, I would be on a certain winner!

Our much maligned yet highly essential water closet has, perhaps, generated more stories than any other house fitment throughout the ages. Few would deny that it is known by many names and, in Courtney Street, it was consistently referred to as the **Petty**. Perhaps it was derived from the Northumbrian **Netty** although we cannot be sure which name came first. Another line of thought takes us over to France where their toilet is known as the "little room" which in their language is *petite chambre*. Hence in its journey over the English Channel ***petite*** may have been corrupted to **Petty** which again is pure speculation.

As a child in that era it was all that I knew and, according to parents and grandparents, I was very fortunate to have a modern water toilet in our backyard; which was their cue to launch into life with an earth closet and the spectre of night soil collectors. As they warmed to their theme I would be told about life in back to back houses and how they would have to hold their breath when the collection man carried the bin, and its ghastly contents, through the house followed by a flotilla of excited flies. Even worse was their much repeated and graphically added-to account of a time when the pan fell off the carrier's shoulder, in the middle of the living room which, out of respect for my readers, I will end there. Perchance you have just finished a meal or, even worse, you may have been looking forward to starting one! Terrace talk always maintained that the older end of Courtney Street, beginning with Arthur's Terrace, started life with earth toilets. As time went by these were progressively converted to water closets which led to the demise of what was a wooden box, with a hole in the middle, with a bin of ashes as the receptacle.

Literally from such ashes arose the toilet unit we know today with a seat that can be raised or lowered at will. According to street legends, upheld by several older residents, some earlier tenants viewed their new water toilets with suspicion, yet were elated at the sight of the toilet seat. In an instant it was removed and fixed to the bedroom wall as a frame for a cherished yet faded sepia photograph of aunt whoever, frowning down at them from the depths of her mid-19th century best dress. Critics regularly poured scorn on this claim but there were those who, to quote, swore on their mother's grave that they had seen and touched several of those extraordinary picture frames. In fact one old lady, in her view, sealed the authenticity of toilet seat picture frames by claiming she had seen one with Christmas decorations draped around it so that, as they say, is that!

Perhaps you have read enough about toilet related topics so I will skim over a most unusual event that dominated the winter of 1938. You will recall the infamous Whitechapel murders of the 1890s, committed by the so-called Jack the Ripper that still captures media attention? Well Courtney Street had a junior version of this mystery in which someone, under the cover of darkness, would sneak into backyards and smear jam on the seat of unlit toilets. I will leave to your imagination the effect this had upon many night time victims who sat upon it and, despite intense vigilance and terrace end speculation, the culprit was never caught; which was perhaps as well. Suddenly the jam attacks stopped as mysteriously as they had begun and exploits of the *Phantom Jam Smearer*, like those of its Whitechapel counterpart, are counted among the great unsolved mysteries of all time.

Finally I must admit that our toilet in the yard, although primitive by modern standards, was infinitely better than all I heard about the infamous earth toilets. But I tend to forget this when reality often reminds me of ever damp walls and bulging plaster, with flakes of distemper falling on a scoured stoned floor that never fully dried. A distinct chill of winter was a permanent resident despite changing seasons in the yard outside. It had a small frosted side window that served no obvious purpose; because light and ventilation were provided by a substantial gap between the top of the door and the upper door frame. Such a design was, of course, ideal for those who enjoyed being snowed or rained upon whilst attending to those essential needs of nature. Electric or gas lights, of which there was a mixture in the 1930s, did not extend to the 'petty' although a blend of instinct and light from the back kitchen window was just sufficient to guide those taken short.

As a point of historical interest I must record that many men, under the cover of darkness, preferred to open the kitchen door and discharge their cause for concern straight into the yard sink. Conversely there were some hardy souls who would visit the toilet in the small hours of the morning, although the vast majority preferred the option offered by chamber pots which, to this day, still survive as ornamental plant pots or modern art receptacles for large decorative candles.

The backyard toilet could, if it were able, boast semi-detached status with the adjacent coalhouse and that together they formed an effective partnership essential to the well running of any house in any street. It would be hard to deny such a claim and, in parallel, the objectives of this book would not be fully met if, for whatever reason, I failed to release my memories of those 'two rooms in the yard.' Hence let us now turn our attention to the coalhouse.

Tales from the coalhouse.

Whatever the weather, save if there happened to be several inches of snow on the road, the Co-op (Corp) coalman would arrive in the street and alert all interested parties with his bellowed version of 'Coal' which, to my ears came out as "Coo-well... Coo-well." Having first tethered his horse to a lamp post he would then serve his regular customers, of which my mother was one. She knew it to be 'his day' so on the first burst of "Coo-well" she would open the coalhouse door, unlock and open the yard door to the passage then station herself in the yard to count the bags as they were delivered. Not that she distrusted him but.....well times were hard.

As a young boy I was amazed at the strength of the coalman as he shuffled down the narrow passage with an enormous bag of coal on his back that almost doubled him in half. His faltering steps, reflecting the weight he was carrying, caused him to ricochet from wall to wall as he made slow progress to our backdoor where he slowly turned into our yard. Having carefully positioned himself he drew a deep breath then tipped his bag into the coalhouse. His last act was to recover his cap which had followed the coal to its destination. In winter time coal levels were dangerously low but, as summer approached, stocks would build up and were contained by fitting a series of boards edgewise upon one another, to form a sort of dam; thus preventing an avalanche of coal when the door was opened.

A coalhouse was not complete until it had shelves bodged out of old lard boxes fitted high up on the back wall, upon which tins of tar, paint and my dad's last for mending boots found refuge. Several Courtney Street tenants found more unusual outlets for the back wall of their coalhouse which, if practised today, would have landed them in severe trouble. The first was rabbit hutches fastened to the coalhouse wall in which the unfortunate animals eked out their lives in a cold, black cavern of coal and cobwebs until their weight gain earned them a place in the cooking pot. I know this for a fact because a school friend would, as a favour, proudly open his coalhouse door for me to 'admire' his dad's rabbits munching coal dust coated lettuce leaves. He was probably aware of my sensitivity when he invariably added that the 'one on the left' would be the next on their dinner plates. That was my cue to instantly leave the scene on the pretext that mother was waiting for me. But that was not the end of it.

There was another coalhouse attraction that fascinated all children and many adults, and drew them in from the length and breadth of Courtney Street. In one of the mid-terraces there lived a merchant seaman who at the end of one trip brought home with him .....a monkey! Yes, you read correctly that a monkey came to live in Courtney Street and it spent most of its time attached to a lead nailed to a coalhouse shelf. It was not impressed by a procession of street viewers and would, in its way, hurl offence at them in the form of monkey chatter. When that failed to drive them away it would leap from the shelf and, with uncanny accuracy, hurl lumps of nutty slack at their fast scattering figures. In fairness it must be recorded that its owner often walked the street with his monkey on his shoulder which greatly pleased the creature, in that it happily accepted and ate chips nervously handed to it by passing admirers. In fact the owner of the Sunkist Fruit Store in Dansom Lane proudly gave it a ripe banana which, to the applause of fascinated viewers, it carefully peeled and ate. In the longer term I have no idea what happened to Courtney Street's adopted monkey, other than an unconfirmed report that the hurdy-gurdy player had failed in his quest to engage it as part of his street act.

There is justification to argue that in every community of human beings we will find a wide assortment of behavioural patterns from which a special group will graduate to earn the status of "characters." Courtney Street was not short of these partisans of odd behaviour and, to the fore, were a couple that my grandmother nicknamed 'Dick and Liddy'; thus making it easy for me to protect their real names. Liddy is best described as a bundle of fading shawls from which, without warning, a pale thin face would suddenly pop-out, peer suspiciously around her, and quickly retire behind a veil of frayed edges. Nevertheless despite her apparent fragility, complicated with a speech deformity, she held full control over Dick and he was quick to conform to her every word.

By contrast Dick was a well-built, happy-go-lucky man who asked little of life other than access to a glass of whatever, as long as it contained alcohol. He was happy to take on casual work and for a couple of bob (10 pence) he would often help the milkman to push his heavy cart, particularly up the slope leading to Dansom Lane railway crossing when the road was icy and slippery. He also enjoyed helping the coalman and would happily deliver bags of coal which, because of his strength, were no problem to Dick. He was not a scholar and his only claim to academic fame was when, out of context and not knowing what he was talking about, he would stand up in the pub and bellow, "A verb is a doing word." After those words of advice, which was the last remnant of his school knowledge, he would solemnly sit down in anticipation of a free drink; and he was rarely disappointed. Dick was well liked because he generated and attracted laughter which, together with essential living requirements, was very scarce in the 1930s. He was a good worker providing he was slowly and carefully told what his job was all about. There was little point in giving him written instructions because he couldn't read and he was a total stranger to decision making. His main work outlet was that of a temporary assistant coalman from which I am able to share with you a 'happening' which captivated the entire street and, in the process, led to Dick receiving several free pints in return for his version of the event. As a lad I, too, was intrigued to hear this exciting account in which I was not disappointed because parents and neighbours were very happy to repeat the same unusual story, over and over again, to anyone who would listen. This was a great help to me and I was able to put together several versions and finally commit to memory the following, which is a fair representation of what happened on a memorable day in 1938 ....

..........Dick and his coalman boss had completed a busy morning delivering coal in several streets off Holderness Road and had stopped for a midday break at the top end of Courtney Street. The horse, complete with its nose-bag, was fastened to a lamp post and the coalman again reminded Dick that he was going to disappear for a while, but would return later in the afternoon. In the interim it had been agreed that, after lunch, Dick would deliver the last remaining ten bags of coal then sit on the cart to await his master's return. He assured his boss that he could easily finish the work off, more so, because he knew the houses having delivered there before. The coalman's last act before he left was to give Dick some money with the instruction to go over to Lipton's and buy something to eat.

With several glances at his fast disappearing boss Dick began to slowly walk towards Lipton's until the coast was clear. Then he immediately swung around on his heels and, dodging between moving traffic, he was through the door of the Nags Head pub in record time. Around one hour later he emerged from the pub seemingly without the same confident control of his legs that had marked his entrance. Back at the coal cart he sat for a while on the driving bench and then, quite suddenly, his mind became clear as to what was expected from him. With all haste he leapt off the cart, quickly hoisted a bag of coal onto his back, and began his afternoon schedule of deliveries ....

............which, as it happened, coincided with Mrs Thompson (not her real name) sitting down in her kitchen waiting for her tea to mash.

Suddenly she became aware of someone kicking the backyard door; but before she could do anything about it the bolt flew across the yard as the door burst open to admit a man with a bag of coal on his back. He twice turned a full circle, as if looking for something, and then he opened the toilet door and promptly tipped the coal in and, to compound her horror, he followed it and lay flat on his face without visible movement. Nervously clutching her pinny she whispered at the prone figure, "Are you alright?" and the absence of an answer sent her screaming up the passage and into the street. A sawmill worker responded to her cries and, after a few words with her, he went to investigate the so called dead man in her toilet. A few yards behind him Mrs Thompson, now followed by a group of interested neighbours, paused in the yard doorway and looked on anxiously as the sawmill worker cum medic examined a blackened figure who appeared to be at ease on its bed of coal. Standing up he gave his diagnosis that was brief and to the point, "Nowt to fret about misses, he's as drunk as a village parson. I'll help him back to his cart!"

Naturally the ripple effect of this incident must have lapped upon every Courtney Street doorstep and, over seventy years later – it is now lapping upon ours! It certainly elevated Mrs Thompson into the public eye and, according to the winds of gossip, she would recline on her black horse hair couch in the best traditions of Marlene Dietrich, without a cigarette holder, and relive her experience time and time again. Her theme was that divine intervention had compelled her, against her intent, to immediately vacate the toilet. "It was," to use her reported words, "As if a cloud of goodwill had gathered me up and safely set me down on this couch only seconds before the back door burst open and a large man, with a bag of coal on his back, literally spun into my yard. He then, as if possessed by the devil, flung open the petty door and emptied his bag of coal upon the very spot where, moments before, I sat in contemplation. After this he was struck down as if dead!" Thus delivered it was her cue to pause and sob until her glass was filled from the communal jug of beer.

To a large extent I can appreciate her concern. Let us imagine ourselves sitting upon that same toilet, perhaps reading a square of newspaper taken from a nail on the wall, when suddenly the door is thrown open and a sack of best Barnsley nuts suddenly lands in our lap! Surely some of mankind's most horrific nightmares are fermented from incidents such as that?

But Mrs Thompson had the last laugh when she ended her account with….. "And the crux of the matter was that I did not deal with that coalman and, more to the point, I had not even ordered any coal. It so happened that the silly bugger got the wrong house; and my old man said, as he happily shovelled it into our coalhouse, that he will not get it back!"

The Old Lamp Lighter of Long, Long Ago.

The tale of the Phantom Jam Spreader was but one example of the need for effective public lighting which, although in place, was more labour intensive than it is today. At set intervals along both sides of Courtney Street were lamp posts that, in common with most other streets in Hull, were fuelled by coal gas which, if left to burn as a jet, would have very little luminosity to offer its surroundings. This was overcome by containing the flame within a mantle which glowed very brightly when heated but, because of the nature of its chemistry, it rapidly became very fragile even after a short period of use. This fact quickly became known to those of a destructive nature when they discovered that the impact, of well-aimed snowballs on the lamp casing, was sufficient to break the mantle within and plunge the area into darkness. These acts of vandalism were, fortunately, minimised by the regular presence of the street policeman, whose measured tread and nonchalant flick of his shoulder cape left nothing to doubt that he was a man who must never be trifled with. His almost guttural command of, "Cum ere you lot," had a twofold effect upon the miscreants before him. They either froze to the spot in fear or took to their heels as his, "I know where you live," reminder reverberated in their ears. They ran on knowing it was only a matter of time before their dad was involved, because the street Bobby knew all who lived on his beat like unto the back of his hand. Courtney Street and indeed all other residential areas had much to thank the no-nonsense beat policeman for. His friendly advice and down to earth manner of keeping the peace was highly appreciated, and he was looked upon as an extended family member of many law abiding households.

The street gas lights, thus protected, continued to dispense a wide pool of flickering yellow light to the advantage of both pedestrians and road users alike. It must be remembered that these gas lights did not turn themselves on automatically but relied upon an appointed lamplighter and his long pole with a hook on the end, to reach up and activate a lever switch, which turned on a jet of gas that was immediately ignited by a pilot light. This procedure was reversed at an agreed time following the onset of dawn and, naturally, the entire practise was dispensed with during war years when the blackout became a way of life – which is a later story. Perhaps, in our journey, we should not forget the lamp lighter men who controlled those beacons of guidance regardless of storm force weather which, at times, they preferred over a following of young boys with their incessant questions and requests dominated by "Giz a go mister." I feel certain that his memory was honoured when, in 1946, Jim Ed Brown wrote and had published a song about a street gas lighter. It had an attractive melody that still lingers in my mind; and its lyrics began with:

> "He made the night a little brighter wherever he would go,
> The old lamp lighter of long, long ago."

Its popularity was confirmed by the radio singer Dorothy Squires as her voice drifted through many open windows, and it was well used as a slow foxtrot at the nearby Abbey Street dance hall; which again is another story.

As an aside quite a number of Courtney Street houses in the 1930s were without electricity and relied upon gas lighting that, in turn, depended upon the gas mantle as described above. Due to their fragility they often had to be replaced which alerted a terrace end 'think tank' to conclude that a war with Germany, which was gaining momentum, would decimate their availability. This, much to the amazement of local shops and the delight of their suppliers, set off a chain of panic buying that continued for several months.

In his Master's Steps he trod

I have always believed that a great source of learning is to be alert to your surroundings and mentally record all that you see and hear. That is why I particularly looked forward to going for walks with my dad who enjoyed nothing more than, to use his expression, 'stretching his legs.' Apart from his company there was, for me, a great bonus of knowledge to be gained from his desire to explain the background and purpose behind many of the sights we saw and he never failed to answer, in detail, my unending stream of questions. We explored High Street and the Old Town and, knowing he had my interest, he would put on his best mysterious voice and tell me that a certain old building was haunted by the ghost of an ancient sea captain. He obviously told it well because despite myself I found myself walking closer to him and, somehow, my hand had taken hold of his! Then there was the joy of spending time on Hull Pier watching the paddle ferry arrive and depart for Lincolnshire, after which we would walk along Princes Dock side when dad would describe the nationality and purpose of the many ships moored there. My special joy was to run between the dockside railway lines pretending to be a 'puffer-train' – but I don't do that now! On other occasions we would go to East Park where I had the joy of running myself into the ground, while dad sat on the grass puffing away at his pipe.

He regularly took me with him when he visited his mother who lived in long gone Parrott Street which ran off Selby Street and, as a special treat, we would take the tram to town, and walk along Anlaby Road to Selby Street which, in those days, was just before the railway gates. Again, I was introduced to landmarks new to me including the ivy covered former Union Workhouse which stood on the site of the present Hull Royal Infirmary. I would listen in awe as he told me, from what he saw when a boy, how poor families were split up and sent to the Workhouse which, from its title, meant they worked hard for minimal food and poor living conditions. He explained that the days of the Poor Law had gone and the building was now used as a Council run residential shelter for elderly and infirm people. I clearly remember looking at its residents sitting on the front lawn in the shade of weeping willow trees; no doubt feeling thankful that they no longer had to crush stones or pick oakum (Ref.6).

Come march with me

Then we went on other walks, or perhaps I should say political parades, which by their nature were different but no less instructive to my developing mind. These organised weekend processions were composed of many men from Courtney Street and other areas of Hull. Some were chanting slogans and others held banners proclaiming "We Want Work" or "Food for our Families" together with several other placards displaying variations on these themes. I remember in one parade there were two men carrying a gibbet from which swung a stuffed dummy with "Means Test" pinned to its chest. Another enjoyable feature for me was that I met up with several of my school mates who were also proudly marching with their dads.

Obviously we had only a limited understanding of what it was all about although I knew it was organised by the Communist Party which, according to the many dads around me, was the only party that cared for the working classes. The parade ended with a mass meeting held on Corporation Field which, in the 1930s, was a moderate sized plot of land fringed with fruit market buildings and situated directly opposite Park Street Technical College. When everyone was assembled we were addressed, through a hand held megaphone from a central stage, by a slow moving queue of guest speakers. Little that was said made sense to me at the time but, as I got older, I was able to look back and reconstruct topics that were bothering them. Two main areas of contention inflamed the passions of several speakers, almost to the point of hysteria, and these were the anticipated war with Germany and the evils of the Means Test system. Whatever ones views were it had to be conceded that it was no small feat of oration that led the large gathering to conclude that threats of war and the Means Test, were both designed by the bosses to intimidate the working classes!

Nevertheless the Communist viewpoint was gaining momentum. Terrace end debating groups and clusters of drunken men meandering home were also quick to denounce all this talk of war as propaganda, started by the bosses, in order to bring the working classes into line. Nevertheless the topic was not dismissed out of hand and, if anything it gained momentum both around the fireside and out in the street. Naturally I paid great attention to all that was being said and, more and more, I was aware that a wind of impending war was rattling many doors and windows in Courtney Street. Despite themselves most households were soon caught-up in a drive to horde as much non-perishable food as possible and anything that could be stockpiled, money permitting, was duly added to the pantry top shelf and held in reserve. If any food commodity had a reasonable shelf life then it was bought; even down to jars of mustard which mother loved *only if it was German Mustard!* Cans of precooked meat sold under the trade name of **SPAM** had suddenly appeared on display stands, at a reasonable price, and were soon challenging tinned corned beef and condensed milk for pride of place in most war orientated pantries. As ever my curiosity was whetted and I just had to know what SPAM stood for. I lodged my question with several adults and never lost heart despite a run of, "How the hell should I know" based answers, until one of my Courtney teachers advanced his belief that it was derived from **SP**iced h**AM** – I cannot confirm the accuracy of his definition but it was, without doubt, a clever and most impressive answer!

Time to get my hair cut

In my immediate life I gave up trying to understand why almost every adult had to talk incessantly about war related topics when, to my mind, there were far more important matters much closer at hand. Take for instance the fact that it was April 1938 and my 7th birthday was imminent, yet I still had no idea if my weeks of campaigning (or nattering as mother called it) had persuaded anyone to buy me a clockwork train set. They could go on at length about Adolph Hitler and someone called Benito Mussolini, who probably had an abundance of train sets to play with, yet my needs were never mentioned. That was not until my mother suddenly confronted me with the fact that my hair wanted cutting before my birthday and that she was, there and then, taking me to the previously mentioned Courtney Street barber. Her policy was to open his shop door and thrust me in with instructions to, "Take plenty off." After which she paid him and left me to wait my turn in a small 'salon' that was filled with men, pipe smoke and boisterous conversation. I immediately recognised the usual faces sitting on what was *their chair* because, to some elderly men, it was their only social outing which they keenly looked forward to. Even their elderly dogs slept on *their* bit of floor and, by way of coincidence, flicked their ears in unison as hair clippings constantly fell upon them.

When I was a little older I realised that Courtney Street was unique in that it had a barber's shop that was really a social club, with the option of having a shave or haircut if one felt like it. Throughout this the vocal yet likable Courtney Street barber commendably held together two or three independent debates, whilst either shaving or trimming the hair of an equally vocal customer. He wore a brown dust coat that was fraying at the cuffs and, as he bent over, his trusty comb always hung dangerously from his top pocket yet, while I was there, it defied gravity by remaining in its appointed place. He did not have a wide range of appliances yet his essential items were at hand. The sink contained his shaving soap and brush whilst above it hung his sharpening strop which honed his cut-throat razor to the standard required. When not in use his prime tools of trade, namely his razor, scissors, hand clippers and hair brushes were within easy reach on his bench as they awaited the call to serve either the living or the dead. It was all the same to our street barber who accepted most jobs, even if they were only vaguely related to hairdressing.

I never knew when it was time to sit in his dreaded chair, and come to think of it neither did anyone else. The Courtney barber, despite his continual chatter, had an unerring memory for whose turn it was; which he probably activated whilst vigorously shaking a thread-bare sheet taken from the neck of the last customer. Before the dislodged hair clippings had settled upon customers and dogs alike his voice boomed out, "OK young-un, it's your turn." Throughout the relatively short process I loathed almost every moment of what was being done to me although, in fairness, I was impressed by the fast opening and closing motion of his hand clippers. I also noticed that as hair built up on the back of his hand and coat cuff he would scatter it around all present by a deft back-flick from his wrist and over his shoulder. "There now, what do you think to that?" he roared as his two brushes, astride a left side hair parting, flattened down what was left of my Brilliantine soaked hair. In front of me was a wall mirror which, probably, was a refugee from the mid-Victorian era. In its prime it may have been a work of art but now, almost deprived of its silvered background, it offered a passable likeness in only three small islands of reflection; which were more than enough to confirm my worst fears!

In some Courtney Street houses, and I know this to be a fact, there were mothers who took pride in cutting their offspring's hair themselves. Where the boundary between skin and hair line fell was dependant not on some expensive implement but, rather, on the humble kitchen basin. This was placed on the subjects head, in helmet style, and any exposed hair was promptly cut away; whilst remaining stubble was removed with ' mister's' cut throat razor. When released into the street he would immediately be taunted with, "Hey, all of you – come and have a laugh at basin crop!" I mention this as a combination of social history, and my thoughts as a despondent seven year old, obliged to gaze at myself in the Courtney barber's ancient mirror. Who would condemn me for comparing the image before me with victims from the fore-said kitchen bowl procedure? There would be little to choose between the traumas wreaked by either process; other than the fact that my lack of hair was, in my view, consistent with the use of an egg cup rather than a conventional basin! When outside his shop I had to endure the gauntlet of laughter and shouts of "baldy" as I slunk home in a severe sulk, vowing that when I grew up I would let my hair grow onto my shoulders. However, as if in response to my anguish, the Courtney Street hairdressing salon suddenly closed; although he continued to live in the back room where he eventually died. In later years mother told me that the Courtney barber had such a strong liking for beer that he often had to be called out of 'Vicky Vaults' when his shop was full. It was not long before he realised that his 'salon' was unnecessary when all he had to do, with the pub landlord's permission, was to turn up in 'Vicky Vaults' in his brown professional dust coat together with the tools of his trade. Apparently the venture was a great success because his old and new clients appreciated not having to sacrifice drinking time in order to have their hair cut and, according to the pub landlord, his trade increased accordingly!

Life went on regardless

Under normal circumstances my birthday would, like many others in Courtney Street, have been an open and quickly closed event except for the glorious fact that I did receive my clockwork train set. It was a model of the then famous 'Silver-Link' that, when fully wound, would whizz around its narrow diameter track with such velocity that it often shot-off and had to be recovered from a jumble of footwear and piles of newspaper that lived beneath the sideboard, much to the alarm of several painted faces on the coach windows.

It was at this stage of my narrative that I felt drawn, after my reference to newspapers beneath the sideboard, to pause and talk a little about heaps of old papers that were familiar sights in almost every Courtney Street house I was invited into. They were not restricted to underneath the sideboard because an equally popular storage spot was beneath chair cushions or down the back of the couch. But why did the residents of Courtney Street have such an attachment to old newspapers? In 2012 we have a dedicated recycle bin for such items though, in their way, I suppose street residents were also into recycling – but strictly within their own homes. In order to support this view I made a list of the many outlets for old newspapers that were active in our and other houses I visited:

1. Making spills to light dad's pipe.
2. Tear into squares of toilet paper to hang on a nail in the 'petty.'
3. Lining cupboard shelves.
4. Used as padding beneath a table cloth.
5. Stuffed under doors and into cracks to protect against cold draughts.
6. Swotting flies – a regular summer time activity.

7. Ignition support for wood and coal when lighting the fire.
8. Making paper logs by tight rolling sections of newspaper and firmly tying with string – with the aim of replacing scarce wooden logs on the fire. Sadly they would burn away faster than a log; but after all they were better than nothing.
9. A double sheet of newspaper, spread in front of the fire recess, was often used to 'draw' a reluctant fire by inducing an up draught of air. Often the paper itself caught light giving a few moments of frenzied waving, stamping and cursing!

Having reached and passed my seventh birthday I was aware that, to a noticeable extent, my interests where dramatically changing, for example my attention to such comic characters as Desperate Dan, Pansy Potter – the strongman's daughter and Lord Snooty and his gang, to name but a few was fast waning. More and more I wanted to know what was happening on the 'Home Front' and beyond – meaning that I stepped up my 'wigging-in' sessions both at home and particularly at the terrace or passage end. Another valuable source of information was listening to neighbours talking over the backyard wall, or when they were sitting out on the bedroom window ledge and washing the partly lowered window in front of them, whilst all the time loudly berating alleged failings of some political character. I had developed a liking for listening to the radio, and news bulletins were a great attraction; more so when I was beginning to understand some sort of pattern emerging between national and European news highlights. It is true that Rediffusion radios were a great asset in many Courtney Street houses and, in later years, I developed the view that entertainment programmes were on the increase in this period of uncertainty, as if trying to hide the contrast between waning peace and advancing war. Every Saturday evening we would be glued to the radio listening to Henry Hall, in his hesitant voice, telling the country that "This is Henry Hall speaking and tonight is my Guest Night." He retained this same opening such that it rapidly became his national catch phrase. He played popular songs of the 30s and featured stars of the entertainment world including Elsie and Doris Waters and Flanagan and Allen.

Come and join our 'do' ....

It was traditional for households to look forward to family sessions in front of their radio although such events were restricted to the weekend. Weekdays, except for occasional treats, were dedicated to the rigours of school, work or job seeking which despatched many younger families off to bed by nine o'clock. Elderly men often assembled in the pub and, for the umpteenth time, related extracts from their lives whilst spending several hours sipping away at the same pint of bitter.

But times were changing. Perhaps it was an increasing threat of war with Germany that introduced escapism in the form getting sloshed either at home or in the pub. Both from my restricted observations fortified by 'overheard' conversations there was no doubt that 1938 was witnessing an upsurge in house parties. Along the length of the street it was becoming a regular weekend feature to see many steamed up house windows that, being dark with the light behind it, took on the appearance of an opaque curtain. But this was no ordinary covering because it had a serious role to play; and that was to hide from public view the frenzied party within. For one can never be sure how a sensitive passer-by would be affected by the sight of drunken bodies intent upon shouting, swearing, jumping up and down in the name of dancing whilst roaring out what, to them, was a popular party song. Also we must not forget the pianist who, with loud pedal hard to the floor, dutifully accompanied them on a honky-tonk piano oblivious to the fact he was playing a totally different tune to the one being 'sung.'

By tradition these social gatherings began in one of several local pubs and, when sufficiently merry, they would depart with enough beer to last them through the house 'do' ahead. If the pub did not have a 'beer off' then they would call in the previously described Courtney Street establishment, which competed with the pubs by giving away a packet of crisps if a certain purchase price level was exceeded.

From time to time it was the turn of our house to host a family 'do' with relatives from Craven Street making up the numbers. Their warming-up preliminaries always began in the *'Full Measure'* pub in Cleveland Street and I never knew what time the house party broke up because I was long asleep in bed, totally unaffected by the din going on below. It was not unusual for neighbours to add to the numbers, and the beer supply, by calling in on the way home from their Saturday night in the pub duly waving aloft their bottle opener – just in case we had lost ours! As an aside the Courtney Street nickname for a bottle opener was a *'Door Sneck Lifter'* because to lend it out also meant that its owner was invited to join the party!

Occasionally, I was allowed to stay up for the start of a house party, and it never failed to amaze me just how many bodies could be packed into the ground floor of a Courtney Street sham four house. When the celebrations were in full swing I would sit under the kitchen table, out of the way of adults, who were uncertain just where their legs were leading them in that packed maze of uncertainty. But even my haven of safety had its problems because of the build-up of empty beer bottles around me – which were stored there awaiting the recovery of one old penny per empty returned. There was one occasion when I was tempted to dip my finger into the beer dregs and taste what they so much enjoyed – urghh! – and the experiment was never repeated! As ever the provider of music was Jim at the piano who, with great gusto, would belt out his repertoire of boozy family songs; including the recently introduced '*Beer Barrel Polka*', also known as '*Roll out the Barrel*', that lasted throughout the war and beyond. Even today it is unnecessary to remind most people of its almost immortalised chorus that contained the words:

Roll out the barrel, we'll have a barrel of fun
Roll out the barrel, we've got the blues on the run
Zing boom tararrel, ring out a song of good cheer
Now's the time to roll the barrel, for the gang's all here.

For posterity I will add that, during the war, the second line was altered to read:

"Roll out the barrel, we've got the **Huns** on the run,"

This was truly a party song, to end all party songs, that was best delivered when vocal chords were lubricated with beer courtesy of Moors and Robson's or Hull Brewery, it matters not which, because the result was equally mind-boggling.

Please pause and imagine an indeterminate number of bodies happily packed into a sham four house when, all of a sudden, they would begin to jump and sway together in the best traditions of a Red Indian war dance, whilst energetically roaring out words to the Beer Barrel Polka. Add to this the sound of Jim playing the piano with its loud sustaining pedal hard down to the floor, and bottles of beer dancing in unison on the table top, and you have begun to create the atmosphere of a typical Courtney Street house party. From the din of rattling bottles above my head I quickly formed the view that '**Beer Bottle** Polka' would have better described the potential of this tune!

Feeling tired I would await a lull in the dancing when I would judiciously creep through a forest of unpredictable legs, make my way upstairs, and fall into bed clutching my ageing Jelly Legs. I once remember drifting off to sleep to the sound of a strident female voice leading a sing-along, to the tune of John Sousa's famous two-step march '*Blaze Away*' which, as far as I am aware, was written without official librettos. For those who know the tune they may also remember the opening words that our party loving vocalist sang me to sleep with:

"All of a sudden a bloody big pudding came rolling down the stairs,
It rolled round here, and rolled round there – and bounced of all the chairs..."

......but, in due course, the morning arrived and I was my usual happy and talkative self despite the sight of my shaking and pale faced mother, who had no stomach for alcohol, crouched over the back-yard sink quietly murmuring a mantra composed of, "Never again ...please God never again..." And she totally ignored my plea for a slice of bread and jam!

Don't miss the Saturday night sports!

These do's were not regular events in our household but the street as a whole, more so when faced with a possible war, really let rip in what became known as '*Saturday Night Sports.*' Obviously I was tucked up in bed and asleep while all this was happening, but my previously mentioned strong sense of curiosity was ever to the fore. As time went by I mentally collected several anecdotes related to Saturday night activities from my parents and other adults, most of whom had no idea I was 'wigging-in' to what they were saying but, nevertheless, they donated valuable data for this narrative.

The sports began after the pub's last order bell had run its course and 'chuck-out' had commenced. Most men happily staggered out, some with their arms around each other's shoulders, and all with a vague idea of where they were heading as their sawdust contaminated footprints meandered into the night. Others who had come to rely upon the bar for essential support were propelled into the street by a couple of tired barmen, whose thoughts were on a quick tidy-up then home to bed. Nevertheless they would good humouredly acknowledge a swaying figure, with arms like flailing tentacles seeking something to hold on to, as it tried to say, "Goo – goo – night gaffer," before it sank into a heap on the pavement. "He won't stay there for long when the beat Bobbie comes," they agreed with a grin, as they locked the door and shot the bolts.

There is common ground for agreement that life has many imponderables that the average person addresses with either a scratch of the head, or a shrug of the shoulders, followed by a keen desire to change the subject. Ask any street member how young birds find their migratory way from East Park to central Africa, or how salmon from the depths of the ocean can cover immense distances in order to spawn in some distant Scottish highland stream, and a few mumbled half-words followed by an apologetic "Dunno" is the best to be hoped for.

But there were far deeper problems than that to baffle the wives of Courtney Street. For example why did men who lived at the Tin Mission end of the street travel all the way to the 'Nags Head' rather than use

'Vicky Vaults' which was much closer to home? Conversely why did the Holderness Road end menfolk, rather than cross the road to the 'Nags Head' pub, prefer to walk almost a mile to the 'Vicky Vaults'? Therein rests an enigma set to test renowned analytical minds, or kitchen sink plain logic, to their respective limits without reaching a satisfactory conclusion.

But it was an undeniable fact that two groups of drunken men were going to enter Courtney Street, from both ends, and meet somewhere in the middle. At times there had been trouble, and even the occasional fight, mainly when Hull Kingston Rovers had not produced the result expected from them leaving Hull FC to hold the bragging rights. But law and order, in the form of the regular beat bobby who knew them all, drunk or sober, was there to keep the peace. His usual spot was at the passage end that ran between the back of Wesley Terrace and the sawmill wall were, with his Woodbine surreptitiously smouldering behind his back, he judiciously surveyed all before him. He was not a spoil sport and he even smiled at some drunken antics, or allowed his foot to tap in rhythm to music from passing mouth organs, which were very fashionable in the 30s. According to more than one source he even joined in with an intoxicated choir singing the 'Happy Birthday' chorus to a limp drunken figure lying across his mate's shoulder! But the revellers knew, from experience, what to expect if they overstepped the mark; like the time a reveller, out to impress, boasted that he still could climb to the top of a lamp post in record time. Now street lights were a sore point with most beat bobbies who remembered well the roasting they received from the desk Sergeant which concluded with a warning that *they* would be held responsible for any further broken lights in their streets of duty. In quick bounds our upholder of the law was over to the lamp post and spectators quickly made way for his person and voice as it thundered out, "Hey, Tarzan ...if you brek that bloody mantle then you'll have my boot up your arse! So get down now and get yer self off home – cos ya missus is out looking for yer."

Thus the socialites noisily sang their respective ways along the street and, according to my informants, as they got closer to home there was a dramatic change in the songs they sang and staggered to. For example '*Yes, we have no bananas*' became '*There's a long, long trail a-winding into the land of my dreams* .... 'And '*Roll out the Barrel*,' faded in favour of '*If you were the only girl in the world, and I was the only boy.*' Perhaps a faint light of diplomacy had managed to break through their fog of intoxication?!

In due course sanity, although struggling hard, was beginning to return to Courtney Street as Saturday night sports drew to a close. Yet, before it could be handed back to wandering dogs and cats that had been 'chucked' out for the night, there were residual pockets of activity to be resolved. I was assured that there was always the solitary man left sitting on the kerb edge being noisily sick into the gutter; and that there was always a head from the window above ordering him to 'clear off and throw-up outside his own house.' I really think it unnecessary for me to add that the actual words the irate woman used were far too 'expressive' for this book!

Then there were two characters that are still very clear in my mind, even to knowing their names, yet for obvious reasons I will not reveal them. It is enough for me to say that in build they were close images of that famous comedy duo Laurel and Hardy hence, for convenience, I will refer to them by those names. They were great mates and, in the week, they spent much time working together on their allotments and, by way of reward for their efforts, looked upon it as their right to get drunk every Saturday night. In consequence their passage home was laboured, uncertain, and inconsistent with the ideal of walking in a straight line, but they would persevere and reach the end of Burleigh Grove which was their traditional stopping place. Being on the shorter side meant that Laurel hitched the back of his coat over the railing spikes and, as if on a coat peg, he was held in an upright position despite the desire of his drunken body to find rest on the pavement. By comparison Hardy was tall and bulky and able to lean back on the metal fence from which position he always began his loud monologue as if speaking in a foreign tongue, which, in fact, was the Hull accent pickled with copious amounts of beer. Whatever he was trying to say remained a mystery but, almost at set intervals, he would look down at Laurel and immediately become lucid through his recurring expression, "Now you know me and I know you." Laurel would knowingly nod his head and, for the umpteenth time, resume patting his coat and trousers pockets searching for his beloved Park Drive cigarette which, according to my informants, was always stuck behind his right ear. Apparently this ridiculous double act could go on for some time until Laurel, without warning, would suddenly unhitch himself from the railings which meant the time had arrived to move on and local residents could at last relax to the fading voice of Hardy confirming the fact that, "Now you know me and I know you!"

And then it was Sunday

Who knows – but this day could have begun with a sparrow fluttering into the street and, by way of making its presence felt, it may have performed one or two minor acrobatics before landing on top of a lamp post. Let us pretend that from its new vantage point it surveyed the familiar scene and fluffed out its feathers, to greet the approaching dawn, as dew-enriched rays of sunlight tentatively crept around timber stacks in the wood yard. With justification our feathered friend may have considered himself to be the first visitor of the new day, but this was far from the truth. Whilst the sparrow's head was still beneath its wing and the first light of dawn was struggling to paint the edge of our eastern horizon, there were already shadowy figures at work along the length of Courtney Street and surrounding areas.

There was a rumour that parts of the street were haunted and, if so, these may simply be departing phantoms of the night. But let me assure you that these flesh and blood figures were early morning foragers, busily searching for discarded beer bottles, which were then carefully stored away, awaiting times of acute need, when their one old penny deposit value would be claimed with haste.

But it did not end with bottles because, since time immemorial, drunken men have been noted for losing all manner of objects that would challenge, and defeat, the most creative of minds should they try and predict all that could be found. From the onset I must add that some found items were a mystery to my young mind and, when I asked my parents for clarification, they would respond with, "you should not have been listening-in to what people were saying." Needless to say I now know them to be totally inappropriate for inclusion in this book! It could be guaranteed that treasure trove in the form of coins, cigarettes and tobacco would always be found and, as ever, they would immediately be given a good home. Among less predictable findings was a pair of braces, ear trumpet, single sock, false teeth and, of all things, a monocle!

Sunday was, as far as possible, strictly reserved as a day of rest. Unless they were shift workers most men remained in bed until dinner time whilst mother steadily made progress towards preparing, and serving-up, the mid-day meal, courtesy of a three-deck pan and steamer balanced on the open fire. In common with other children I was not allowed to *'rive about' (indulge in rough play)* in the street on the Sabbath and had to amuse myself in the back-yard which, in my case, was not a problem because I preferred my own company. I had a number of friends but we never seemed to share much in common; which is no criticism of them because, in all probability, it was me who was the odd ball. Also I would be foolish if I claimed that Sundays in pre-WW2 Courtney Street were noted for an atmosphere of idyllic tranquillity but, on balance, it was the quietest day mainly because shops and factories were closed and, following the tumult of Saturday night sports, any day would be quiet by comparison.

Very occasionally there were Sunday morning upsets that were likely to be off-shoots from the previous night's high-jinks. One such incident remains vividly in my mind as a result of my mother asking me to go to the passage end to see if the Corp (Co-op) milkman was in the street. From the kerb edge I detected his presence but I was more interested in the sudden sound of a window breaking, followed by a door being violently wrenched open and a female voice screaming obscenities at a certain someone who, she claimed, had spent all her money in the pub leaving nowt left to buy food for the kids. Quickly people poured out of their houses as a man staggered out of Claremont Avenue, with his hands to his face, which was not sufficient to stem the flow of blood from running between his fingers. Horrified I watched him sink to the pavement as neighbours rushed to his aid whilst others tried to calm his, by now, berserk wife who, I later learned, had thrown a valve set radio into his face. White faced and in a state of shock I ran and told my mother what had happened to which, without a word, she closed and locked the backyard door and led me into the house whilst stressing 'that it was nowt to do with us and we'd best keep out of it' Mother knew full well how to soothe my distress and, after I'd eaten my second slice of bread and jam, she quietly asked me, "Was the milkman in the street?"

The inevitability of a war with Germany was constantly at the forefront of most Courtney Street minds but, true to their nature, they stoically kept it to themselves except when it became the theme for terrace end 'seminars'. The dreadful fear of a new conflict, when the horror of the 1914-1918 war was still active in many minds, was beginning to affect people in other ways; particularly on a Sunday when the local Salvation Army band marched into Courtney Street. Normally a few elderly ladies and one or two curious children would stand and listen to them but now, all of a sudden, times were changing. Adults of all age groups, together with their children, listened attentively to an address delivered by the Band Captain and then sang heartily from hymn sheets that were handed round. I remember one Sunday, when their closing hymn was 'Nearer my God to thee,' my developing mind slowly grasped the prophetic nature of its words with regard to a forthcoming war. And I was not alone with my thoughts because, as we dispersed, I heard one man say to another, "It makes you think, doesn't it?"

Also active on all days of the week was the Hull City Mission who where a team of evangelists that went door to door with the message of salvation. One caller was an aptly named lady called Mrs Holy who had a profound effect upon my mother so much so that, with immediate effect, I was despatched to the Courtney Street Baptist Church (Tin Mission) Sunday school. I must admit that I enjoyed it because I was learning, in better detail, the meaning of strange teachings that were not fully explained during the morning school assembly. One of our

Sunday school teachers was a kindly man who we greatly respected despite being in awe of his appearance which, of course, was no fault of this own. Always with affection, yet never to his face, we would refer to him as 'Mr Gorilla' which we looked upon more as a status title than anything else; however many years later my adult mind reclassified it as being thoroughly offensive!

Another teacher who took our Sunday class from time to time was a lady named Mrs Flowers and, before you ask, that was her correct name. She was a very compassionate person who, during the week, would call and help out households that were finding it difficult to cope. On one occasion she took to me HRI outpatients department when I fell and cut my forehead whilst playing in the backyard and, for being a brave boy (ha-ha), she gave me a scripture book covering the last journeys of St. Paul; which is still in my bookcase.

November 13th 1938 was a momentous day for me when, along with several others, I was presented with a Philip, Lord Wharton Trust Fund Bible for committing to memory, and subsequently reciting to all present, no less than seven psalms. Needless for me to add that there is no way I could now repeat that feat. The chapel was run by a Mr and Mrs Finch who were central to the needs of the street. They ran a Life Boys brigade which I did not join mainly because their style of uniform was not to my liking. At Christmas they arranged and held a children's Christmas party and, during the summer, they organised a day trip to Withernsea for the Sunday school children. Unfortunately I missed the 1938 outing but was able to take part in the July 1939 trip which, sadly, proved to be our last opportunity for enjoyment before the war began in September 1939.

July 1938 – Annual school sports day

Our school morning assembly always ended with prayers and as these words of devotion were being delivered, from the rostrum, a well-practised 'whisper message' was passing rapidly along a line of eager young ears. Normally these clandestine messages failed to rise above well-known facts such as, "So and so has smelly feet" or "A. N. Other is daft." but, on this occasion, I was intrigued to be informed that the teachers were 'playing with us like a cat plays with a mouse!' To me this was a new expression which perfectly summed-up the situation we were in. It had long been talked about and, considering the fast approaching school summer holiday, we hoped that every morning assembly would release the date we were all looking forward to but, alas, another assembly was drawing to a close and we were still none the wiser. When back in the classroom a more adventurous boy put up his hand and got as far as, "Please Miss, when will ..." only for teacher to cut in and, in no uncertain terms, tell us that if our work and behaviour did not improve then it may not happen at all! Once in the playground we immediately got together and quickly concluded that our only remaining option was to write to the Prime Minister and ask him to intervene if matters did not go our way. Thus agreed we moved on to the next stage which was to find someone to compose the letter, provide an address to write on the envelope and, finally, produce a postage stamp. The outcome was a total impasse which drifted on until ordered to be silent in the line-up prior to marching back to our classrooms.

Thankfully our long awaited good news arrived at the next morning assembly when it was announced that *the School Sports Day was on* and would take place the day after tomorrow! Despite being in the hallowed presence of our class teachers and being aware of the solemnity of the occasion, our previous worries and concerns were immediately cast out in the form of a spontaneous cheer of shameless delight. Trying to look severe the Junior School Headmistress furiously beat the table with her cane, and reminded us that there was still time to cancel the event. The sudden silence was deafening. With hindsight I believe the sight of so many pairs of shocked eyes, and mouths frozen in open mode, were sufficient to explain why so many teachers, with hand to mouth and looking down at the floor, struggled hard to avoid an outbreak of uncontrollable laughter which, to say the least, would have impinged upon their dignity.

On what was to be one of the warmest days of 1938 our school sports day had finally arrived as groups of lads joyfully approached the Boys entrance gate, cheerfully swinging their lunch in named carrier bags which, without fail, had to be immediately handed to teacher on arrival. As I approached I could not help noticing a forlorn Annie standing at the Girls gate, silently gazing at the scene of joy before her, which prompted me to walk up to her and ask if she was alright. I fully agreed with her grumble that it was not fair that boys could have a sports day whilst she had to attend a daft sewing lesson. Pressed for time because the school 'line-up' bell was ringing meant I had to think quickly on my feet, so I asked her if a bite of one of my jam sandwiches would make her feel a bit better? My offer was quickly accepted and, as her teeth sank into it, she added that she got up too late for her breakfast. With that I told her to keep the sandwich as I turned and ran for the line-up. My last sight of Annie was of her ravenously devouring one of my precious jam sandwiches which I had given away as a reflex action and, much to my surprise, I did not regret doing it. In no time at all the buses arrived and we were carefully counted as, in single file, we climbed aboard under the watchful eye of a teacher who quickly diffused squabbles as to who should sit alongside who. Our destination was the Maybury Road School playing field which, on an annual basis, was made available to school children from local industrial backstreets for fun and games, together with purging factory smog from their young lungs. For us a school with a playing field attached was bliss beyond words and, when we were finally set loose, we just ran and ran until our legs and breathing could take no more and we collapsed into gasping heaps of total delight. During this stampede of joy one of my friends received a bee sting on his nose which he totally ignored in favour of running, and falling, in this grassland paradise. How different all this was to our small and unsympathetic concrete playground, that had happily grazed the skin off unwary knees belonging to many generations of boys who had fallen upon its unyielding surface. Fortunately I still have a photograph taken during this 1938 visit to Maybury playing fields which I have reproduced opposite:

The victim of the bee sting, which can be seen on the left side of his nose, is the lad kneeling on the front row with a football in his right hand. I can be located sitting at his left side and sporting one of those terrible haircuts to which I referred earlier! Some of my immediate colleagues also present in the above are Brian Palmer, George Rennard, Brian Larvin, George Turner, Neville ???, and ??? Wilde. It is interesting to note that the bus driver was on hand to intervene when, for whatever reason, one of the boys suddenly became rather vocal. Also of note is the front row lad wearing his wellies on this hot summer's day which, as I remember, he kept on under strict orders, from his mam, that if he lost them he would walk in his bare feet for ever. Nevertheless he ran with them on, albeit in a series of loping bounds that threatened to upend anyone close to him. When the day ended it was unanimously agreed that it had been the best event of the year and, as if to prove the point, it was both talked and argued about for many days to follow. History will never know who scored the only goal in a twenty-a-side football match and if, in fact, the goal itself should have been allowed. A consensus of opinion was evenly split, between the respective teams, as to whether someone had widened the goalmouth by surreptitiously moving a pile of coats, that were acting as goalposts, or if the vanquished were simply suffering from sour grapes.

September 1938 – Peace for our time

For several decades I have been interested in the history of both world wars and, in particular, events leading up to the start of WW2. However it is a massive topic which, for the purposes of this book, need only appear as a summary of events well known and understood by parents and terrace end debating groups alike. Hence my outline of factors that led to WW2 may bridge the gulf separating peace and forthcoming war and, as a dubious bonus, show why the terrors that would soon fall upon Hull, and many other cities within the UK, were doomed to happen.

Both Britain and France suffered badly through the horrors of trench warfare in WW1 and, consequently, were not thrilled with the thought of another major conflict within the same lifetime. Therefore when Hitler and his Fascist party gained momentum from the late twenties onward the allies, by agreement, followed a process of appeasement in the hope that Hitler, in time, would be satisfied just with the recovery of land lost within the 1918 Armistice agreement. Our then Prime Minister, Mr Neville Chamberlain, was dedicated towards a peaceful solution which in any age is a good thing; except had he first read the book Mein Kampf (meaning My Struggle), which Hitler wrote in 1925 whilst in prison, he would have realised that within Fascist dogmas the concept of world domination was not an option but, rather, a number one requirement. Obviously world occupation was not viable but, through intimidation and other nefarious means, Hitler intended the Fascist philosophy, with its inbuilt racial supremacy, to spread and be accepted on a global basis. In direct violation of armistice agreements Germany was re-arming on a massive scale and, surreptitiously, widening its borders. From all accounts Hitler was not interested in an all-out war with Britain and at no stage did he ever declare war upon this nation. His main dream was to match Britain, who was then a major colonial power, by creating his own empire in Eastern Europe; with Russia as his number one conquest.

Additionally he also feared the numerical strength and tenacity of the British navy, which he had good right so to do.

It is a fact that Hitler had always considered Austria to be part of Germany so in March 1938, after much deep and violent intrigue, his troops entered Vienna and Austria became part of the German Greater Reich. On the pretext that ethnic German population was suffering in the Sudetenland area of Czechoslovakia, the war drums began to sound in that region. With that, Prime Minister Chamberlain had a meeting with Hitler in Munich, in September 1938, to try and diffuse the rising tide of European tension that had attracted concerns even on the world stage of events. In Chamberlain's view the meeting was an overwhelming success and he returned with news that the Czechoslovakian problem had been resolved and a non-aggression pact between Germany and Britain had been signed by Hitler and himself. Back in England Chamberlain was ecstatic in his belief that peace was now ours. He waved the signed agreement at the press reporters declaring that we had 'peace for our time' and were now able to sleep safely in our beds. This agreement is well remembered for its satirical value because a few days after its signing Hitler's forces moved into the Sudetenland region and, in March 1939, went on to occupy the whole of Czechoslovakia.

In parallel was the highly emotive situation surrounding the former German city of Danzig, which at the end of WW1, was placed under League of Nations control and was classified as an open and self-governing city because of its significant German population. Additionally the Polish nation, much to the disgust of its German citizens, was able to use Danzig, later to be known as Gdansk, as its Baltic port. Hitler, during his many frenzied speeches, vowed to take Danzig back under German control; hence the stage was set for the invasion of Poland. At last Britain became fully alert to Hitler's true intentions and, together with France, a pact was made with Poland that, should Germany invade them, then the allies would declare war on Germany. When this pact was made public one of our neighbours cleverly described it as, "World War One Part Two!" As a point of interest it is reported that in 1940 someone asked Hitler about the non-aggression pact he had signed with

Chamberlain and his reply, with disdain, was that it was merely a piece of paper that meant absolutely nothing.

The drive to improve our fighting capability continued with great vigour throughout 1938 and into 1939 wherein it became a matter of National survival against what were seemingly unmanageable odds. On land we were faced with a well disciplined and thoroughly mechanised German army, who were soon to show their strategic skills in what became known as the 'miracle' of Dunkirk. Our air strength was limited numerically but we had a world beater in the Spitfire which, together with the Hawker Hurricane, played highly significant roles in the Battle of Britain. The German navy had a large fleet of submarines that would play havoc with our merchant shipping in the Battle of the Atlantic. Their surface warships were fast and well-armed but they sailed alone, or with a supply vessel in the area. Their main role was that of predators which was put to good effect in the early months of the war. In turn we had a large navy which, together with the RAF, eventually cornered such ships as the Bismarck, Tirpitz, Scharnhorst plus others and sank them. Fortunately for us the German navy never had an operational aircraft carrier. However, the Nazis had plans to build a total of four carriers and had almost finished one of them. Her name was the Graf Zeppelin and though launched in December 1938 she was never over 80% completed. Construction delays, lack of aircraft, and bitter disputes between Air Marshal Hermann Goering and the Navy ensured that the ship was doomed to become scrap metal.

Back in the world of Courtney Street and district its menfolk discussed finer points of the tense European situation within the noise and sawdust of 'Vicky' Vaults bar, or in the more genteel surroundings of the Nags Head snug, without ever offering a faint light of guidance for our Nation to follow. I say this without hint of satire or criticism because, in my view, the Allied High Command and the Cabinet itself were equally perplexed over how to respond should Germany invade Poland. Soon they, and indeed the entire world, would find out when one of the most horrific conflicts in the history of the world became a reality.

But, as ever, lives in Courtney Street moved on so, for the moment, let us return to the antics of the younger generation ......

October 1938 – A few words about the School Playground

When in use the school playground was a place of tradition that must never be taken lightly. I say that because some adults, who lived close to the school, described children as a horde without coherence or purpose, intent only on acts of pushing, shouting and other forms of aggression. I penned those words several decades after this criticism was made hence, in the interests of delicacy, I have modified the remarks allegedly used! To me it is obvious that complainants gave the schoolyard only cursory glances because, were this not the case, they would have instantly been captivated by the efficiency of the playground duty teacher.

She was truly an inspiration to watch and an example to be followed by all who desire to progress; in the true meaning of the word. For example imagine this young woman holding a saucer containing a full cup of tea in her left hand whilst her right hand, with the speed of a striking cobra, drew from a heap of writhing bodies a young aggressor by his coat collar and, after a few words, would send him on his way – yet all this happened without spilling a drop of her tea. I feel certain this awesome feat, had it been portrayed in oils, would have hung with pride alongside many of the world's masterpiece works.

Further it must be remembered that playground activities followed traditions handed down from earlier generations that, at times, could encourage boisterous behaviour. Some activities were more physical than others but all were seasonal in their application. For example there was a time of the year for playing 'conkers' (seeds of horse-chestnut trees) wherein two players, each with a conker threaded onto a piece of string, took turns in striking each other's conker until one broke. Obviously the one with the hardest conker would win and this was often achieved by either soaking it in vinegar or painting it with clear varnish. This was a regular accusation made by many losers hence occasional scenes of conker-related playground violence were not unusual.

Fancy a game of marbles?

A popular mid-year activity was marbles which was dominated by a copious number of *instant rules* that had to be declared before the game began. The way it was played in Courtney Street, and no doubt in other streets, was at odds with National rules wherein it is played in a circle. We played it either in the street gutter or along the side of the school playground wall. Having mentioned the existence of rules really demands that I give some instances which, as far as I remember, were as follows:

No Nowts. This meant that the game was free from any rules be they traditional or otherwise. In order for this to be effective **No Nowts** had to be accepted as the first shout to be heard before the match began.

Anys. This is the direct opposite to **No Nowts** meaning that any known rule is permissible. Obviously these two options controlled the direction of the game hence preferences must be loudly declared, and accepted, with maximum haste. There is little need to add that the one who called the first was often the subject of heated debate and, again, violence was not unknown.

Kisses. In simple terms a marble was 'booled' (rolled) along the ground with the objective of hitting the other player's marble which, if achieved, meant it became the property of the successful 'booler.' The strike had to be a head-on collision unless the cry **kisses** had been made; which then granted victory to glancing contact between the two marbles.

Bombs To overcome rough surfaces a **bombs** claim allowed the player to stand astride his opponents marble and, in bomb manner, drop his directly upon its target. For this to be valid the height of the drop must equal the distance separating the marbles at ground level. Such a rule, by its very nature, was not immune to argument and occasional fisticuffs.

There were several other rules that have escaped my memory – the reason being that new ones appeared at the start of most opening seasons, only to fade away before period ended.

Other more vigorous playground games reserved for the colder parts of the year were **Tig** and **Riallyo** whose season was, by the Headmistress, often cut short due to their inherent ferocity – more so with the latter game.

Thoughts of Hull Fair

By contrast there were periods of relative peace and orderly playtime behaviour when one of the annual events grew near. Heading this list was Christmas with outrageous speculations being made as to what would be received, closely followed by birthdays. For many the month of October dominated playground debates because of its close proximity to the start of Hull Fair. Past experiences were regurgitated and duly exaggerated after which they were compared with what was expected from the forthcoming event. For the first time I became very interested in listening to the many accounts because October 1938 was very special to me because I was going to Hull Fair for the first time. The following script form of what I heard filled me with unbridled excitement over what joys lay ahead:

"Hey Alfie, me mam said she's taking me to Hull Fair and I can't wait," shouted Ben from the other side of the playground.

"I'm going," claimed another – "And me as well," replied a third, "Cos my mate down our terrace said that a man with two heads will be there."

"I bet he's very clever with all those extra brains," added a more studious lad in the group.

"Not as clever as a monkey that's going to be there cos it can write down the five times table," shouted a voice from the back.

"More than you can do Smiffy," quipped the comic of the crowd.

And so the banter went on and I was enthralled to drink in every word of it. Mention was made that Father Christmas would also be there; although no one could give a tolerable explanation as to how he could be at both ends of Walton Street at the same time. However, such debate was quickly by-passed in favour of spending more effective moments reliving past adventures at the fair. I was really smitten with the delight that lay ahead of me without knowing that when I made my *second* visit to the fair, I would be sixteen years old.

November 1938 – "Please Miss, someone has pinched the school gates"

We were having a revision lesson that centred upon our two to twelve times tables in which, for example, our teacher would say, "six times eight," and then point to any child at random expecting to receive the correct answer. If this proved to be the case then a rapid, "Then what are eight times six?" would baffle some and raise the arms of others. Those with their arms and fingers stretched rigidly in the air, as if trying to touch the ceiling, were following the age old premise that such contortions showed an act of enthusiasm no teacher could possibly withstand. On this occasion the matter was left unresolved when suddenly every pair of eyes in the room, including teacher's, became fixed upon the window and a noisy 'something' that was happening outside. "It sounds like a Gerry tank miss," muttered a boy on the back row as he slid lower in his seat, as if seeking safety beneath his desk. The noise outside, which reached a crescendo as it passed the school, was composed of men shouting and much loose metal rattling as, seemingly, a convoy of lorries slowly moved by. Quickly the teacher walked over to the window, climbed on a chair and relayed the news that it was only a group of workmen. In response to someone who muttered, "We'll see better at playtime," her quick reply was that unless they behaved themselves there would be no playtime.

It was home-time and with bated breath the entire class left the security of the school and gingerly stepped out into the street. The sight of more than normal terrace end debating groups suggested that things were not right and the acrid smell of burnt paint rather than routine factory emissions added to our uncertainty. Jangling his pocket of marbles the current champion, half-heartedly, asked if anyone wanted a game. But it was to no avail because he, and indeed everyone else, could not escape from the fact that something terrible had happened and it was up to us to find out what it was. Those lads who lived at the top end of the street had turned right and drifted into their open plan terraces without showing any sign that things were amiss. With that the rest of us began our slow walk towards the Dansom Lane end and noted that the stench of burnt paint was getting stronger until, with Granville Avenue on our right, and Arthur's Terrace on our left, we stopped as one and gawped in amazement. The terrace railings had disappeared! In panic we ran on until I reached Leonards Avenue and noticed that, in common with all other houses with front gardens, the metal railings were no more. I learned that the men we heard passing the school were armed with oxyacetylene and other cutting equipment and were under orders to remove all metal railings and gates, even those around Tin Mission, because the metal was urgently needed to build tanks, battleships and aeroplanes. I well remember that, as a boy, I was astounded as I gazed down Leonards Avenue as if I had never seen it before. The much beloved metal railings proudly shining in their coat of black paint were gone for ever, and all that remained were small metallic stubs serving as mocking memorials to something that once was. The stone kerbs which had supported those metal sentinels now seemed devoid of purpose, and rather reminded me of a line of aching gums mourning the sudden loss of their teeth.

Next day when we went to school we found that the gates and anything else metallic had, for safety reasons, been removed after the school had been cleared of children. Probably each teacher dreaded the sight of us filing into the Assembly Hall knowing that every tenth child would stick up its arm and announce, "Please Miss, somebody's pinched the school gates!"

From metal railings to war work

From an historical viewpoint it had been hinted that the country was in critical need of various grades and types of metal to help with the construction of tanks, ships and aeroplanes as our defence against the rising tide of fascist aggression. The public had also been urged to donate household metallic items ranging from pans to dolly tubs, and general unwanted metal within the range of door knockers to old bikes and all would be melted down to help with the rearmament cause. Perhaps this gentle persuasion approach had not worked too well? Because, all of a sudden, Courtney Street and the entire district became the target for a pre WW2 blitz in the form of mechanised teams of men, armed with metal saws and oxyacetylene cutters, who quickly removed metal railings and gates from public buildings, parks, churches, schools and houses. Many Courtney Street residents took the patriotic view and waved the flag accordingly. Whereas others, including those whose rose bushes had disappeared with the railings, likened the authorised work force to the armies of Mussolini who had invaded defenceless Abyssinia in 1935.

Several papers have been written on the philosophy behind this urgent drive with a consensus of views being that most requisitioned metal, including Edwardian iron railings, was unsuitable for a wide range of advanced military requirements. This is perhaps the reason why a land-mark hill of rusty metal railings spent the duration of the war in a field off Cleveland Street, gazing forlornly at St. Saviour's Church on the opposite side of the road. Another point of view suggested that the entire affair was to boost home-front morale into believing that they were taking an active part in the Nation's drive to put Hitler firmly in his place.

From my observations and mental notes I firmly believe that the Country had decided that war was inevitable and work output should increase accordingly. I learned from my mates that more and more dads were finding work and many factories, including the Courtney Street Saw Mill, were working overtime. My father was working longer hours and it was beginning to show. Although the extra money was useful he seemed, when at home, to be permanently tired which meant I had to play quietly – or else! He often stressed that he dare not seek work elsewhere because, according to a letter from the management, the Tannery had been declared essential war work and, as a result, he would be exempt from any future call-up into the armed services.

Often I would voluntarily '*get up the dancers,*' which was a Street expression for 'get off to bed,' earlier than I needed to have done due to the panoramic view, from my back-bedroom window, of the Humber Saw Mill which, as I mentioned earlier, extended from Burleigh Street to the bottom of Upton Street; in the process of which the site ran parallel to the length of Courtney Street. The fact that they now worked until late in the evening meant that often the site was flood-lit so, from my bedroom window, I had a clear view of cranes lifting tree trunks and other large wooden items. Literally I was spoilt for choice because there was also the goods yard with steam engines shunting wagons that, at times, collided with a noise like thunder. Occasionally I would notice a crane come close to the fence between Courtney Street and the wood yard and furtively lower a section of wood to someone waiting on the Courtney side. Clearly, in modern terms, a '*guvvy-job*' was afoot!

The birth of 1939

When one is about to recall a day from the past it is almost instinctive to add that it 'only seems like yesterday' as a prelude to explaining why it had made such an impact upon the storyteller. Such is my attachment to the last day of a certain year, more clearly presented as Saturday 31st December 1938. Like many of my present age what I did last week remains an unfathomable mystery, yet I can recall that November 1938 was sunny and warm and, by contrast, we had snow at Christmas.

Whilst wigging-in on a group of adults I heard one of them declare that the 31st December 1938 felt decidedly different from any other last day of the year. Several nodded their heads in agreement, and one lady believed that it had a strange atmosphere about. With a hint of mystery in her voice she concluded with," that it was as if we had reached the end of a way of life."

Later I and my friends, as usual, met to play in the street but our hearts were not really in the last marble contest of 1938. One of our younger group members had, suddenly, started to cry for reasons he openly admitted that he did not know. He denied that we were the cause for his distress and, as more tears began to fall, he promptly turned away and ran home. It was indeed an odd day. In fact one of the lads, who had a poetic turn of mind, added that it felt like being at the pictures as the curtain fell at the end of a happy story. Soon we split up because some were going to relatives' houses to 'see in the New Year' whereas there would be just mam, dad and myself at home. Jim was full of joy at the prospect of being allowed to join other 16 year olds at a New Year's Eve party in Kent Street. Having left school last year he was now working in Reckitt's box making department and was also busy writing songs with his friend, Frank Hardy, who provided the lyrics. In his own mind he was now a 'grown up wage earner' whereas I was a mere almost 8 year old child; hence the gulf between us was even wider. So after dinner I spent a little time in the terrace walking along railing- deprived concrete kerbs and, without losing balance, I managed to leap most of the gaps left by missing gates. But, if truth be known, I wasn't really interested in my task and, for once, I was happy when mother opened the door and called me into the house.

"One of your favourite songs on the wireless," she said as she turned up the volume of the ever popular 1920s melody 'The Laughing Policeman,' as its hilarious and highly contagious laughter chorus began. In no time I was literally rolling on the floor beside myself with laughter and my mother, with her pinny to her mouth, was trying to control hers. Even my father, who was not noted for sustained outbursts of merriment, came out of the yard and immediately joined in with the laughing policeman! Whenever I think back to this happy scene my mind habitually modifies a well-known expression to read, "A family that laughs together, stays together," which in the face of all that was before us was no bad thing. As it happened the Laughing Policeman lifted the curtain on a new experience for me in that, for the first time in my life, I was going to be allowed to stay up and see the New Year in. Retrospectively I often wondered if my parents had a premonition that this was our last New Year together under the mantle of world peace. Further to this may have been their apprehension that if we all managed to survive then we would discover, perhaps to our great regret, that life would never be the same again.

"We have some freshly baked mince pies and, before you ask, there are some jam tarts with pastry fingers for you to pick off!" added mother with a wry grin on her face. That was excellent news which added to my delight of already having seen two bottles of Tizer, my favourite fizzy drink, part hidden on the pantry floor behind some bottles of beer. Already I had decided that if there was something odd about today then we could do with more of it! No grumbles about Tan Yard, washday or talk of walking miles to stock-up on this or that in case war is declared. Instead mam and I played Snakes and Ladders and later dad told me great stories about his adventures in India when he was a serving soldier there in 1920. Then we listened to all manner of programmes on the radio including the humourist Gillie Potter who always began his witty talks with, "Good evening England, this is Gillie Potter speaking to you in English." Then, in his well-modulated voice awash with subtle humour, he would talk about a variety of topics including an imaginary village called Hogs Norton where Lord Marshmallow was the area squire. When mention was made of the good squire relaxing in front of his large baronial fireplace, 'upon which a sofa was merrily burning,' mother would glance at our little Yorkist stove and immediately collapse into laughter. At another stage a sing-song developed led by the then popular duo Anne Ziegler and Webster Booth followed by foot-tapping to the songs of George Formby describing his exploits in a Chinese laundry and with his Little Stick of Blackpool Rock. Then it was time to listen to a relatively new programme to which I had become a fan. It was called 'Bandwagon' starring the ever popular "Big Hearted Arthur Askey" who generated lots of laughter from his several catchphrases including "Hello Playmates" and "Before your Very Eyes."

"Are you sure that you can keep awake until midnight?" mother asked after the clock had struck ten and I had just delivered my second yawn. I must admit that the warm glow of flickering firelight, and sparks gently pirouetting up the chimney, were incentive indeed for me to close my eyes; but on no account was I going to lose my first opportunity to greet the New Year in. So to demonstrate my intent I leapt to my feet and announced that I would walk around the backyard and get some fresh air. In the cold and clear night air I was soon fully awake as I listened to far distant sounds of drunks shouting and singing. But, for me, a calming peace had descended and, for a few moments, angry talk and fear of war to come had been wiped away. The tranquil stillness of the night also added echo content to the sound of shovels scraping in coalhouses, near and far, as the endless appetite of house fires was met, and seemingly acknowledged, by many columns of smoke drifting aimlessly from lines of house chimneys. To be able to study the behaviour of the night was a new and fascinating experience for me until suddenly the spell was broken by a command from within, "Come in now or you'll catch your death of 'cowld' (cold)."

It may have been the suggestion that I could get a cowld and become badly (ill) that brought back to my mind something I heard yesterday in the playground that worried me. "Dad," I asked whilst warming my hands before the fire. "A couple of lads at school told us that when the war starts all children will get *vackerated*, what does it mean and will it hurt?" At first I was puzzled that they both burst out laughing until they explained that the word was *evacuated* and, as dad began to fill his pipe, I knew he meant to expand upon the word. Ever keen to learn I poured a liberal portion of Tizer into my cup, sat back and listened as dad went on to tell me that, if a war with Germany did begin, then many important targets in Britain would be bombed and a lot of people would be killed. With barely a pause he went on to explain that since Hull was an vital sea port then it was very likely that we would get bombed, hence the government had decided that all children would be evacuated from Hull and other danger areas to safer places in the country. "Where is the country?" I asked in all innocence. "You remember when we went to Withernsea on the train and you looked out at all those trees, fields and village houses passing by; well that is the country." Momentarily my mind went back to earlier in the year when, for reasons I cannot remember, I went with a friend to a house in Severn Street that had a rear garden in which there were flowers, bushes and a tree. From that moment onwards my mind was set on living in a house with a tree in the garden, so that I could build a tree house and live almost like an urban Tarzan! So far I had not overcome the logistics of bringing this to pass in Leonards Avenue but, could it be, that an opportunity was now unfolding itself? “Dad,” I said with rising excitement. “If I was *vackerated* to the country then would I live in a house with a garden and a tree?” “I expect so,” he muttered with a shrug of his shoulders, “But at least you would be safe.” Without lifting her head mother muttered almost to herself, “And without anyone to love you like we do.” Quickly dad added that nothing had been decided yet because all this talk of war was still a rumour; probably started by Hitler to try and frighten us.

“That’s early,” mother exclaimed as a ships buzzer broke into our silence as we studied a flake of soot waving to us from the fire grate. “There’s only four minutes left of the year so I’ll be on my way,” remarked dad as, clutching a piece of ‘lucky’ coal, he let himself out of the back yard door; thus symbolically taking 1938 out of the house. Quickly mother slipped the bolt into place as, with a grin, she remarked that we didn’t want any new-year jam on the petty seat! Mum and I then stood in silence as the last moments of the old year, together with its laughter and tears, slowly left us and took its place in the realms of memory. Suddenly new life returned as the radio struck up with ‘Auld Lang Syne’ to the background of cheering crowds as the front door opened and dad, together with 1939, came into the house. Immediately the three of us, with our arms around each other, welcomed the New Year as only a united family can. In no time we had our coats on and when mother had finished her ritualistic rattling of the front door – ‘just making sure that it’s locked’ – we joined others at the terrace end. There was a well-attended ‘do’ going on in a middle house that led to a permanent overspill onto chairs in the front garden. We later learned that they operated a rota system of place changing to ensure that everyone was warm – part of the time! The fact that Hull was the third major port in the land was borne out by an ear-splitting outburst from a massed choir of ships’ buzzers ranging from deep basso profondo tones courtesy of large ocean-going ships to ear penetrating hoots from lighters and other small craft. In parallel was the rapid tolling of a solitary, albeit cracked, church bell that probably originated from St. Andrew’s in

Abbey Street or St. Saviour's in Cleveland Street. Added to this unruly struggle of competing clamour was an unwavering scream from factory sirens with background shouting and singing from drunken revellers. This symphony of discord progressively stunned the human mind and drove berserk every dog in the neighbourhood as, without exception, they howled their protest at the light of the moon and the gentle blink of watching stars.

I had often heard the noise made by crowds of drunken men and, on odd occasions, I had seen one or two tottering along the street, but never the multitude of befuddled merrymakers now before me as, with difficulty, they made their way home. One well inebriated man heading towards Dansom Lane stopped, swayed before us and, with a lop-sided grin, slowly wished us each a, "Happy New Merry!" With that he did a complete turnaround, as if searching for his intended direction, and then began to wobble into Leonards Avenue. Quickly dad pointed him in the direction of Dansom Lane and with a brief, "All the best mate," gently pushed the grateful reveller on his way. It was some weeks later, when the same man was seen coming out of a neighbouring house, that mum discovered he actually lived in Leonards Avenue! Goodness only knows how long it took him to find his way back home in his then drunken state.

I was so pleased that, for the first time, I had seen the entry of a new year and as I stood between mum and dad, holding each of their hands and watching the antics around me, I knew that 1939 was going to be a special year; although I never would have guessed just how special it would be.

May 1939 – The buzzers are blowing

Come on now – get up. Can't you hear the buzzers blowing? That would grow to become a familiar message that quickly became a way of life after war was declared. But at the moment we were still at peace and I was already way past my 8th birthday. As a belated present I was looking forward to the annual Tin Mission day out at Withernsea, which Mr

Finch had promised would go ahead despite strengthening rumours of war. But before then Courtney Street, and the rest of Hull, were braced for the first public testing of an air raid alert followed by the 'all clear.' In fact it had developed into an exciting new topic that quickly dominated terrace-end debating groups whose numbers had been swelled by new members, who were keen to have their say on the contentious topic of air raid sirens and the fact they were going to be tested sometime this week. It had not gone by unnoticed that many of these devices had already been fixed to factory roofs and other buildings throughout Hull. Some experienced debaters had argued that they were a total waste of time and money, because 'Gerry' would never reach Hull since our lads would have shot them down long before they reached our coastline. Another seasoned stalwart was heard to say, "And God help 'em if their buzzers wake up our Nora's bane cos then they'll have a real war on their hands!"

In fairness it was a well-publicised fact both in the Hull Daily Mail, and via a touring van fitted with a megaphone, that on a certain date and at a fixed time, we would experience the sound of an air raid siren. This event was simply to familiarise us with the tone of this all important reminder, lest we should ignore its efforts to tell us that enemy aircraft would soon be overhead. Perhaps the originator of the word 'ignore,' in this context, did so with tongue in cheek? It would have stretched the ability of the most naive among us to accept that any creature, composed of flesh and blood, could possibly ignore such a high pitched full bodied howl that rose and fell, as it battered away at our sorely tested ears drums. Some people in the street, in their anguish, maintained that the siren was enough to wake the dead; which was to me a blatantly obvious remark. For instance if someone had told me that when the siren had reached full pitch then display dummies, clothed or otherwise, had leapt through Waistell's tailors' shop window and fled down Holderness road, with their hands clasped to their ears, then I would have accepted it without quibble. Even when the test period was over the siren was not immediately stilled because its departure followed a slow descent down the harmonic scale, until it finally left us in the form of a deep throated groan that remained in our minds as an epitaph to what our ears had suffered. The event concluded with the siren being reactivated; only this time to tell us that the enemy had left and it was safe to leave the street shelter. This was known as the '*all clear*' which had all the auditory horrors of the '*air raid alarm*' except it did not rise and fall at the zenith of its activity. By contrast it maintained an equally intrusive yet constant blast upon our aural senses. Needless to add that under real air raid conditions the siren quickly became an accepted part of our lives, which is more than can be said about the attentions of the Luftwaffe.

June 1939. Take your Gas Mask off, Caney .....

.... "But I've not got it on," I replied having again fallen for their ploy. As with one voice their cry of "You could have fooled us!" taught me to be more careful in the future.

The use of poisoned gas, as a weapon of warfare, was adopted with appalling effect in the trench warfare of World War One, and many feared that it would be used again if we went to war against Germany. Within British High Command there was a justifiable fear that gas attacks would also be launched against our civilian population as part of relentless air attacks upon our cities. In Great Britain the Government decreed, as early as 1936, that it would manufacture sufficient gas masks for the whole population and distribution began, direct to each household, in early 1939. The masks were carried in cardboard boxes with long string shoulder handles and it was a prosecutable offence not to keep one on your person. Babies were enclosed in a cradle-like respirator and air was pumped in, using a hand-pump, through a special filter that removed poisonous gas from the air intake. Younger children were provided with Mickey Mouse styled masks to add an element of play to the donning process. As the war progressed the fear of gas attacks waned and laws, regarding the carrying of gas masks, were relaxed and, as a bonus, the holders proved ideal for carrying a wide range of personal items.

Imagine the task set to all teachers, courtesy of an unknown person of authority, that it was their responsibility to ensure that children, in their care, carried their gas masks when on school property. Additionally, as part of the classroom syllabus, they had to have daily gas mask drills to ensure that children could quickly put on their masks almost as a reflex action. That was easier said than done as I well remember from my classroom days. Some children just got on with the task whereas others, with no small showing of skill, created problems as if under obligation to do so. "Please Miss," objections to wearing a gas mask were diverse and included a rubber induced feeling of sickness, loss of access to one's nose when it needed blowing or scratching, partial loss of visibility due to high levels of condensation or well-rehearsed panic attacks when their face was encased in a tight fitting second skin. These objections were effectively countered by a threat to fit the complainer with a *Mickey Mouse* gas mask designed for toddlers! Eventually the drill would get underway and, as far as I can remember, included the following distinct commands:

1. Remove your mask from its cardboard box.
2. Slowly and carefully put your mask on your face.
3. Check that the mask fits snuggly to your face, adjust straps if necessary.
4. Breath normally and await further orders.

The advent of gas masks produced new problems for all teachers regardless of the lesson in progress, and would range from a command to pay attention and leave your gas mask alone, to the more serious question of, "Where is your gas mask?" when teacher noticed its absence. Invariably the missing unit was recovered from the school toilet or found hanging on a peg in the cloakroom. I clearly remember one classical occasion when, after a prolonged search by teachers and pupils, the missing respirator was seen to be lying on the sloping roof of the Junior School and was duly recovered by the disgruntled caretaker. When questioned by the headmistress as to how the gas mask came to be where it was found the owner promptly responded with, "Don't know Miss." And when asked what he would have done had there been a gas attack he thought for a few seconds then, devoid of inspiration, he again reverted to, "Don't know Miss." In street terms many of the children I knew never took seriously the publicised role of the gas mask and preferred to use it as a multi-purpose play toy or, if the occasion demanded, it was an excellent weapon either in defence or attack when swung above the head in the fashion of a mediaeval flail.

August 1939. A question of character

Earlier in my narrative I touched upon two street 'characters,' known as Dick and Liddy, who blended well into street life mainly because, in working class areas, they were accepted without quibble. In 1930s Courtney Street, along with many other streets, there lived a marked cross section of 'characters' whose bizarre behaviour both annoyed or entertained yet, curiously, could never be fully ignored. There was one middle aged lady who was dubbed 'Mrs Cumming' because when passing people in the street she would always say, whether invited to or not, "Sorry I can't stop. I've got to get home because they are coming." No one ever found out who her visitors were and, to be fair, no one seemed interested enough to find out.

In general some characters were quiet and retiring whereas others were renowned for weird ideas, which they thrust upon anyone within vocal range. One man, who was thought to live in Burleigh Street, would either walk quietly along the street or when 'that way out,' which several claimed stemmed from the phase of the moon, he would accost people with the claim that he was a new prophet sent from distant space, and that he was here to save everybody. Such offers were usually met with a shrug of the shoulders and, without breaking step, the dissenter would mutter, "Don't know nowt about that mate" as he disappeared into the distance. Courtney Street people rarely allowed themselves to be drawn into impromptu debates, centred on extreme subjects, and quickly adopted a stance of 'neutrality through ignorance' that was symbolised by the above mentioned shrug of the shoulders.

Religious belief

Most street members were tolerant and respectful to religious groups and, in particular, to the previously mentioned Hull City Mission and the Salvation Army who, in several supportive ways, remained active throughout the war years. From what I learned directly or through the *wigging-in* technique indicated that most people held onto the Genesis Creation account, together with respect for their neighbour, except when circumstances demanded otherwise. It was then that the concept of an 'eye for an eye' as taught in the Book of Exodus could quickly be applied with spectacular results!

At the ungodly end of the scale there was a 'character' named Robert, who lived in one of the mid-terraces, who regularly proclaimed his belief that life began when a large rock, from outer space, hit the earth many millions of years ago. From within this rock emerged a multitude of microbes that, liking our climate, began to mutate into the various types of life, human and otherwise, known to us today. Robert, who was not noted for brevity of speech, persisted in openly evangelising his version of 'The Origin of the Species' to the dismay of those he met up with; and many terrace end meetings immediately disbanded to the cry, "Hey-op, Rock Bob's heading our way!"

Enter Gypsy Boswell

Conversely there were street 'characters' who were both accepted and even encouraged to display the fruits of their oddity. Such a person was a lady known locally as Gypsy Boswell who, as far as I remember, lived in Marion's Crescent. I am even less certain if her surname really was Boswell, which matters little in a street where nicknames were common place. Nevertheless street talk was adamant that she was from a travelling family, and that her late husband had a rewarding income from sweeping county manor house chimneys. Not surprisingly he died relatively young from bronchitis leaving his widow in reasonable comfort. Nevertheless Gypsy Boswell supplemented her funds by making and selling wicker mats and baskets to Holderness Road shops who, in turn, kept her busy through their regular orders. In parallel she would happily set aside her weaving and tell the fortune of anyone who called upon her. She never made a charge for this service and was reported to be unerringly accurate in many of her predictions. According to my mother she also had many regular clients who sought her advice on a wide range of topics ranging from flitting to another house, or would auntie whoever, on whom they had taken out a life policy, recover from her present illness?

But it was August 1939 and the street was awash with rumour and counter-rumour of the imminence of a war with Germany. Reportedly Hitler, whilst frothing at the mouth, was dementedly screaming that his patience was exhausted over the Danzig crisis together with many alleged attacks, made by Polish soldiers, over the frail border with Germany. Consequently a small number of Courtney ladies, including our next door neighbour, arranged to call upon Gypsy Boswell and ask her to foretell if war was imminent. Her main speciality was tea leaf reading which began by asking each of the ladies to drink their cup of tea and leave behind a small residue. After a mandatory three turns of the cup, whilst held in the left hand, it was upended and the liquid left to drain into the saucer. Sharp intakes of breathless amazement went around the room as Gypsy Boswell carefully scrutinised the residual tea leaves and pointed out many shapes resembling tanks, rifles and other warlike paraphernalia that left little doubt, in the minds of those around the room, that war was imminent. "But when will it happen?" gasped someone who was first to recover her voice.

With that Gypsy Boswell produced a tin box from a table drawer and, with due solemnity, removed a pack of Tarot Cards. At this stage allow me to remind you that my narration is totally dependent upon what I was later told, or heard, which was minimal with respect to the complex feed-back from Tarot readings. Reference to a range of cards symbolised by a *wheel of fortune* or *a hanged man*, together with many more odd situations, failed to bond with those seeking answers; except when the **nine of swords** emerged as a crucial card for all present.

"It could mean the ninth month which is September, "muttered Gypsy Boswell almost to herself. A cry of "Bloody hell that's next month!" was immediately followed by apologies for what, to the perpetrator, was a sacrilegious outburst. "But," she continued whilst clutching the Tarot Cards to her bosom and ignoring the interruption, "Before number nine can come to pass it will have to be preceded by one of the four Horsemen of the Apocalypse representing war; and you will know him because of his red horse."

With that the session was closed and, following the tradition of a good hostess, Gypsy Boswell passed round fresh cups of tea to all present. In due course the ladies wandered home convinced that war would begin in September but at a total loss to explain the part to be played by 'that there hossman from the Arpokerlist!' As an aside I must add that the name 'Apocalypse' first came my way expressed, phonetically, as **Arpokerlist** leaving me with a challenge to identify both the word and its origin which, in due course, I found in the Biblical book *Revelation* set amidst its wealth of prophecies appertaining to the end of the world.

September 1st 1939. The Galloping Major

My previous section brought into focus just four names from several well-known Courtney Street characters but, for reasons that will soon become obvious, I have urgent need to introduce you to yet another; better known as the Galloping Major. I became aware of him during some of my earliest *wigging in* sessions from which I heard, in graphic terms, that good or bad luck could emanate from him during his dramatic horseless gallop along the length and back of Courtney Street. No one knew who he was or where he lived although rumour had it that he sort of 'disappeared' into Waller Street which, according to one of my earlier sections, was a street noted for deep and dangerous intrigue!

Reasons for his spasmodic gallops, during which he faithfully reproduced horse-like mannerisms, were not clear. I believe this to be a good thing because clarity of any situation minimises the advance of creativity, through which tales bordering on the supernatural are readily generated and expanded on. For example there was a worried lady whose house fronted Courtney Street who owed a month's rent and, to the sound of the major galloping by, she rushed out only to find a ten shilling note lying on the pavement. Conversely, a woman startled by the clatter of his boots looked up from scouring her doorstep and, in doing so, knocked over her bucket of water. Who, other than the Galloping Major, could be blamed for a passing man slipping on the spillage and breaking his wrist? Yet despite my overwhelming sense of curiosity there were times, even in my early informative years, when I dismissed the entire business as a legend without foundation; although my meeting with the fabled Courtney icon was closer than I thought.

It is one of the peculiarities of the human mind that a certain date, in one's life, will arrive and remain as a beacon within a quagmire of quickly fading memories. For me Friday the 1st September 1939 was such a date because, as I arrived home from school, a sudden and unexpected party burst into life on the small square at the end of Leonards Avenue and, joy upon joy, the entire terrace was invited to it. The event was a wedding reception and 21st birthday party of John, a young man from the terrace who, by special licence, had married his school day sweetheart who he publically fawned over with unashamed passion. The reason for the haste was that the bridegroom was an army reservist, who fully expected to be ordered to duty at a moment's notice, thus adding a story book romance flavour to the occasion – and errant tears from older ladies who thrived upon such unrestrained tenderness. However, my attention to top table adult activities was minimal because I was distracted by the sight of several bottles of my beloved Tizer, seemingly begging me to drink from them, which I resolved to do as a matter of priority. Thus when a series of halting and slurred speeches had been delivered, and the couple had departed to Southcoates station for a two day honeymoon in Withernsea, attention was given to the serious matter of eating and drinking. As the piles of sandwiches decreased I noticed that men of the group, as if by prior arrangement, had furtively gathered around the respective fathers of the married couple who, in unison, announced that there were matters to be discussed that could best be done in 'Vicky' Vaults. Several female voices reminded departing family males that they had been 'supping since dawn' and that they should stick to drinking shandygaff (Shandys); which was received with silent contempt. Mother had long since taken her leave in order to get dad's tea on the table and the remaining ladies of the terrace were regaled, for the umpteenth time, by our neighbour who had attended the fortune telling session at the house of Gypsy Boswell.

For my part I joined up with a few of my mates as we watched, with keen interest, the antics of two Council workmen who were measuring the road, at fixed intervals, from a point beginning at Albion Avenue and ending at Granville Avenue. In due course, having become thoroughly fed up with our repeated, "What yer doin', mister?" advised us they were measuring up for three street air-raid shelters that were to be built there.

Agog to be the first to tell my mother about this breaking news I turned for home only to stop in my tracks, as if frozen to the spot, as a sudden burst of cheering and clapping came from the Holderness Road end of the street. Very soon the object of their attention appeared in the form of a bedraggled youth, wearing a thick woollen jersey despite the warmth of the evening, who was furiously galloping down the middle of Courtney Street. He wore a pair of hob nail boots that added an impressive amalgam of sound and sparks as he literally thundered along the road. His hair was wet with sweat and his eyes bulged, not unlike the appearance of a panic driven horse, as spittle became foam adhering to both sides of his face.

As if to release inner fears or simply to warn of his presence he, at regular intervals, threw back his head and gave vent to a series of highly credible neighing cries that put cats to flight and caused every dog in the district to bark their response. But that is where their defiance ended because it was blatantly obvious they were happy to maintain a safe distance away from those flailing feet of spark emitting iron. But, as in most situations, there has to be the exception and on this occasion it was a dog, perhaps new to the area, which launched himself at the Galloping Major, who undoubtedly he was, with the intention of literally ending his gallop. Although I searched hard I failed, abysmally, to think of a word more expressive than *spectacular* to describe what happened next when, in response to an ear-splitting whinnying cry, both his metal clad feet left the ground as a joint side kick aimed at the advancing dog. It was a mercy that he only caught the dog with a glancing blow but it was enough. With a yelp it ran, tail between its legs, and settled for sniffing at animal scents around the base of a lamp post; whilst the victorious Major, without loss of momentum, continued his relentless charge towards Dansom Lane. He momentarily marked time outside Tin Mission then, duly snorting in horse fashion, he turned and commenced a breakneck gallop back towards Holderness Road. A few dogs that had followed him at a discreet distance formed the view that they were the object of his charge and promptly fled into the nearby wood yard.

It was at this stage that the spectacle of the Galloping Major was matched by a dramatic incident that occurred at the top of Leonards Avenue when a horror driven scream gained the attention of all in that area. There stood the trembling form of our neighbour with her left hand clutched to her chest, as if appeasing an overworked heart, whilst her shaking right arm, with extended first finger, pointed at the retreating form of the Galloping Major. "Look at his jersey," she cried in a trembling voice. We duly did as told. "What colour is it?" she added with rising urgency. As one we replied, "Red," although in truth some did narrow it down to "Mucky red." She struggled to regain her breath and, with great effort, gasped out that we had witnessed the *Red Hossman from the Arpokerlist,* as predicted by Gypsy Boswell, meaning that we were now at war with Germany! Totally confused I drained all I could from a lone bottle of Tizer and slowly walked home wondering what was for tea.

Although I have been able to share with you my personal viewing of the Galloping Major I am still at a loss to explain his historical background. According to many adults they knew him in their childhood days yet, to me, he was a young teenager. Was he from a family of extroverts who specialised in impersonating horses, or was he a ghostly figure destined to spend eternity galloping up and down Courtney Street? On the premise that it takes all sorts to make a street I am prepared, for the moment, to accept the former option – unless any readers know differently?

PART FOUR

SEPT 1939 TO MARCH 1940

THE PHONEY WAR (SEPT 1939 – MARCH 1940)

Within the confines of *normal circumstances* I would have expected terrace end gatherers and pub bar supporters to have energetically debated, argued over, or perhaps resorted to fisticuffs in order to drive home their views on Gypsy Boswell's prediction – and the seemingly supportive role played by the Galloping Major. But we were far from being in normal circumstances. In rapid succession a series of unshakable facts had stunned Courtney Street and, indeed, the entire nation. Although it was not her nature to do so I would have imagined that Gypsy Boswell, if asked, would have claimed a fait accompli based upon three realities beginning on the 1st September when Germany attacked Poland, the 2nd of September when Britain demanded they withdrew or face war with the allies and, finally, at 11am on the 3rd September when Prime Minister Neville Chamberlain, told a packed House of Commons, that Germany had ignored our ultimatum thus meaning that we were at war. Already the recently formed British Expeditionary Army was on its way to join forces with our allies along the French-Belgian frontier with Germany. After Mr Chamberlain had completed his explanations the announcer gave out a list of directions for men of all service reserves to report immediately to their nearest depot or Mercantile Marine office. Thus Gypsy Boswell's predictions had come to pass and, as far as I know, she was never again consulted except in her capacity as a maker of wicker baskets.

For the first time I began to experience what I later discovered to be a melancholy state of mind as I slowly wandered towards Tin Mission and the awaiting Sunday school. We had now been at war with Germany for three hours and the only indication that anything was different was the fact that I had my gas mask case slung over my shoulder. I had heard on the one o'clock news that German aircraft were bombing Polish cities whereas, in stark contrast, the only activity above my head were two starlings arguing over perching rights on a lamp post. Before our classes began Pastor Finch addressed us on the horrors of war and the need, at all times, to pray that heads of nations would seek peace. Following his talk we struck up with the hymn 'O God, our help in ages past ....' and then moved on to our lesson which, to the best of my memory, was on our forthcoming Harvest Festival service.

On leaving I met up with two lads I knew who lived further down the street but went to St Mary's School, in Wilton Street, because they were Catholics. With arms outstretched they were acting the roles of opposing fighter aircraft, engaged in a dog-fight, with full vocal sound backing including the roar of the engines and rat-a-tat-tat of machine gun fire. "I wish I could be there to see the real battle," gasped the one who had stopped to recover his breath. "What real battle?" I asked with rising interest. "Haven't you heard Caney? At dinner time German troops landed at Hornsea and Withernsea and our army is pushing them back into the sea!" which prompted them to renew, with even greater intensity, their mid-air combat. Shaking my head I slowly walked home knowing full well that had the invasion story been true then Pastor Finch would have told us about it before we split up for our class work.

I chose to include this short scenario because I believe it to be a standard template for other false invasion reports that, in explicit terms, claimed comparable enemy landings that always happened along coastal areas local to Hull. Perhaps these were the result of an over active imagination or, dare I even suggest it, that our geographical knowledge may have been restricted to just Hull and district? It must be remembered that in the 1930s holiday breaks, for the majority, were day trips to Hornsea and Withernsea hence we lived in a much smaller world. I know this as factual because more years than I care to admit came to pass before my geographical knowledge embraced most of this country and several other parts of the world.

Monday 4th September 1939. Courtney Street at War

When I began to compile my war memories I gave much thought to what my first reactions were to the awesome transition from peace to war. I knew about peace in the same way I knew about life around me in Courtney Street but war; well it was something I thought only happened in other countries and that it was all about hurting people and making them cry. I did not like it and I knew that Pastor Finch at Tin Mission, who knew God better than I did, thought in the same way. So next Sunday I resolved to ask him to contact God and give him my request to stop all wars, so that we could be happy and have another terrace end party.

Then I realised that family life would never be the same again. I was fortunate that my dad would remain at Tan Yard on essential war work but many other mothers and fathers, together with courting couples, were faced with immediate separation due to conscription into the forces. The enormity of family break-up was beyond my level of comprehension but it had made its mark on all ages, and its pathos extended even to radio music through the regularly played song *Goodnight Sweetheart* written by Ray Noble, Jimmy Campbell and Reg Connelly; and made popular through the voice of Bing Crosby and other well-known singers. This song was to be a tribute to many separated couples and, in memory of that age, I will share the theme lines with you in the hope that some of you may remember the music:

> Goodnight sweetheart, all my prayers are for you
> Goodnight sweetheart, I'll be watching o'er you
> Tears and parting may make us forlorn
> But with the dawn a new day is born
> So I'll say goodnight sweetheart, sleep will banish sorrow
> Goodnight Sweetheart, when we meet tomorrow
> Dreams enfold you, in them, dear, I'll hold you
> Goodnight sweetheart goodnight.

Evacuation of the vulnerable

On August 31st, 1939, the government had decreed that evacuation of all vulnerable people from cities likely to be attacked by German bombers, including London, Birmingham and all major ports, would begin forthwith and, by the time war was declared, it was in full swing. It was designed to ensure the safety of children, disabled adults and others in similar categories by transferring them to countryside locations. Jim was too old to be evacuated whereas, according to Government sponsored appeals of the time, it was absolutely imperative that I be whisked away into the country until the danger was over. However evacuation was optional and parents had the right to refuse to part with their children. You may recall that the topic of evacuation, in the event of a war, had been discussed between the three of us and, at that time, the prospect of living in a country house, with a tree in its garden, was a bonus that appealed to me. But it was also true that mum and dad could not agree on the evacuation topic and it was, more or less, left up to me to decide if I wanted to go. I suppose I must have given my consent because, all of a sudden, all documentation had been completed and, much to my mounting horror, I realised that I was to be evacuated the following morning. I can clearly remember standing in my pyjamas, in the back kitchen, after having had a full wash down in the sink. All clothing mentioned on the evacuation list had been packed in my suitcase and a label bearing my name and school had been fixed to my jacket and, as a special going-away treat, mother had even included a bar of Fry's Five Boy chocolate wrapped up in my spare socks.

But all of a sudden I became aware that our light hearted turmoil centred around the packing process, urgent ironing, boots to be blacked (polished) and much laughter when dad asked if I wanted to take his Tan Yard clogs with me, or should they pack my now thread-bare Jelly Legs, *had been nothing more than a pretence*; designed to keep my spirits up. I lost count of the times that mother, with a loud sniff, suddenly broke off what she was doing and scampered up the stairs, only to return with the news that she was developing a cold. And why did Dad keep going into the yard in order to blow his nose and return with renewed determination to, somehow, continue with his comic act; which was never his strong point! But now it was early evening and the three of us, as if worn out with pretence and hard work, sat in silence in the back kitchen. I suddenly felt that I was waving goodbye to my childhood that had begun in Blanche Grove and developed into boyhood here in Leonards Avenue and, by return, I was going to live with total strangers who may either love me or hate my very presence under their roof.

But first of all I had to deal with the fact that this was my last night with mum and dad who I loved so much. For a few moments I stared at them both and, as if in slow motion, I watched a single tear leave my mother's eye as it sought a place upon her lap. The sight of mother's lone tear went straight to my heart, causing me to bite my lip and run over to the kitchen window. In mounting panic I studied the back yard – my first and only real playground – as I tried to burn into my memory every crack, chalk mark and scurrying 'black clock' that I must soon leave behind. Then mother's arm was around my shoulder and, with a break in her voice, she asked what was bothering me. My reply came in the form of a stifled cry, enveloped within a torrent of tears, as I flung myself into her arms and all I managed to blurt out was, "I don't want to go, I don't want to leave you both. I don't care anymore about trees in gardens cos this is where I want to live." In my highly charged emotional state I was shushed against saying anything more as the arms of both parents held me close, and gently assured my sobbing body and inconsolable mind, that we would see this war through together. That was enough for dad, who later admitted he'd been having second thoughts about me leaving, and he promptly grabbed his coat and departed for Williamson Street School, which was open all night as our local evacuation centre, to tell them to remove my name from their list. Soon he returned and we sat around the fire in silence after mother had summed up our future in the words, "If we have to die then it's good that we die together." Suddenly dad rose to his feet, looked at the clock, and then at me followed by "Up the dancers me lad – it's long past your bedtime." With a grin I said "Thanks dad," and was up the stairs two at a time. Although I had not been anywhere I felt I had come home – and I was here to stay.

Normally my journey to school was quick mainly because the men had gone to work and it was too early for mothers to set off shopping or even wash the doorstep. Also pavements were usually populated with junior and senior boys and girls who, in varying degrees of interest and attitude, headed towards their respective school gates. But today was different because it was Courtney Street evacuation day. Already I could see several single deck buses parked outside our two schools, awaiting the pleasure of snuffling mothers and crying children who, from a distance, resembled a pulsating mass of emotion held together by interlocked gas mask cases. Stir into this scene the sight of harassed teachers dashing around holding up names tags which had fallen off evacuees' coats, all to the wavering accompaniment of a clockwork gramophone playing *Rule Britannia*, courtesy of a group of flag waving elderly ladies. Hold this scene in your mind for it was truly a sight to remember!

I found out later that around two thirds of the school population left on the coaches that day, together with many of our teachers, which meant that remaining classes were larger in number and an even greater strain on facilities and teachers' tempers. At our morning assembly the Head Mistress, with no lack of dramatic voice control and rhetoric, proclaimed to us that ill-behaviour on our part was tantamount to helping Hitler win the war, and would always end with, " and we don't want that to happen – do we?" As ever we would enthusiastically respond, in a traditional vacillating school child voice, "No, Mrs Hardwick." (I cannot remember her real name). Because of staffing shortages the junior school reverted to mixed sex classes meaning that, for a time, I again sat next to Annie who I first shared a desk with in the infants school. Soon the teacher decided to split the classroom, with boys at one side and girls at the other, for reasons best known to her. However before this happened I discovered that Annie was still living in the same terrace but with her grandparents. Apparently her father was a reservist so he was already in France and her mother was on war work in a Hull factory. Nevertheless their plan to send Annie away from Hull, as an evacuee, may well have solved their custodial problem had the child agreed to it. In colourful terms she told me how she had stood up to her mother even to the threat of kicking her foster parents, refusing to eat, and if all else failed then she would join forces with Hitler! It would appear that her mother had more on her mind than her daughter's tantrums so Annie, courtesy of her grandparents, got her way. Then, almost as an aside, she confided in me that she had no intention of doing what she had threatened but it meant that she was able to win her case and remain in Courtney Street with her friends.

Civil Defence takes the offensive

As an eight year old boy, with a very strong sense of curiosity, I was at a total loss to understand how quickly Courtney Street had managed to prepare itself for a much publicised onslaught by enemy bombers. I suppose one disadvantage was that I lived in an age wherein children should be seen and not heard, which meant I rarely got a straight answer to a direct question which, nonetheless, brought me to my ever dependant *plan B* – the art of 'wigging-in' and listening to the radio. Through this time honoured technique I was able to piece together that, since mid-1930, Britain was satisfied that a war with Germany was inevitable and had, quite sensibly, put into action plans for both National and Civil defence; the latter of which was in an advanced stage of mobilisation. Fortified with this information it came as no surprise when I awoke on the second day of war to find that the windows of many shops, houses and office buildings had been decorated with criss-cross strips of sticky tape which, as I was later told, would lessen the blast force of a nearby exploding bomb that, otherwise, would shatter glass into thousands of lethal fast-flying fragments.

Courtney Street and the Blackout

Then there was the ***Blackout*** that took immediate effect when Hitler invaded Poland on the 1st September 1939 – some 48 hours before we declared war on Germany. This feature was designed to make sure that Hull, and all other inhabited places, remained under the cover of darkness in the event of a surprise attack by enemy bombers. It also brought into Courtney Street use a new expression that went along the lines of, "Do you know when *lighting up time* is?" Each day became more and more characterised not by its position in the week, or even what the weather was like, but by the all-important *lighting up time*; for which severe penalties faced anyone who flouted this new law against blacking-out the city. At this appointed time every semblance of light had, until the morning, to be hidden away from enemy sight. For some Courtney Street households this was a new and totally unaccustomed way of life because they, and their families before them, had never had curtains to close when the lights were on; and they cared not a fig that passers-by could *gawp* in at them. But in an instant times had changed. Houses, flats, offices and factories all needed to have proper window coverings. These could include shutters if thoroughly sealed, but most common were special curtains or blinds which the Government freely supplied, in the form of thick black material, to every applicant. Depending on the ability of the householder this material could be made into conventional *black-out blinds* or more attractive curtain designs as long as the finished covering conformed to legal requirements. And that is where the real problem began because *black-out* curtains could not simply be drawn together because sections of light may escape at the edges. My mother overcame this by fixing eye-rings to the curtain, and hooks to the wooden window frame, which meant the daily putting-up of black-out blinds, over the net curtains, was a wearisome process – to say the least. Also a dark curtain had to be fitted over the front door and woe-betide anyone who opened that door, without first turning off the house light, for they were likely to hear the air-raid warden shout, "Turn that light off – have you forgotten there's a war on!"

Obviously at my then age I never went out alone in the blackout and even with an adult it was a scary experience. Particularly on a cloudy night the darkness was intense and as a child I was terrified and clung onto the hand of whoever I was with. Revisiting my fears with an adult mind it felt as if I was trapped in a thick black fog and seemingly surrounded by forces of ill-will. Sometimes they would feel very close to me causing me to hit out with my free hand which, to my then mind, led me to believe that whoever it was had, laughingly, just stepped out of the way. I hated my new experience of total darkness even to the degree that a visit to the petty became a postponed challenge that necessity eventually had to over-ride! Use of public highways became a nightmare because any vehicle driving in the dark had, by law, to partly shield its headlights, and torches had to be covered with tissue paper in order to dim the light. All street lights were turned off for the duration of the war as were lit signposts and previously illuminated advertising hoardings. This may well have confused Luftwaffe pilots but its effect upon Saturday night drinkers was, to say the least, catastrophic and worthy of a pause in my narrative whilst I share with you the following over-heard tale that I have edited into a readable account: –

If perchance you happened to be slowly and carefully feeling your way along Courtney Street during the black-out, long after pub last orders and final chuck-out had occurred, you may have wondered why a myriad of tiny fireflies were slowly oscillating their way towards you. Knowing that no such creature would ever venture into Courtney Street you may surmise they were static electrical sparks produced from the highly charged black velvet night around you? "Surely not," you may muse and elect for a down-to-earth conclusion along the lines, "I don't know what the heck they are but they are certainly confusing me!"

As they drew closer then detail would replace conjecture as it became obvious these were, in fact, glowing cigarette ends faithfully following the unsteady gait of alcohol befuddled smokers. It truly was a scenario of the unexpected. For example a static glow of varying intensity, hovering some 15 inches above ground level, was indicative of a drunken smoker lying on the pavement puffing away at his cigarette whereas, from time to time, a glowing cigarette end would vanish to be followed instantly by a thud and an oath – meant that the smoking reveller had walked into a blacked-out lamp post. The blackout would prove to be a productive patron of new experiences for many in Courtney Street before the war finally ran its course.

The experience of total darkness was exciting for many because it was their first glimpse of a virgin night sky wherein the moon and distant stars could display their natural brilliance unhindered by reflections from city lights. As with most advantages there was the downside in the form of confusion, fear and danger trying to get from start to destination. Many of our neighbours came to instant grief when stepping out of their darkened house into a blacked-out Leonards Avenue seemingly awash with limb threatening obstacles. The first challenge was 'find the kerb' which, since the metal railings had been removed, was no longer a safe haven to hold on to. In fact it is fair to say that, invariably, the kerb was first to find an unwary foot and, with apparent glee, quickly deposited its owner onto whatever was awaiting him or her. Other adventurers, attempting to be wary of the kerb ahead, would misjudge the distance to the once entrance gate and prematurely turn left or right into the waiting branches of a rose bush or similar growth. Each such misadventure was accompanied by an outburst of full throated obscenities that had my mum and dad rocking with laughter in their chairs. In fact dad often said it was more entertaining than listening to the radio! Since the first of September road accidents had increased so much that a 20mph speed limit was introduced and **white lines were painted down the centre of roads – which are still with us today.** White paint was also applied to kerb edges and the base of lamp posts but accident rates remained high throughout the blackout period. One of the more unusual safeguards recommended to male blackout walkers was to leave their shirt-tails hanging out so they could be better seen in dimmed headlights.

Although I never saw it applied in Courtney Street I was assured that some men did adopt this precaution and, on one occasion, it almost resulted in serious injury – or even worse. It was one of those accounts that drifted on for a while although rarely openly talked about lest the ears of 'banes' should be corrupted by it. Most mothers used the silent word cum lip reading technique which was a challenge to my curiosity although, with my now advanced expertise at *wigging-in*, I was able to finally extract, edit and store the entire episode in my mental social history file awaiting the advent of this book. In order to flavour its readability I have given the lead characters' names which, for obvious reasons, are entirely fictitious:

Shirt Tails in the Blackout

Matrimony had done George Brown no favours. Those who knew him in his single days would well remember his cheerful and friendly disposition but, seemingly, his new wife would have none of this. In their courtship days he was known as 'laughing George', a popular guest at any party worthy of the name; but all this changed after they were married. There was a malefic down side to his wife's nature that gained momentum after the marriage vows had been exchanged and the church door had closed behind them. With no small amount of skill, she managed to make his life a living hell. As the years passed by he became a morose yet steady man, who held down a steady job, as a steady-minded insurance agent cum collector for a local company. His income was as dependable as his nature which meant that he and his wife Martha lived in relative comfort. There were no children of the marriage.

As time went by Martha developed an obsession that George was having an affair and no amount of denial from her husband made the slightest impact on her views. Eventually her mania reached such proportions that she would wait for him to leave his office and walk him home, *to keep an eye on him*, caring not that her actions raised occasional eyebrows in the neighbourhood. However he was allowed out every Monday evening in order to attend his R.A.O.B. meeting of which he was a lifelong member but, true to tradition, she would be waiting for him outside the Lodge when his time came to leave. However the onset of the blackout meant that Martha dare not face the unlit streets alone despite her conviction that George, somehow, was having a clandestine affair with his 'floozy' despite his pleas of innocence. But her husband always arrived home at the same time, and in his usual melancholy state of mind, which changed not as they drank their traditional cup of cocoa prior to retiring for the night.

Then the evening for the Buffs' Annual General Meeting arrived which, by its title alone, meant that it was a special occasion which had to be marked with an above normal intake of alcohol. By tradition the business side of the meeting was quickly concluded and jollities began which, in the early months of the war and before air raids had started, were almost like a return to peace-time life; but that was until the time came for George to leave and face the darkness outside. Regardless of the blackout which was intensified by heavy cloud overhead George, by instinct, knew his way home. However, in the interests of personal safety, he had agreed with his colleagues that since they were all a little tipsy they should walk home with their shirt tails on full display. Consequently as good Buffs they would be safety conscious through which road traffic would see them better. Thus George promptly pulled his white shirt out of his trousers and with the tails swaying below his knees, and his coat over his arm, he began his careful walk home that was achieved without mishap – until he knocked on his own front door.

With the interior light turned off the door was opened and George entered to his wife muttering, "You're late – you've been with that woman again." With that she switched on the light and beheld her husband standing before her in an attitude of wild abandonment with his shirt resembling a long smock and an alcohol-fired grin marking his enjoyment of the fact. This initial meeting was based on sound conjecture but what followed was clearly heard by most people in the terrace. To say that Martha went berserk was a profound understatement. From a fusion of oaths and hysterical shrieks came remarks such as, "Why did you bother to put your trousers back on?" and "Did she keep you warm in bed?" followed by Martha declaring that she would put an end to it.......

By now several alarmed neighbours were standing in the terrace, wondering what to do, when, without warning, the front door burst open and George, in a blaze of light, staggered out clutching his arm which was bleeding badly from the attentions of a carving knife. Neighbours and at least two Air Raid Protection (ARP) wardens, attracted by the uproar and rare sight of an electric light openly competing with the blackout, were quick on the scene and Martha was contained before she was able to complete her threat to "Kill that two-timing bastard!" Matters then moved quickly. George was taken off to the Infirmary and his wife was arrested and detained in the police station. George, who had the unspoken sympathy of his neighbours, soon returned home and was cared for by his rescuers whereas his wife, having mentally passed the point of no return, succumbed to a heart attack whilst creating in the police station cell.

Had this rather sad story ended at this stage then it could not have justified a place in this book. However I was so amazed by the startling epitaph to this tale of woe that I felt it a matter of historical duty to secure a place for it, within the archives of Courtney Street history, from which now I leave you to draw your own conclusions......

....George Brown suffered no lasting ill from his injury and soon returned to work and two months later, after a very short engagement, he married his work colleague Jean Summers who, through the years, had accompanied him on all his insurance rounds.

Meet the Air Raid Protection Wardens (ARP)

My above passing reference to Air Raid Protection wardens reminded me that I should not allow these important public characters to simply drift in and out of my narrative without formal introduction. After all they did play a vital national role when Britain was under almost constant aerial bombardment and many of them lost their lives in the line of duty.

As far back as 1937, when war was seen as a distinct possibility, a large number of volunteers were recruited and trained to be Air Raid Wardens. Hence when war was declared the scheme was up and running and its ranks were quickly swelled by many more volunteers from men and women in reserved war work, or others who were only partially active for whatever reasons. The Wardens were trained in first aid, basic fire control and were also responsible for enforcing the blackout. They helped in policing roles too, particularly in protecting bomb damaged property from the attention of looters which, unfortunately, did happen and I will touch upon this outrage later. For identification purposes they were issued with arm bands, steel helmets with 'ARP' stamped on them, a hand bell to tell people when it was safe to leave the shelter, a rattle to sound in the event of a gas attack and a whistle to summon help if needed – not forgetting their own gas mask! All this ancillary equipment was packed in a shoulder bag which, more so for older volunteers, was no small weight to carry around. Local command posts were required and, for the Courtney Street neighbourhood, a sturdy concrete ARP station was built on a plot of spare land between Tin Mission and a dental laboratory fronting on to Dansom Lane. As a point of general interest the ARP post was close to one of several static water tanks that would play an important role when the incendiary bombs began to fall.

Our very first air raid alert

Whilst typing the above title it immediately struck me that its construction appeared to radiate the same level of loving tenderness that one might have expected from the announcement, "Our very first child!" Without doubt both events could claim originality whereas their paths of development would be in stark contrast. Birth is the joy of new life and an air raid siren became symbolic of approaching death which, despite our optimism, could not be denied.

Regardless of the seriousness of our plight I must admit that as an active eight year old I was still, secretly, looking forward to the first non-practice sounding of the buzzers; which was the general expression for the sirens used in Courtney Street and, I imagine, in many other places. My repressed excitement approached bursting point as mum and dad prepared the house in accordance with advice given in several civil defence leaflets that came through the letter box.

Until street air raid shelters were built then interim places of safety, in the event of an enemy raid, were to be found beneath the kitchen table or within an alcove formed by the boxed-in bedroom staircase. After a brief experiment it was unanimously agreed that the underside of the kitchen table was inadequate for a family of four, whereas 'under the stairs' as it became better known, was ideal. Although Leonards Avenue houses did not have a meter cupboard beneath the stairs, a sort of inner sanctuary of safety, there was sufficient space to sit on an assortment of cushions and stools. As a final move the kitchen table was tipped on its side so as to effectively box us in on three sides and, should a raid become severe, we had some old blankets to crawl under as a cover against flying glass. We each had our designated jobs to do before we went 'under the stairs' and mine was to cover the goldfish bowl so that nothing could fall into it. After one or two trial sessions we were fully prepared and ready for Hitler to do his worst.

The first opportunity for us to prove ourselves came to pass at around 3am on the 4th September 1939 when I awoke to dad's voice bellowing, "Everybody up – the buzzers are blowing." In record time we were dressed and, according to plan, we were soon huddled beneath the staircase wondering what would happen next. No one spoke and we each listened for the slightest sound that would betray what was happening outside. In a short space of time I found total darkness to be stifling, and the steady tick of the house clock ominous, as fear quickly replaced my former boyhood quest for an adventure. My confidence was not helped when I recalled explicit radio reports of bombing raids upon Polish cities, and Hull Daily Mail pictures of terrified women and children running from burning ruins in Warsaw. Perhaps mother sensed that I was upset as she put her arm around me and despite the darkness she, with unerring accuracy, guided a piece of 'Five Boys' chocolate into my mouth. Yet silence and darkness continued to cocoon us in its unreal world of oppressive isolation in which the slightest sound was an omen of doom. Once or twice I forgot the rule and began to say something only to be stilled by 'shhh' warnings, which carried a hint of further action if not obeyed. Thus as self-appointed Trappist Monks we silently gave our mind to all that was happening outside albeit that, within a period of around two hours, all we heard were sporadic blasts from an ARP warden's whistle and a voice of authority bellowing, "Close those curtains." Then without warning my cotton wool life of isolation ended as the air raid siren began its gradual build-up to an unbroken level of ear-splitting decibels that flushed my mind '*clear*' of everything; except for the fact that the '*all clear* 'was sounding. Nevertheless our household did suffer a war related casualty in the form of Jim hopping around on one leg howling that he had cramp in his left foot.

There was never any doubt that great effort was being paid to the creation of new regulations designed to give maximum attention to the needs of war-torn members of the public. Some never got off the ground and many others were ignored when the Blitz was at its height. However one that did stay the course was that morning school attendance could be missed if an air raid alert, lasting more than one hour, had occurred after midnight. Thus freed from school attendance meant a morning discussing the incident as perceived and exaggerated by children, who had been ordered to stay at the terrace end in case the buzzers went again, whilst their mothers, with arms folded in grim contemplation, relived the night's events in discreet debating groups. For once I did not wig-in to adult conversation having become enthralled by several topics raised by my peers including, yet again, renewed enemy activity along the east coast betwixt Withernsea and Hornsea. There was one rather verbose lad, whose nickname was Billy-Boy, who would not have been out of place shouting the odds at Speakers Corner. He went on to proclaim that last night's buzzers were because a lot of German bombers had been shot down over Spurn Point, and that only one had got through on its way to Hull. But it ran out of petrol and crashed into a field just outside Withernsea. At that point a passenger train, as if on cue, passed on its way to Withernsea which prompted, with no small measure of sarcasm, a heckler to comment that if Withernsea was under attack that it was odd that the trains were still running. With a degree of derision in advance of his age Billy Boy carefully stressed, as if talking to someone who was hard of hearing, that Withernsea station had not been captured by the Germans which was the reason that our trains were still going there. As his opponent drew breath to reply Billy Boy quickly added that all he said was true because it came from his dad, who was a bus driver for the East Yorkshire Bus Company, so he knew about and saw all that was happening.

September 1939 to May 1940. The Funny War

It was not long before the written and spoken media were describing present hostilities as little more than a *phoney war* because, as far as this country and western Europe were concerned, nothing of any note had happened. British and French troops had taken up positions on the Franco-German border and there, more or less, they remained. Certainly Germany was not alarmed by this threat at their back-door and, although outnumbered by the allies, they did not feel the need to divert forces from their Polish offensive. The plight of the Polish people was horrendous more so because of another dodgy peace treaty, this time between Germany and Russia, that contained a secret agreement for the Soviet Union to invade Poland and thus set-up a buffer zone with Germany. Under the leadership of Generalissimo Joseph Stalin Russian military might poured over the border and advanced rapidly into eastern Poland and, true to tradition, the Poles openly fought until they were swamped. After this they continued as an underground resistance movement that was very active until the end of the war and, as if to press their hatred of their attackers to the full, many of their fighter pilots found their way to Britain and a place in the forthcoming Battle of Britain.

The media may well have been confused and so was I! As an avid follower of news bulletins I had a fair idea of what was happening and any gaps were filled through my relentless *wigging-in* sessions. But quite suddenly the expression '***phoney war***' had become very fashionable and I had not the remotest idea what it meant. It must be remembered that in those days a dictionary or thesaurus were strangers to most houses in Courtney Street and our only book, other than the Bible, was the 'Family Doctor' which was hidden away from me because of its rather *sensitive* content. Then I suddenly realised that the word 'phoney' when said quickly, with all the richness of the Hull accent, was not far removed from the word 'funny' which was enough for me. The next day was a busy one for teacher in her oversized class but I managed to briefly catch her attention with my question, "Please Miss, do you think this is a funny war?" She gave me a glassy look and told me to ask her again at play time – which did not materialise because I overheard a teacher say that Miss was resting with a bad headache. At home I waited in the yard for dad to come home from work and then fired the same question at him. His response was less polite and went along the lines, "Don't give me any of your stupid jokes because I'm tired and want my tea."

But phoney or funny, whatever the case may be, there was an attitude of don't rush at things – just sit back and see what happens. From what I have read of that era there was a belief, from Prime Minister Chamberlain downwards, that Hitler did not want a war with Britain and its allies, and when his conquest of Poland was over then all would slowly return to normality. After all Hitler had made no attempt to attack Western Europe with his *Blitzkrieg* tactics that had laid Polish cities to waste and, according to a news programme I heard in October 1939, he had even offered to enter into peace talks with us. However this marking-time philosophy allowed Britain to build up her strength should the need for all-out war ever become a reality.

In later years I formed the view that our Government had overlooked the fact that Germany was also getting stronger, both in confidence and military might, which was an awesome combination; more so when Italy, who were a military driven nation of doubtful fighting ability, under the dictatorship of Benito Mussolini, had signed a 'no holds barred' pact with Hitler. Before I move on I will add that, at times, our House of Commons was a battlefield in its own rights with cries for Chamberlain to resign before it was too late. There was a strong move from many key members, including Winston Churchill, who recognised that Hitler had world domination in mind and we should not waste another moment trying to appease him.

Barrage Balloons and Sandbags

In Courtney Street, and indeed throughout the country, the phoney war had effectively diluted a determined fighting spirit that sprang to life when war was declared. From time to time, and for no apparent reason, the buzzers would sound but enemy aircraft were not involved and even Billy Boy had conceded that enemy action against Withernsea had ceased! However I must stress that regardless of an absence of bombs and bullets in our midst there had been no let-up in national security which, if anything, was intensifying as time went by. For example we had hovering above our heads bloated and heaving bags of hydrogen called barrage balloons, whose metal mooring cables were designed to deter low flying aircraft from attacking our city. There were times though when these obese monsters would break loose, and their trailing metal hawser would short-circuit power lines causing serious disruption to the war effort. Then there was the memorable occasion when, in a strong wind, a local balloon broke free from its moorings and its straggling metal chain destroyed a whole line of house chimney stacks. The response from several soot covered residents was severe and their anger fired comments were totally unsuitable for this book. But, in fairness, their fury was justified and I will recognise their wrath through one of the milder expressions delivered by a little old lady of some ninety years who, whilst waving a clenched fist at the errant balloon, was heard to ask, "Whose blooming side are those gasbags on?"

Elsewhere around us much was happening. Seemingly overnight all pillar box domed tops had been painted with a yellow gas-sensitive paint, which would turn red if exposed to the merest whiff of mustard gas, thus giving an instant warning to put on our gas masks. Every day more and more sandbags were appearing in front of shops and public buildings as an additional defence against explosions and flying splinters. Now this was really a first class idea because it was not unusual for bags of sand to split and discharge their contents on to the pavement. Passing adults may mutter the odd 'tut-tut' and walk around what was, to them, more mess on the pavement; but in my eyes it was a seaside beach born again – and there for the taking. In the blink of an eye those grains of happy memories were scooped into my pockets and taken home where I would relive summer trips by making sand castles in the backyard. There were always tense moments when I arrived home with my pockets filled with sand, and the sight of my bulging pockets immediately set mother off *chowing* at me. The threat, "If you *traipse* sand through the house then I'll *bray you*," was a risk well worth taking and, as the war progressed, my backyard sand castles grew larger – that was until it rained hard when, much to my chagrin, sand castles and memories attached to them quickly disappeared down the yard sink and immediately blocked the drainage system. Horrified I watched the water level in the yard creep up until the petty floor was flooded and dad, despite the heavy rain, had to start digging out the blocked yard sink. To say that he was annoyed would fail abysmally to describe his true feelings and, when his task was over and two buckets were filled with wet sand, I had little difficulty in resisting the temptation to ask him if I could have my sand back!

Despite the intrusion of sand bags, yellow pillar boxes, sticky taped windows and barrage balloons Holderness Road and district had been revitalised by the daily sight of smart looking men and women, resplendent in their service uniforms, as they proudly socialised in areas once noted for empty stomachs and no work. All service personnel now had the advantage of a regular wage, paid to their dependants, some of whom were also employed on war work in local factories. Therefore household incomes had never been so high but an increasing dependency was being placed upon aging grand-parents to care for children during the day. But phoney war or not there was now a very much 'live for the day' attitude that was much to the fore and service personnel, who knew their days may well be numbered, were making the most of their new found public admiration. Most of them were mainly on post basic training leave, prior to being ordered to wherever the War Department saw a need for their presence, so they had understandable intentions of grasping enjoyment whilst they could. They were particularly welcomed at the Abbey Street dance hall and were never short of partners, in the many popular *excuse me* type dances, ranging from the Saint Bernard waltz to a slow fox-trot – whilst not forgetting the up and coming palais-glide that became very popular in WW2.

What's on the news today?

The expression, "As long as I know what is going on around me then I can put up with anything," was the proverbial bottom line sought by most street discussion groups. But a wind of change had set in and, since September 3rd 1939, that cherished conclusion had evaded all interested parties be they around the home fire, at a wind-swept terrace end or leaning on a pub bar. Naturally I became curious. So through long established processes I discovered their problem was a simple one to express, but impossible for them to answer. For example the concept of being citizens of a country which was officially at war with another major nation baffled many due to a perceived lack of physical aggression between the two adversaries. Not that anyone wanted any form of hostility but it was a common belief that, throughout history, war depended upon violent action in order to justify its title. As one street philosopher later said in my presence, "A war without hurt is like a dentist without pincers," and to substantiate his claim he gave a wide toothless grin to all around.

There were many street dwellers that bothered not with a radio or newspapers, and when they set foot outside they would immediately ask of the first person they met, "What's on the news today?" The response could take minutes or considerably longer but the conclusion was ever the same – simply nothing aggressive was happening in Europe. In fact the general direction of many conversations was beginning to slip back to the 'peace-time' stage set of weather and rats in the backyard. Nevertheless communication was still alive but whether it was effective or not was another matter. For example declaration of war had coincided with the appearance of a Sandwich Board man who, with total disregard for the weather, walked the length of Courtney and surrounding streets. He was a thin faced morose man with straggly wisps of white hair hanging from the edge of his cap and down to his shoulders. From a cursory glance it appeared that facial muscles had failed him in that his lower jaw would not fully close, and the resultant gap revealed his only tooth situated centre right in his upper gum. It was a prominent tooth that someone, of active mind, was quick to describe as a milestone along his path of life! The message on his Sandwich Boards was simple and to the point in that the front advised everyone to 'BEWARE' whilst the rear qualified this with 'YOUR END IS NIGH.' If anyone should ask him for clarification of this cautionary message they were met with a sniff and quickly given a crumpled leaflet that came out of his pocket with the speed of a Wild West gunfighter as he, without breaking pace, trudged slowly on his way.

Another popular source of communication, to be found outside several newsagent shops along Holderness Road, were news placard boards carrying headlines such as, "Air Attacks upon German Harbours – much damage caused." However radio programmes did not share this level of euphoria and, as the winter of 1939 approached, both sides settled down to propaganda warfare in which the RAF reportedly dropped millions of anti-Hitler leaflets over German cities and had several planes shot down and damaged in the process. As a point of interest I read, in later years, that the British Government had banned all bombing attacks on German land targets due to a high risk of incurring civilian casualties. Clearly we were novices to modern warfare and, did we but know it, our British fair play was soon to be swept aside by levels of airborne brutality, committed by both sides, that would scar history until the end of time.

Moreover I remember hearing on the radio that Hamburg was one of the cities showered with leaflets. This was the city used as a base for the notorious German propagandist William Joyce who was Irish by blood, American by birth and carried a British passport. His nick-name was Lord Haw-Haw and he broadcast nightly news bulletins, in English, to the British people. As a lad I heard several of his broadcasts that always began with, "Germany calling, Germany calling," which at its peak had a reported audience of around six million listeners. I hasten to add that his attraction was not through the quality of his transmissions but, rather, in the ludicrous way he tried to drive home blatant lies. Many listeners reported that his broadcasts helped dispel the monotony of war-time life in Britain; in fact my father thought him to be as funny as the comedian Arthur Askey but, on reflection, he would add the rider,

"Well – not quite!" At the end of the war Joyce was arrested by British Military Police and taken to London where he was tried and found guilty of treason. He was hanged at Wandsworth prison in 1946.

National Registration Day

Much publicity had been given to a date in late September which bore the title 'National Registration Day' when every householder had to fill in a form giving details of the people who lived in their house. I remember my dad grumbling about it in terms of "not another bloody form to fill in," although at school our teacher told us how important it was for the Government to know who lives in what and where. No one seemed to be too sure as to why this information was needed and, more so, why a threat of prosecution hung over the head of anyone who refused to comply. For those who had difficulty with reading and writing a team of volunteers was available to help and, to avoid embarrassment, confidentiality was assured. Nonetheless I felt a degree of private embarrassment because, for the first time, my *wigging-in* skills were of no avail since no one, regardless of social standing, had the remotest idea what the forthcoming National Registration Day was all about. In fact it was several decades later, when I was involved in researching my family history, that I began studying census returns that had been compiled every ten years beginning in 1841. I found that a National census was held in the year 1931 but, soon afterwards, every record of it was destroyed in a fire. Thus in 1939 the Government were restricted to outdated 1921 census information, and the stark fact that a 1941 survey may well be out of the question. They realised there was an urgent need for a 1939 National Registration Day which was virtually a census, albeit out of sequence. With hindsight it then became obvious that the Government needed the data for three main purposes: –

1. To enable a National Identity Card system to be introduced through which all non UK subjects were identified and, in the interests of national security, processed accordingly. I well remember my Identity Card which, by law, had to be carried

around by every citizen and had to be shown on demand by police officers or other authorised persons. It was mandatory to commit to memory its unique number which, together with my National Service Army number, I can clearly recite today; because to forget such detail does not bear thinking about both then and now! In relatively recent times attempts have been made to re-introduce the Identity Card scheme but, at the time of writing, the 1939 to 1952 National Identity Card remains unique in British history.

2. The National Registration requirement would help the War Office identify members of the public whose ages would necessitate their registration for compulsory enrolment into the Armed Forces.

3. Finally to establish names, ages and health issues for every member of the public who would, according to their status, be issued with a ration allowance book.

What colour was your Ration book?

When the historic day dawned for every eligible person in the country to receive a Ration book then my level of curiosity hovered around 'melt down'. My nature called for immediate answers which were not forthcoming because parents had this unfortunate tendency to prevaricate, or if I pushed hard, I would be ordered to *stop nattering* and go and play in the back yard. Teachers were not much better because they were too busy to talk and they would see me at play time – which they never did. However I did briefly establish that it would not have a noticeable effect upon my intake of bread and jam; until mother added that she could not be absolutely sure of this. At times parents could be more irritating than I was supposed to be but, as ever, they had right and might on their side. Then there was the matter of the ration books themselves. “Mam, why is mine a different colour from yours and dad's?” was a question that I could not get out quickly enough. Through persistence and *wigging-in* I soon learned that my blue ration book entitled me to more meat, milk and fruit than the buff coloured version held by all adults. Needless to add I was not allowed to even handle my ration book, and my request to take it to school in the event that I may feel hungry was dismissed without comment. Despite being denied the opportunity to examine these books I did work out that they were full of coupons which were cut out and used to buy a fixed amount of rationed foods each week. For example each time sugar was bought the sugar coupon was handed over to the lady at Maypole. This meant that if all of the sugar coupons were used up early in the week then you had to wait until the next week for more. Despite a growing scarcity of food I must admit that throughout the war years I never once felt hungry, yet in later years, when I became a parent myself, I often wondered if my parents suffered hunger pains on my behalf?

Rationing was progressively introduced and began in early January 1940 when a weekly adult allowance of butter was fixed at two ounces (50 grams) with sugar at eight ounces (200 grams). I distinctly remember the amounts because dad went livid at the news and wished Hitler a not-so-happy New Year – or words to that effect. As the war progressed practically everything that was available was on ration including clothing and furniture. Fortunately the various amounts that made up a weekly food ration per person could be augmented with un-rationed extras like bread, cereal, potatoes, fruit and vegetables: ever assuming they were available in the shops.

Make-do and mend

Even after the passage of over seventy years the expression 'war time spirit' still comes to mind when I am faced with challenging projects, which rely upon hard work and dedication for a desired outcome. Such was the response in those early months of the war when clothing, bedding, curtains and many more essentials were in short supply and much was done to encourage women to repair family clothes or 'recycle' old clothing, by unravelling the wool of aging jumpers and knitting it into something useful for all members of the family. In Courtney Street a 'Make do and Mend' group was opened in Tin Mission and the noise of pedal operated Singer sewing machines, and clacking knitting needles, became a regular feature at that end of the street. According to a poster on the mission notice board the organisers would, from time to time, invite a guest demonstrator who would encourage the ladies to be inventive and produce dresses and skirts from old curtains and, in turn, curtains or table cloths from barrage balloon material (a sort of rubberised fabric) that was always lying around the area particularly after an air raid. As a last resort when ladies stockings were not available then many women would work in pairs and draw lines down the backs of their friend's legs to give the impression they were wearing stockings. That was the limit of my knowledge of what happened within these meetings, mainly because mother did not go and neither did the neighbours she regularly talked to; hence I was left without many juicy little anecdotes that are dear to my heart!

However there was one incident that was related to the make do and mend group who, as I mentioned, used our Sunday school hall for their activities. Despite clearing away all their belongings the ladies had, on this occasion, failed to notice a pin lying on the floor. It would appear that the caretaker had also missed this object when she inspected the room before the Sunday class began. Then as we filed in we were told to sit on the floor because the teacher wanted to do some group work. As many parents are aware it is not the nature of children to sit still and one boy, in the midst of writhing-about, managed to impale his lower quarters on the afore mentioned pin. He immediately leapt to his feet and, clutching his bottom, raced around the room yelling his head off. In due course he was taken home and his angry mother was heard to ask if they gave the banes pin cushions to sit on!

Birth of the Black Market

It is a sad fact of life that whatever the situation, be it for good or bad, there will always be someone who will cheat in order to make money; and even the wartime rationing system was quickly abused by a rising tide of self-motivated enemies of the state. These miscreants were often referred to as *Spivs* and they made handsome profits from those who had the money to pay over the odds for rationed commodities. This practise became a National problem and was known as the *Black Market*. It was vigorously attacked by Ministry of Food Inspectors, supported by the police, and when convicted the perpetrators received hefty fines together with hard labour prison sentences. In fact there was a move in Parliament to add several strokes of the birch to their tariff, but I do not recollect if it ever came about.

Throughout the war years, despite my traditional watching and *wigging-in*, I was never aware of ration fiddling on the scale reported in other parts of the country. However there was one incident I will share with you which I 'overheard' at a terrace end and it involved a new milkman in the area. It had been noted that he always had surplus milk available, at extra cost, which the spokeswoman alleged came about because he diluted his milk allocation with water. This particular meeting ended their business by agreeing to pass their suspicions to the police after which the milkman was never again seen in the street.

My personnel view is that shady dealings, involving rationed items, just did not happen to any great extent in the area where I lived. For if we are to accept that affluent households readily attracted operators from the Black Market then Courtney Street, and district, would be to them what a sunny day is to Count Dracula!

Home for Christmas

At the risk of becoming boring on the topic I must stress again that I, despite my early years, was an avid listener to radio news items relevant to our war with Germany. I mention this because I was alarmed at a growing attitude among the public that there was something phoney about this so-called war, mainly because bombs were not falling in their back yards. Increasingly, the Government was being criticised over its handling of the crisis with Germany both on the battle field and within the confines of our shorelines. More and more I heard adults complaining that Hitler was being constantly appeased whereas they were being pressed to evacuate their children, endure the blackout, eat less because of food rationing and risk being fined for not carrying an Identity Card on their person; all in the name of a war which, according to many, did not exist as far as they were concerned.

But from what came out of our radio I was convinced that members of the Royal and Merchant Naval Services were very much aware that there was a war in progress because they had been in the front line from day one. I had started to keep a childlike diary of events in which I remember recording the fact that a liner was torpedoed, with the loss of over 100 lives, on the very day war was declared. A few days later another passenger ship taking evacuees from Britain to Canada was sunk with the loss of around 90 children and many adults. As part of a staple diet of maritime carnage several of our merchant ships were sunk and the Royal Navy were initially outgunned by the powerful German battleships *Scharnhorst* and *Bismark*. However I was able to record one item of good news in that three of our light cruisers, despite one of them suffering severe damage, had doggedly followed and managed to disable the German pocket battleship *Admiral Graf Spee* forcing it to shelter in Montevideo harbour, wherein she was subsequently scuttled.

In and around where I lived aggression was still restricted to neighbourhood arguments over whose son had been throwing stones and broken Mrs Whoever's window, or why the coalman had delivered only two of the three bags of coal paid for? But change was in the air. At first it was barely noticed because it began as a mere trickle that soon, as Christmas 1939 got nearer, became a torrent of returning evacuees, both young and elderly, who had decided that enough was enough. Many said they were fed up with quiet villages and rural tranquillity and longed for the noise and bustle that characterised the East Hull Street of their birth. Others, looking around them cynically as they got off the coach, would ask if their house was still standing after all the promised air raids had come to pass. Apathy was gaining momentum within public circles and was encouraged, perhaps unwittingly, by the news media.

I mention this because I clearly remember seeing, in a national newspaper, a cartoon depicting a gigantic figure of John Bull standing on the White Cliffs of Dover and launching handmade paper aeroplanes towards Berlin, which was indicated by an arrow on the horizon. Each paper 'plane carried the caption, "Watch out Hitler – here we come!" This was obviously a satirical attack on the on-going leaflet dropping over Germany which was still under serious debate in Parliament and held in utter contempt in the streets. Nevertheless indifference was spreading and many residents had stopped carrying their gasmasks and identity cards. Some Air Raid Wardens would half-heartedly challenge these law breakers only to receive the now hackneyed reply, "What war?" The same laid-back attention was also given to blackout regulations that had slavishly been followed when initially introduced. If, on a now rare occasion, a warden would shout, "Turn that light off" it would immediately be followed by words to the effect, "What the hell for?" We still had the occasional, and for no obvious reason, air raid alarms in the early hours of the morning which raised no more than a yawn, scratch and an immediate return to the land of sleep.

"Mam – is there any school today?"

.... was a regular weekday question when the time came to get out of bed.

This change in our life style had been brought about by the sudden return of many former evacuated children whose presence had given an unforeseen social problem, of massive proportions, both to Hull and nationwide education authorities. It was nationally estimated that around 70% of the original evacuees had returned home placing an even greater burden on schools that were desperately short of teachers. Some had remained in the country with residual evacuees and many younger teachers had been conscripted into the forces. Retired teachers responded to an urgent call for them to return but, despite their presence, there was still a teacher shortage problem of mammoth proportions. Inevitably classroom overcrowding led to the temporary closure of Courtney Street School and many others throughout Hull and the country.

Sadly numerous pupils within my age range were wartime statistics in that we, particularly during the period 1940 to 1944, were denied regular school attendance at the most formative stage of our lives. The authorities did their utmost to keep some form of education alive by opening one school local to a group of streets. Thus from time to time, when Courtney Street School was closed, we would all pile into Buckingham Street, Estcourt Street, Chapman Street or Mersey Street schools which appeared to open on a rota basis, depending on teacher availability. Despite good intent it was difficult for the authorities to operate a structured educational programme but it went some way to keep us off the streets.

And then it was 1940

Certainly these and many other concerns carried most of Courtney Street through an austere Christmas despite cries that matters could have been far worse if beer had been put on ration. Then, almost apologetically, the year 1940 quietly entered our lives without the midnight sounding of church bells which, by law, were to be rung only to alert the public that the nation was being invaded by enemy forces. The weather for January was unforgettable in that it was very cold and, as if to prove its presence, it covered the inside of my bedroom window with frozen condensate that, due to an arctic blast blowing through badly fitting frames, remained ice-covered for several days at a time. In our house we prepared ourselves for exceptionally cold bedrooms by pre-heating our beds with metal shelves from the Yorkist side oven. At bed time I would change into my pyjamas in front of the fire prior to a mad dash up the cold stairs followed by a quick dive beneath the now warm blankets. Entombed within my cavern of comfort, with my knees pulled up to my chin, I felt safe and secure against a raging gale that shook the house and rampaging frozen rain as it sought to break every window in its path. True to promise January remained very cold and freezing rain eventually turned to heavy snow by the end of the month. An increasing number of houses were running short of coal due to priority demands, for all types of fuel, from nearby war-based industries; and the now added feature of snow blocked roads had further worsened the plight of some householders who were reduced to chopping up spare chairs for kindling, or trying to borrow a bucket of coal from neighbours.

Help from over the fence

On several occasions I heard adults talking about workers in the Wilmington and Southcoates coal depots who, at the height of that bitterly cold winter would, at strategic points, shovel spilt coal over the fence for shivering householders to scoop into their buckets. Had their Robin Hood activities been discovered then they would have faced the sack and possible prosecution. Nevertheless their actions, and risks, were matched by workers in the Burleigh Street wood yard who, when out of sight of supervision, would throw logs over the fence destined for fuel starved fire grates. Yet there was at least one local victim of the deep freeze status of January 1940. One cold morning there was a flurry of police and ambulance activity and many adults trudged through the snow to the terrace end to discover the reason why. In no time at all the news was out and the entire street was stunned to learn that, a few terraces from where I lived, an elderly lady had been found dead in her house huddled over an empty fire grate. The house was devoid of coal and her food, consisting of half a loaf of bread, had been gnawed out of recognition by ravenous mice. Even the water in her kettle had frozen as solid as a rock. Alone and confused she had literally frozen to death and, at her feet, lay her old and loyal dog who had died with her. It would appear that her last act was to try and keep the dog warm by covering it with a shawl. A few days later every able-bodied person was out with their spades or shovels clearing the snow so that the funeral could go ahead; and a wreath bought by door to door collections was the sole floral tribute on her coffin. Perhaps these actions were an amalgam of love and a disturbed conscience although, officially, this tragic event was recorded as an instance of death by natural causes.

That winter of sad memories seemed as if it would go on for ever until, all of a sudden, a sparrow landed on the backyard wall with a piece of straw in its beak – as if looking for a place to build its nest. At last the spring of 1940 had arrived and, in the first rays of its feeble sunshine, many people had firmly decided that, after a delay of over six months, war was never going to happen. As if to confirm their view several national newspaper headlines were advising readers to, "Forget Hitler and take your holiday." With that daily trips to Withernsea again became popular and, in part, a leaner version of our pre-war life style was beginning to return to the street; except when urban battles were in progress.

War in the streets

To some extent many East Hull streets were becoming an almost daily battle field for marauding children, whose parents were in the forces or on war work respectively and schools were intermittently open and closed. Perhaps out of boredom, and influenced by accounts of military warfare, some streets had formed their own youth gangs who, in turn, launched attacks upon similar groups representing neighbouring streets. Matters reached crisis proportions when two children were badly beaten and had to be detained in hospital. The resulting public outcry led to the streets being regularly patrolled by air raid wardens, and the police, who quickly dispersed gangs of mischief bent children. In the event of cheek or disobedience from gang leaders they were not slow to administer a judicial clip around the ear, or a boot up the backside, which worked wonders in restoring order. For my part I kept well clear of gangs or membership of the same. I had one or two special mates, and the names Jimmy Watson and John Hobson spring to mind, but for the most part I preferred my own company and spent much time creating story situations using a few lead soldiers and an ageing block of plasticine. As ever Tin Mission tried to amuse and occupy the time of jaded children by running Punch and Judy shows followed by talent contests which, on one memorable occasion, won for me the princely sum of one shilling (five pence) for my piano rendering of the Fairyland Waltz from my tutor book.

Back to school with the best teacher in the world

Dates and days around this period remain lodged in my mind mainly because we were going back to school on a regular basis after the Easter holiday; and I was not alone in looking forward to our return. After many weeks of dull monotony, with threats from mother that she would find something for me to do unless I got from under her feet, it was a constant shuffle between the house and the passage end. There was a dearth of adult gossiping groups hence I was denied my cherished moments of *wigging-in*, and even my few mates had nothing imaginative to talk about. Thus it was a welcome relief to us all when notes came through the door, advising parents that we would return to school, on Monday 8th April 1940. After my mother, with eyes turned to heaven, had unashamedly raised her voice in gratitude to God for his intervention, then went on to explain that the teacher shortage problem had been greatly eased by an influx of trained teachers who had previously left to become fulltime housewives together with others who were fresh from teacher training college.

Thus we lined up in the playground on that first Monday back and, with a spring in our step, we marched with elation towards the assembly hall and into the acrid stench of floor polish that filled the entire building. After we had taken our appointed class position we listened to our headmistress give a patriotic address followed by some prayers and then, in memory of those seamen fighting the 'Battle of the Atlantic' we sang the hymn, "Eternal Father strong to save ..." When the service ended we were introduced to our new teachers some of whom, even to us, looked too young to stand in front of a class of children of indifferent behaviour. With exhortations for our good conduct, delivered with known voice inflections that signified trouble for wrongdoers, we were dispatched to our respective classrooms. Against a hectic background of getting new registers sorted out, and then finding that some children were in the wrong classroom, our replacement teacher did very well. She spoke in a gentle yet compelling way and when she read us a story we were spell-bound. Her voice enthralled us and every word just had to be listened to. Her every vocal emphasis, that gave life to the character or situation she was talking about, was a new experience for each of us. Later in the day she told us it was our turn to tell a story but in written form, so we moved on to a lesson we knew as 'Composition.' This was one of my favourite subjects and in no time, with head down, I was furiously writing away about a long since forgotten topic. 'Miss' moved about the classroom gently helping those who had problems expressing themselves and I noticed that at one stage, because we were so quiet, the headmistress surreptitiously peeped into the room – just to be certain that all was well!

PART FIVE

APRIL 1940 TO JUNE 1940

APRIL 1940 AND THE WAR IN EUROPE BEGINS

With every justification I walked home from school in one of my happiest moods for some time. Together with the rest of my class we had, unanimously, agreed it had been our best day at school and we mentally urged tomorrow to come quickly so that we could re-join our new teacher. In fact one of my class mates yelled across the road, to a member of another class, that our teacher was better than his. Much to our surprise he agreed with us and asked if we had spare desk space for him! As I approached Leonards Avenue our one-legged newspaper delivery man pulled up alongside me and thrust the Hull Daily Mail into my hand with the request, "save me getting off my bike." Nodding my agreement I walked on thinking how great life was turning out. First of all it looked as if the war was going to fizzle out and soon things would be back to how they were. Already Courtney School was getting back to peace-time ways and, as a bonus; I had the best class teacher I had ever known.

Still in raptures I half-heartedly looked at the front page of the paper and I was transfixed with the super large print headline. In a flash peace and our new teacher faded to the news that dark war clouds were rapidly sweeping across Europe, fanned by strong German forces massing on their border with Denmark; and that submarine attacks, on our supply ships, were intensifying in the Atlantic. When I got home mother, with a worried look on her face, grabbed the paper from my hands and immediately sat down. After a few minutes, she said that Lord Haw-Haw had been breaking into programmes to tell us that the war in Europe had just begun; and we should demand that our government sue for peace before it was too late.

Goodbye best teacher in the world

With the sun streaming through my bedroom window, and mother shouting up the stairs that it was time to get up, I desperately tried to shake off the gloom that had spoiled yesterday's joys. On the way to school I happily shared my feeling of optimism with my mates as we pushed, shoved and chased one another along Courtney Street until breathlessly we fell into the playground. With confidence restored I even ridiculed Billy Boy who had announced that German troops had landed, yet again, on Withernsea beach. When the school bell rang we quickly got into our lines hoping that our new teacher, after assembly, would start the day by reading us another story – and some had even started arguing as to what that story would be. But soon the hubbub died down when we realised that something was very wrong. It was a fact that our headmistress was a stickler for punctuality yet the wall clock told us that we were ten minutes behind the time we should have marched into the school. Twice a teacher had come out to tell us to be good and that we would soon be coming in. A full 20 minutes after our time we were allowed into the assembly hall but not before, when passing our classroom, I saw our new teacher sitting on a chair sobbing her heart out and being comforted by another teacher whilst the headmistress, crouched in front of her, was gently talking to her. On the pretext that I had to fasten my bootlace I adopted a familiar *wigging-in* position only for the headmistress to suddenly get up and slam the door shut. In the quiet and expectant assembly hall we were told that our teacher had received some very sad news and someone was coming to take her home – which for us was the end of a day that had begun with such great promise. It was many months later that I learned how our new teacher had, the day before, gone home to find relatives comforting her mother. Without a word they pointed to a War Office telegram lying on the table from which she learned that her father had died, with the rest of his crew when their ship, as part of an Atlantic convey, had been torpedoed by a German U-boat. The following morning she decided that life had to go on, and as her mother was being cared for, our teacher came to school and began preparing her classroom. Then without warning, which may have been the effect of delayed shock, she had an emotional breakdown which the staff dealt with whilst someone ran to her house to alert the family. For only one day we had been blessed with an excellent teacher who, because of the war, gave up teaching and we never saw her again.

German occupation of Denmark and Norway

That loss of our teacher was not the only event to emerge from the 9th April 1940 which stood out in my mental diary as a date to avoid building hopes upon. Within hours all newspaper and radio broadcasts were awash with the dramatic news that German land, sea and air forces had invaded Denmark. This small, flat country was totally unprepared for attack and was quickly over-run by fast moving Panzer Divisions. In the belief that further resistance was useless, the Danish government, within two hours of the invasion, surrendered and began trying to work out an agreement with Germany. A treaty of sorts lasted until 1943 when, following repeated strikes by Danish workers and accelerated action by their resistance forces the occupying troops became aggressive – to say the least. Apart from gaining an airfield and docking facilities the 9th April invasion was strategic rather than expansionist because Denmark was a vital stepping-stone for the immediate invasion of Norway. It was a known fact that the German war effort depended heavily upon Swedish iron ore, which was shipped to Germany via the Norwegian ice-free port of Narvik. This arrangement was excellent whilst Norway remained a neutral State. Immediately following the declaration of war British naval units partially blockaded Narvik and even planted mines in Norwegian territorial waters without regard to claims of neutrality, on the basis that 'war was war.' Therefore after this surprise attack Germany resolved its iron ore import problem and, by early June, Norway had surrendered to the invading forces; but not without cost in the form of Germany losing one of their troop carrying heavy battle cruisers to Norwegian shore batteries.

This development created for us at home a mystery as to why Germany did not expand their aggression by invading neighbouring

Sweden, and so gain control of the vital iron ore mines. One member of the terrace, who was noted for her original thought, came up with the theory that Germany had intended to invade Sweden but, due to heavy fog and poor visibility, had turned the wrong way and captured neighbouring Norway instead. Had she, and we as a family, owned an Atlas then the answer may have been obvious. A brief glance at a map of the area would have shown that having taken Denmark and Norway then German military might could decide who entered or left the Baltic Sea. Their new conquests also gave them additional bases from which to attack our shipping in the North Atlantic Ocean. As for Sweden their merchant ships were now restricted to operating within the Baltic meaning they had to trade exclusively with Germany in order to survive. Hence Germany did not invade neutral Sweden because they had no need to. Although I find this conclusion irksome to accept I have, reluctantly, to concede that in terms of military strategy it was, for the enemy, a brilliant success.

Naturally Lord Haw-Haw had a field day in his regular 'Germany Calling' broadcasts to the UK whilst, not to be outdone, our propaganda machine attempted to play down the seriousness of what had happened. The House of Commons Debating Chamber was becoming a verbal battle field in its own right because, since 1936, Winston Churchill had, in his inimitable way, been highly critical of the appeasement policy which allowed Hitler to grow to his current awesome level of seemingly unstoppable military strength.

With regard to thoughts from the street these, in two words, were restricted to *stark bewilderment*. In my wanderings within groups of adults the expression, "Do you know what is happening with this war," seems to have caught on. A group of ladies talking at the end of Blanche Grove blamed the news media for their mental confusion in that, a few days ago, we were being urged to 'forget Hitler and go on holiday' whereas now we had to be on full alert because his armies were on the move. Amongst this group there was a rather vocal woman who, according to local rumour, was never without a dust cap on her head – even at bed time. As the debate drew to its close she took it upon herself to summarise their views in the following words that, apparently, were heard two terraces away, "If we are going to have a bloody war then they should stop messing about and get on with it." Although not quite up to Churchillian eloquence I would, if pushed, argue that her words were equally expressive!

Birth of 'The Mysterious Three'

There was rumour afoot that a type of civilian defence army was to be formed that would be trained to defend their locality in the event of an enemy invasion. I and my two mates knew full well that the authorities, spoilsports as they were, would reject our application to join hence we unanimously agreed to form our own home protection unit. Although only three in number we argued, quite impressively, that we had the courage and loyalty of a vast army who would stop at nothing to defend our street. Further, and after much discussion, we agreed not to be known as 'The Three Musketeers' mainly because someone else had thought of it first. Finally, due to the closeness of tea time, we agreed that' The Mysterious Three' was a much more appropriate description of our cause and agreed to abbreviate it to 'TM3', because of difficulty in spelling the second word. This title was then formerly accepted in accordance with our vows to never divulge it, even under torture, concluding with the standard affirmation, "Cross my heart and hope to die – so help me God."

Our objectives were to identify enemy agents who the Government claimed were all around us; in fact we already had reservations about a new rag and bone man who, to our ears, had a distinct foreign accent. Our other duties consisted of watching out for enemy parachutists, searching for unexploded bombs and noting down anything we considered to be suspicious. We later 'obtained' lengths of wood, designed to be our rifles, which we held against our shoulders as we stood guard at a bridge over Sutton drain or when on sentry duty in the back yard at home. Although it never found a place in the archives of World War Two the TM3 was alive and active and, to our belief, played its part in achieving the final outcome now well known to history.

A time of waiting

In addition to the founding of the TM3 the ripple effect of German successes in Scandinavia led to a vigorous restoration of air raid precautions, in terms of attitude and required practices. Hence, with renewed vitality, blackout regulations were enforced together with the carrying of gasmasks and identity cards at all times. At the same time air raid wardens and police officers were given updated training sessions, which they applied with military precision, upon street residents who were still in doubt as to the need for *all this fuss*.

In some ways the war had brought a measure of prosperity to Courtney Street and district due to an increased demand for general workers, of both sexes, in many war related factories. There was a noticeable absence of men who had, seemingly overnight, been conscripted into the armed services and many younger women had enlisted on a voluntary basis. I suppose, on balance, the street was quieter than in pre-war days although there was still the occasional street or terrace row, that would gather interested spectators until boredom, or the beat Bobbie, sent them on their way. The most spectacular incidents were chimney fires – more so when they happened at night when the blackout reigned supreme. Imagine the sight and sound of a torrent of red hot sparks whooshing out of a house chimney, in the style of a gigantic Roman candle firework, set within many shafts of light streaming from hurriedly opened doorways. To have a pitch black scenario suddenly transformed into a kaleidoscope of light, of this magnitude, did much to reduce air raid wardens into a state of apoplectic frenzy!

We're going to hang out the washing on the Siegfried Line

One of our older teachers had the knack of making her geography lessons interesting by introducing her subject through something topical – like an item that was regularly on the radio. For instance her invitation of, "Hands up all who have heard the song '*We're going to hang out the washing on the Siegfried Line*'" was met with a forest of raised arms – with fingers twitching as they sought to outreach those of their desk mate. This was followed by, "Well done. Now who is going to tell me what and where is the Siegfried Line?" In the blink of an eye all those insistent arms fell beneath drooping shoulders as their owners sought inspiration from faded blots and generations of initials scratched on the desk lid.

For my part I was fascinated to learn that the Siegfried Line, built in 1916-17 by the Germans, was a chain of fortifications along Germany's Western border with France and, to add to the interest, facing it on the French side of the boundary was a similar defence complex called the Maginot Line. The wide space between was known as *'No-Man's Land'* and was impassable due to anti-tank traps and other formidable obstacles; not the least of which were massive guns set within both defence lines covering the area between. Consequently, when war was declared, opposing soldiers settled in their respective fortifications and stared at one another – as the weeks stretched into months of inactivity. Now at this stage of her explanation I am convinced that the teacher, momentarily, fixed me with a meaningful look when she explained that America was the first to describe it as a *Phoney war* which, in her view, was not as apt as *funny war* which had recently come to her attention!

Finally she described how necessary it was to play down the awesome power of the Siegfried Line through such a clever public morale boosting song, whose lyrics compared it to a simple washing line. To me this was fascinating information and it prompted me, at the age of nine, to compose my first and only set of song lyrics which, 72 years later, may still achieve publication courtesy of this book:

> The night was dark and stormy and a poor man came in sight,
> although both frail and weary his eyes were filled with light,
> he struggled on through wood and lea and naught did halt his tread,
> as he headed home to Norway where his wife lay snug in bed.

I did add a not very convincing one finger piano melody to these lyrics after which I introduced the entire project to my colleagues at our next TM3 meeting; with a view to getting their support for my first radio launch. Sadly my enthusiasm was not matched and the selection of

Norway, as the focal point for the poor man of the song, was greeted with sustained derision. Thus after a long verbal battle I gave up all idea of what to me, at that tender age, was a promising career as a song lyricist!

May and June 1940. A time for mourning

We are now approaching a key stage of my account as I relive memories of those savage years in which death and destruction, literally, rained down upon many cities of this country in which, next to London, Hull occupied the second position. There is an abundance of historical WW2 records available, awash with appropriate statistics, to label the extent of damage to life and property resulting from a total of 72 air raids on Hull that left, in their wake, a death toll of around 1200 adults and children together with extensive damage to all types of property. In order that I remain within my literary objectives I will restrict my narrative to those air raids that I experienced and, in the process, observe how they affected the people of Courtney Street and district. To my mind any deviation from this route may well complicate local social and historical outcomes I have in mind for this book.

As far as Courtney Street was concerned the war had slipped back into 'watch and wait' mode whilst French troops crouched behind the powerful Maginot Line, and British forces guarded the moderately defended French border with Belgium. The German troops were, however, massing on their border with Holland, Belgium and Luxemburg (the Low Countries) several miles to the north of the Maginot Line. These three nations were not particularly worried by this because they had repeatedly declared their intentions to remain neutral, in the belief that such actions would prompt Hitler to leave them alone.

As a family we were aware that the May Bank Holiday Monday was approaching and, despite it being on the 13th of the month, we had decided to push our luck and have a trip to Withernsea and try, for one day, to forget the war. Also mother declared it would be good to get away from all the building noise and mess going on in the street because, since early April, an army of men had been busy erecting street air raid shelters. These units followed a standard design of fourteen inch thick brick walls and one foot reinforced concrete roofs. They were planned to hold fifty persons and were divided into several sections by interior walls with connecting doorless openings. Each section contained bunk beds, and public welfare was the responsibility of a volunteer shelter warden who patrolled all the sections with a first aid bag over his/her shoulder. Additionally much of our school playground canopy had been converted into an air raid shelter, which meant several indoor play times until the job was finished.

May 1940. Hitler invades Holland, Belgium and Luxemburg

The Dutch, who knew what was happening on their border with Germany, were still surprised when they were invaded by German land and airborne forces on the 10th May which, to quote my father's words, "had buggered up our plans to go to Withernsea on the 13th." Hitler had grandiose ideas of conquering Holland in 24 hours but his advance was slowed by spirited resistance. Consequently, and as a warning, Luftwaffe dive bombers immediately destroyed the centre of Rotterdam in the course of which almost 1000 civilians were killed. Thus the inevitable happened and Holland surrendered on the 14th May.

When Holland was attacked British divisions immediately entered Belgium to meet the German invaders. However most of the Wehrmacht land based units entered eastern Belgium and, against all expectation, rapidly pushed their way through the densely wooded Ardennes forest previously thought to be impenetrable. In a very short time they burst into France, swung around, and began to advance towards the coast thus encircling, on three sides, British and Allied forces that had no option other than to fall back upon Dunkirk. This classical manoeuvre separated the British and French armies and the latter, rather despondently, were trapped in the now outflanked Maginot Line whose massive concrete set guns pointed only towards Germany and could not be moved. Within a few days both Belgium and Luxemburg recognised the impossibility of their situation and immediately surrendered to the German forces. The now battered and beleaguered French army faced the might of the Wehrmacht supported by an ill-prepared Italian army, who wanting to be in on the act had declared war on France and Britain. Thus on the 25th June an agreed armistice took effect and Hitler had achieved total domination of Europe. On the home front Prime Minister Neville Chamberlain, in his quest for peace, had totally failed to estimate Hitler's intentions and, not surprisingly, was facing mounting criticism in Parliament. These latest acts of aggression by Hitler were the last straw and Chamberlain, in deference to the will of Parliament resigned with immediate effect, and on May 10th, Winston Churchill became Prime Minister of the United Kingdom.

May 1940. Formation of the Home Guard

On the evening of the 14th May we had an urgent radio appeal to all men aged between 17 and 60, who were not members of the regular forces, to become Local Defence Volunteers (LDV) which in July 1940 changed its name to the Home Guard. The obvious driving force behind this was the plight of our forces seeking to escape from Europe, and the real fear that Germany would press home their obvious advantages and invade Britain. For me it meant instant elevation of my playground credibility ratings because it was common knowledge that, on the 10th April, I founded The Mysterious Three (TM3) which specialised in home defence matters. Naturally the three of us felt infinitely capable, because of our prior experience in home defence issues, of advising the Government accordingly; after all the street warden did act on our tip off regarding the foreign sounding rag and bone man – and he duly disappeared from the street. Currently we were carefully investigating a new teacher who had a foreign sounding name.........

Probably it was the fame of the TM3 (my boyhood view) that attracted over one million volunteers to the LDV by the end of July drawn from shop workers, teachers, bankers and other occupations. They received uniforms and were trained in the use of weapons and general military discipline. In the event of an invasion their role would have been to slow down the invading force; otherwise they would guard key factories and installations and even detain bailed out German airmen.

May 1940. The miracle of Dunkirk

As German forces closed in on the French channel ports there were many news reports of heavy gunfire from both sides. In the English Channel British warships, under the cover of protective smokescreens, were bombarding German positions whilst above them Junkers dive bombers created havoc, despite suffering losses to our Hurricane and Spitfire combat planes. However time was not on our side and it was an unchallengeable fact that we could no longer sustain our presence on the European mainland. A large number of British and foreign forces were surrounded and pinned down in Dunkirk and their situation was, by the hour, becoming more and more desperate. From this disastrous situation was born "The Miracle of Dunkirk," when almost 380,000 British and foreign soldiers were carried over the Channel, in a flotilla of 700 ships ranging from naval destroyers to pleasure yachts. Each vessel had to run the gauntlet of several trips to and fro with harassment from the air and shore batteries. Through this now historic act of bravery more troops than ever thought possible were evacuated but all our tanks and large guns had to be left behind.

Who do you think you are kidding Mr. Hitler?

....with acknowledgment to Jimmy Perry and David Croft for their theme song, sung by the late Bud Flanagan, for the popular TV series "Dad's Army."

These words, written after the end of the war, testified to the spirit of the British public of all ages which, within my experience, gained momentum as the war years went by. Without doubt Hitler became the butt of many jokes by the media and local adults; although with children it went further than that. His appearance, gait, and similarity to Charlie Chaplin, even down to his toothbrush moustache, gave endless scope for acts of ridicule that entertained both the street and playground alike. Some years after the war ended I read that Hitler, in his earlier life, was a great fan of Charlie Chaplin although there was no evidence, albeit a lot of speculation, that Hitler copied his moustache style from that of the great comic. In Charlie Chaplin's later years, when asked why he favoured his well-known moustache, his explanation was that it gave him a comical appearance yet was small enough not to hide his multiple facial expressions, so necessary in the era of silent films. What more can I say?!

At school play time, or when walking home along Courtney Street, it was a common sight to see several boys competing, with great difficulty, to march in the goose-step style of the German Army. The Hitler moustache was symbolised by the first finger of the left hand judicially placed between the nostrils and the upper lip, whilst the right hand was rigidly held high in the Nazi salute. To complete the characterisation the actors uttered what where, to them, realistic guttural outbursts meaning 'Sieg Heil' or 'Achtung' except when, for no particular reason, the expression 'Donner und Blitzen' would thunder forth. Onlookers and followers, in general, accepted all that was said in a spirit of total bewilderment except for the more studious, who desperately sought a compromise between Germanic expressions and Courtney Street delivery.

Fortunately our new teacher who, like her predecessor, had the ability to make our lessons interesting and instructive taught us how to pronounce these German expressions and, for good weight, explained that 'Donner und Blitzen' meant thunder and lightning and also doubled up as names for two of Santa Claus's reindeer. As enthralling as this was to me there was a serious downside to what I heard. I had the greatest possible liking and respect for this teacher; yet how was it that she was so familiar with the German language? Could it mean that she was an enemy agent? Deep in thought I wandered home determined to raise my concerns at our next TM3 meeting; but that was my problem whereas my peers were free from such burdens of National importance.

Many boys and, indeed, some girls considered it their war effort to ridicule Hitler and his cohorts although, as the war progressed, they struggled hard to find new acts of Nazi based Black Comedy. This mattered little to them because, with minimal prompting, they would re-enact well proven scenarios that gave delight to the cast and baffled several groups of women at terrace ends. From these activities there arose one very incredible happening, which I was a witness to, that began with a routine demonstration of the goose-step way of marching which, to my peers, was symbolic of Adolph Hitler and all he stood for. A particular lad, who was ahead of us all when it came to marching in this style, was demonstrating how to turn round without losing rhythm. For his demonstration he chose to goose-step across an open plan terrace and, as he neared the wall ahead, his regimented foot stamping turn-around would be followed by a sharp upward lift of his bent right leg which, with considerable force from his knee, immediately became parallel to the floor. This was the prelude for him to begin his goose-step-march back. There is no doubt that he had mastered the demands of this difficult marching system and his fame spread accordingly. Lads from nearby streets would call in to watch him in action and they were keen to learn from him. No one would deny or dare to challenge his ability to faultlessly march in German style but – ***when it came to fastening his boot laces*** – well that it was a vastly different matter.

It was a hot day in July 1940 which meant that the sham-four house soon to face him had its front door wide open, and its lady tenant was quietly knitting away in the depths of her arm chair. Deeply intent on marching in time, with regimental precision, he swung around and, as previously described, he sharply kicked out with his right leg to begin his return. And what a splendid kick it was. The power of his knee and leg movement was a tribute to German marching traditions whilst, at the same time, it provided impetus for his loose boot to leave his foot, with the speed of a cannon ball, and pass smoothly through the open door ahead. There was a crash and scream as the goldfish bowl was swept off the sideboard and the household cat, as a reflex action, quickly disappeared down the terrace with the goldfish in its mouth.

The now subdued and ashen faced goose-stepper, who was unable to comprehend why fate had done this to him, stared in horror at the open door not knowing what to expect. When the lady of the house, having tiptoed her way around water and broken glass appeared in the doorway, she demanded, in a voice approaching hysteria, "Who the hell threw this boot at my goldfish?" With that he promptly burst into tears.

PART SIX

JUNE 1940 TO SEPTEMBER 1943

THE BATTLE OF BRITAIN

In this time period we were honoured to have yet another dedicated and efficient school teacher whose name, unfortunately, I cannot remember. What I do know is that, based upon present day teaching standards, she was very much in advance of her age. She never down-played the fact that there was a war on, and she clearly believed that we should have some understanding what it was about. Although I still had lingering concerns that teacher may be an enemy agent I found that, despite myself, I was intrigued by the clear way she could explain matters; bearing in mind that we were a class of nine and ten year old children. Each day, as part of her current affairs update, she would spend time explaining, in terms we could understand, all that had happened since our last lesson. We knew about the evacuation of troops from Dunkirk but, as children, the true seriousness of the situation had made little impact upon us. Her face looked grim and solemn when she explained that Hitler was determined to rule every country in Europe and, so that we knew where they were, she drew attention to them on the classroom wall map. She ended by pointing to Britain and explained, with a very serious look on her face, that we now stood alone against a strong German nation. Surely if she was a German spy then she would be smiling, I mused to myself, but then she left us open mouthed when she explained how very grave the future was; because it appeared likely that Germany would try and invade this country very soon. She explained that heavy bombing raids were happening on our south coast and, again pointing to the wall map, showed how near it was to the French mainland where German invasion forces were massing. She then went on to tell us that, to date, the nearest bombs to Hull had fallen on the port of Middlesbrough.

With that her map pointer moved with unerring speed from the south to north-east coast of England whilst stressing that our Royal Air Force, and anti-aircraft guns, were giving the Germans a hard time. As if on cue her assurance was immediately followed by a loud and window rattling rumble of thunder. Our fear turned into laughter when she added, “There now – what did I tell you!”

Her assessment of the situation became historical fact when, in later years, it was discovered that Hitler had ordered the invasion of Britain but first they had to achieve mastery in the air. This meant an all-out assault on RAF airfields with round the clock bombing raids – mainly in the south of England. Yet as Hitler turned his attention to the British Isles in June of 1940, directing a large force of bombers and fighters first against shipping, airfields, and finally against towns, it became apparent that his air force had great odds stacked against it. The Luftwaffe’s main disadvantage was that it was neither trained nor equipped for relatively long range flights which were a new experience for them. In their victories in Poland and Europe military tactics relied upon close air support for the advancing ground forces and, when German dive-bombers had pulverised areas of resistance, the military immediately moved in and took control. They were therefore ill-suited to the circumstances of this new campaign, known as the Battle of Britain, which was exclusively fought in the air. Also in early massed attacks on Britain several German bomber formations had discovered, to their own extreme cost, that they were unable to defend themselves against our fighter planes; hence the once free-lance Messerschmitt fighter plane was now restricted to providing escort cover. With regard to German successes, prior to the Battle of Britain, credit was mainly due to the Junkers (Stuka) bomber which could, from a great height, nose dive towards its target and release bombs with devastating accuracy. Whilst in dive mode its engines emitted a terrifying sound known, to those on the ground, as the ‘scream of death.’ Imagine the terror and pain to mind and ears as this instrument from hell hurtled towards its target which, to me, was always a certain house in Leonards Avenue. Fortunately our home produced, and much maligned, barrage balloons frustrated the dive bomber because of its thick metal mooring cable that, with consummate ease, could tear the wing off a diving plane. Also the Junkers bomber could not defend itself hence it became target practice for RAF fighter planes thus, due to heavy losses, this once invincible dive bomber was not to the fore in the Battle of Britain. Finally there was our secret weapon in the form of Radar cover. This meant we could use our small stock of fighter planes to best advantage and, as a bonus, manage to totally bewilder the enemy in that, whatever route they chose for their bombers, our fighters were always in place waiting to attack them.

June 19th 1940. The First Air Raid on Hull

From time to time you will notice, as my narration progresses, that I record dates, locations and other details of air raids or particular events. This is a further product of effective training by my aforementioned class teacher. In one lesson she taught the value of keeping a diary which extended to a daily class record. Without excuse or argument we all had to report something, be it about an air raid or other happening on the previous day. Stemming from these lessons in 1940 I became a dedicated diarist and, to this day, I have faithfully kept a diary of events. Sadly through the decades many have got lost, or simply dispensed with, including those relevant to the war years which, had they survived, would have been valuable historic documents. However having once recorded my recollections of WW2 they left an indelible imprint on my memory, which I carefully revived prior to beginning work on this book. Oh, how I wish that my short term memory was as productive!

The heavy thundery showers persisted throughout the day and dad had to trudge home, from Tan Yard, in the pouring rain – which did little for his temper. I remember him grumbling that it was only the middle of the week and Sunday rest day felt a long way off. Having concluded that the news on the wireless was too worrying to listen to, it was agreed that an early night was called for and, in no time at all, we four were hard asleep. That was until around 11pm when I awoke to bright flashes down the edge of the blackout blind, booming thunder and the realisation that thundery showers were still with us – or where they? Sometimes there was a progression of bangs without a flicker of light to induce them and, from a distance I could hear an alarm bell possibly on an ambulance or a fire engine. In one bound I was over to the bedroom window and, carefully raising the blackout blind, I saw an amazing sight. The night sky was an orchestra of swaying barrage balloons and gun flashes; seemingly under the conductorship of a moving searchlight beam.

Then the dreadful realisation dawned on me that I was witnessing my first air raid. Brother Jim was snoring in competition to the noise outside so I dashed into the front bedroom and began shaking my father. "Dad, dad wake up there's an air raid going on – come and see it for yourself if you don't believe me." My father had the ability to be hard asleep and, in an instant, he could be wide awake and thoroughly active. "You're right," he gasped from the window. "They've caught a Jerry plane in the searchlight already. OK grab your clothes and let's get under the stairs." Soon we were all huddled together in our den of safety and, for once, I basked in the glory of being thanked for waking up the household. Dad had heard the buzzers about half an hour before the noise but, as was our procedure, he decided to ignore it – as did most other households in Courtney Street. Suddenly ear-spitting explosions of anti-aircraft shells, literally bursting over the house, prompted mother to throw her arms around me as if shielding me from shrapnel bouncing off the roof tiles. "I'd like to bet that ARP wardens are glad of their tin hats," I muttered from the depths of my mother's protective embrace. Then, for the first of many times, we heard the sound of a falling bomb. It began as a distant whistle which intensified into a deep and rich whooshing sound as if, by satanic intent, every second of its death-bearing fall added to the terror of those awaiting its arrival. When it happened its impact was both felt and heard as the ground beneath me recoiled to its explosive might and, as if taking flight, pans bounced from the top shelf of the pantry and, with an almighty clatter, fire irons fell over in the hearth. I later found that the bomb had landed in soft earth close to Chapman Street railway bridge over Sutton Drain which, as the crow flies, was around a quarter of a mile from Leonards Avenue. The majority of the bombs were incendiary devices that mainly fell upon open ground, although a house in Buckingham Street was hit and set on fire. That was the end of the raid but, as an added precaution, we had to wait for around two hours before the 'All Clear' announced that normality had returned. Our household together with many others then assembled in the street to view the glow of fires in the night sky and listen to the bells of fire engines as they raced around the district. Nothing was said, and even the most vocal terrace end characters were in a state of shocked silence, until it was broken by an ill-timed comment from a man who said, "It's just like bonfire night isn't it?" Immediately he became the focal point for an array of angry glares from which a voice, rich with menace, ordered him to, "Shurrup you unfeeling sod – don't you care about the dead and injured?"

As it turned out no one had died or even been hurt but, had we been aware, it was merely a preview of what was to follow. Mum, dad and Jim, with pronounced and meaningful yawns, quickly returned to the land of sleep whilst I, now fully awake, mentally relived what had happened. I quietly slid between the blackout blind and the window and gazed upon several fires, which glowed with varying intensity on the horizon, whilst two or three searchlights were still scanning a sky now free from hostile forces. Our sentinel barrage balloons, as if assuring me of their protecting presence, slowly revolved pro and anti-clockwise on their steel cables as, in the distance, ships hooters suggested that a convoy may be assembling in the River Humber. I lost all concept of time until I realised that I was cold and the night fires had finally been put out. As I crept back into my warm bed I was aware there was much to think about although, in the silent and mind cleansing hours before dawn, my inner self was soon cocooned in dreamless sleep.

The Mysterious Three (TM3) visit local bomb sites

The wartime system was that an air raid alert after midnight meant that school was cancelled for the morning. So as soon as my cornflakes, bread and jam had been dealt with I was out in the street where I met up with the two other members of our TM3 group. In the best traditions of the Secret Service we never used our real names in preference to our coded titles. My friends were known, respectively, as Agent Two and Agent Three and, on a rota basis, we took it in turns to lead the group as Agent One. It was our new system to keep our discussions free from *wiggers in* by climbing on to the roof of any one of three street shelters that stretched from Albion Avenue to Claremont Avenue. Selected open plan terraces had shelters built between the houses to serve those people living at the Holderness Road end of the street. We considered our shelters to be more superior because of the relative ease of climbing on to the roof aided by two thick metal cables, painted with yellow gas-sensitive paint, which stretched between the shelters. These were in place to prevent anyone from running out into oncoming traffic and were, as a bonus, ideal for standing on and pulling oneself up on to the shelter roof. As an aside they also excelled as aids for budding tight rope walkers despite already having committed one lad to hospital with a broken leg. From our 'secret' vantage point we could lie out flat, or on our sides, which meant we were not seen from ground level, yet we had a commanding view of both approaches to the street. Agent Two, who had no small ability when it came to *wigging in*, was the son of an ARP warden who shared, with his wife, all that had happened during his shift. Had he known that his offspring, with his ear pressed to the bedroom floorboards was recording key points of his address, then he may have been more cautious as to what he revealed. Thus Agent Two gleaned first-hand information of local areas damaged in last night's raid and we unanimously agreed, as part of our duty, to visit and note all that had happened.

Immediately we set off along Dansom Lane, down Endymion Street and into Buckingham Street – which we knew pretty well because of our periodic sessions in Buckingham Street School when Courtney, for war based reasons, was closed. For the same motives we, as required, played host to our peers from 'Bucky.' Due to prevailing circumstances the once noted rivalry between the two schools had eased somewhat but, in the interests of diplomacy, we ceased referring to Buckingham

Street School by its pre-war title of 'Mucky-Bucky'! Road traffic was prohibited from entering the street at either end due to debris and the now dangerous state of a row of houses which had been hit by incendiary bombs. A centre house had been reduced to an unstable shell filled with charred and smouldering wood, sticking at crazy angles, from a muddle of blackened bricks and broken roof slates. Three houses on either side of the centre target had also been damaged mainly because of fire spreading through communal roof voids and by the many gallons of water that had cascaded through the properties. Some people still in their night clothes, with borrowed blankets around their shoulders, stood dejectedly behind safety barriers viewing their once cherished homes whilst patiently waiting for permission to enter and salvage whatever they could. Nearby a WVS van was busy serving hot drinks, soup and sandwiches to victims of the night's events, whilst the local vicar commiserated with those overcome by moments of savagery that had shattered their lives. It was a sad scene. Yet even from the lingering smell of burnt wood, and a stifled sob from someone battling with their emotions, there arose a simple moment of hope when a bird flew off with a crumb dropped near the WVS van. Instantly I saw the point of a recent talk by our teacher when she tried to explain what the expression, "It's an ill wind that doesn't blow someone a bit of good" was all about.

The silence of our return walk was broken when Agent Three found a large piece of shrapnel and a few paces further along I, too, spotted a smaller lump. Thus began an in-depth search for shell fragments large and small which, by the time we arrived back in Courtney Street, had slowed us down due to the extra weight we were carrying. It was not one of our better ideas but we did spend a few minutes, crouched on the pavement, seeing if it was possible to piece them together like a complex metallic jigsaw puzzle. Quickly we gave that up in favour of launching a museum of war relics that, in our minds, would be worth a lot of money in later years. Having agreed to proceed with this we retained better specimens of wartime shrapnel and, as an act of contempt for Hitler, we threw less displayable pieces from Chapman Street Drain Bridge that was our next port of call. Gazing from the bridge we could clearly see a bomb crater, and masses of scattered earth, originating from an embankment that supported the North Eastern Railway line just before it crossed Sutton Drain Bridge. The footpath alongside the drain, on the Montrose Street side, was roped off so we sought a better view by walking on the opposite side, alongside Howard's Row, which was now separated from the drain by a couple of public air raid shelters. It was a very near miss for the German bomb aimer. If the bomb had landed a few more yards to its left then it would have exploded in the centre of the railway bridge. As it happened the explosion dislodged vast amounts of earth thus leaving a gap of several yards over which, almost with an air of contempt, the unsupported railway lines passed on their uninterrupted way.

The ever practical Agent Two brought us down to earth by reminding us that it was time to go home, eat and then get off to school. Nevertheless, and at the risk of getting *'chowed at'* by our respective mothers, we had to pause at the ARP post just outside Tin Mission. Something was amiss, so we mingled with a few adults to *wig-in* as to what was happening. Outside the concrete post stood a very agitated Air Raid Warden accompanied by a Policeman and a Home Guard sergeant who had their eyes fixed upon a pile of sandbags, on some waste ground at the rear of the post. Clearly the Warden was in a state of shock and, by way of easing inner tensions he, probably for the umpteenth time, related what had happened for the benefit of anyone who wanted to listen. Preceded by a loud blowing of his nose he began, "I just returned from my round when a woman, carrying a shopping bag, walked into my ARP post and announced she had something for me. I said, as a joke, "Hope it's a meat pie cos I'm famished". "Not really," she replied as she lifted an object out of her bag and placed it in front of me. What I saw lying on my desk nearly *'sluffed me heart'* cos it was a pigging incendiary bomb! All she would say was that she had found it in her front garden, thought it was a bomb, and that if it went off it would ruin her rose bush. So without further ado she bundled it in her shopping bag and brought it here – then had the cheek to leave her name and address for the public service reward." "Don't get upset Tom," replied the policeman. "If anyone gets a reward it will be you for covering it with sandbags until the bomb disposal team arrives."

With that the three of us, whilst running home, decided that the incident was something we would keep in our records – after all the woman may have been a German Agent sent to plant bombs in ARP posts? After the school register had been marked I was the first to relate our adventures for the benefit of the classroom diary. Teacher was pleased with my report but, as ever, set the seeds of suspicion in our minds when she asked if we knew the colour of the incendiary bomb handed to the air raid warden – was that to feed back to Hitler we wondered?

Blood, toil, tears and sweat

These words were part of the now famous speech given by the then newly appointed Prime Minister Winston Churchill, on the 13th May 1940, when he described what faced our country during the next few years. There were many in Courtney Street who followed this by asking, "So what's new? For years we've struggled to find work, food and clothing for our kids whilst fighting battles with Means Test Inspectors, greedy Landlords and a noisy wireless next door!" But having said that they immediately accepted the future, such as it was, as if argument was a sport belonging to a past age far removed from the horrors of war. It was as if that first air raid had led them to realise, and accept, that at any moment death could fall from the sky and they could do nothing to prevent it.

Years later, I wondered if the almost total absence of young men and women, who were away serving their country, had removed from the street those elements of confidence and enduring strength that are key components in any successful community. Additionally there was, to those at home, the daily dread of a telegram arriving with stark information that a loved one was posted missing or had been killed in action. The once highly popular Saturday night sports that marked pub leaving time, or rowdy house parties lasting into the early hours were no more – although the rigours of the blackout were not designed to help such events. Daylight also had its dangers due to increasing reports of German fighter planes machine-gunning civilians, barrage balloons or whatever took the pilot's fancy. Consequently the once almost statutory terrace end debates had faded away, and people were now only too pleased to get back to the safety of their homes. Thus when evening slowly fell the near deserted street was left to the sound of flapping barrage balloons and the swish of closing blackout blinds, drawn by seemingly disembodied hands specially created for that purpose. It was said that as evening light faded into blackout mode those people left on the street seemed less like human characters and more like silhouettes sliding along the wall and, in the time taken to blink an eye, they simply disappeared. It was as if they had been sucked into a black hole formed by a terrace entrance or an even darker side passage.

As the evening drew on some elderly people, armed with cushions and shawls, would move into street air raid shelters on the basis they would be guaranteed a seat if the buzzers went. It was also a bonus for them to have someone to talk to as well as a street warden who popped in from time to time to enquire how they were. Some not so elderly women also met in the shelter if their husbands were on night work, or if they had had a row with their old man.

On a darker and disappointing side were increasing reports of house burglaries in which the main targets were food, money and ration books. Also bottles of milk were disappearing off doorsteps and coal houses were being raided in the small hours – more so if the back yard door was left unlocked. My father, being ever conscious of household security, designed a unique burglar alarm that may have (or not) been the prototype of modern High-Tec devices. His last act before going to bed was to lean the household steps against the kitchen back door and place metal pans, buckets and whatever came to hand on each of the treads. The theory was that anyone trying to force the door would dislodge the many booby-traps and create a lot of noise in the process. The need to take these extreme actions was a totally new feature to the street bearing in mind that, in pre-war years, doors could remain unlocked and Co-op milk checks left on doorsteps without fear of theft.

These happenings, in direct contrast to pre-war days, led many residents to distrust strangers who, for generations past, had freely walked through the street. Gone were symbolic greetings in the form of a nod or wave and, on no account, were traditional comments on the weather encouraged or even permitted. The street was fast becoming territorial and any transient newcomers, regardless of sex or age, who paused to peer down terraces or passages would be treated with instant suspicion and, if around, the beat bobby or warden would be informed. If they considered it appropriate then those figures of the law could demand to see their identity card and, if not produced, they would be escorted to the police station for further questioning.

September 1940. The Battle of Britain reaches its conclusion

Our classroom scrapbook was now awash with newspaper cuttings and local reports on the progress of the war. Carefully arranged they told a story of how heavy guns were exchanging shells over the English Channel, at the expense of the Dover and Calais coast lines, and that massive air battles were being fought over the southern counties of England. Then there were accounts of convoys of merchant vessels, escorted by warships, battling their way through the Channel but not without loss to enemy submarines and sea mines. So far the epicentre of the Battle of Britain was in the Home Counties of England where the Germans were trying so hard to destroy our air cover to clear the way for troop filled landing barges to cross the Channel. But matters were not going well for Hitler and, as September 1940 approached, the RAF and our battleships were regularly pounding the European coastline after French resistance fighters, through coded messages, had pinpointed the location of enemy landing barges and troop concentrations. The same scrapbook did not contain many references to the progress of the War away from our shores other than references to the Middle East where we had driven the Italians out of Libya, only to be repelled by German forces led by General Rommel. However General Montgomery and his Desert Eighth Army had turned the tide and German forces were being slowly pushed out of Egypt.

During the Battle of Britain relatively small numbers of German bombers paid regular visits to Hull and northern cities and, during the day, low flying Messerschmitt fighter-planes would attack barrage balloons and engage in indiscriminate machine-gunning of the population. In September 1940 I had first-hand experience of such an incident that is still vividly etched into my mind. After an interesting afternoon at school I ran up our back passage, threw open the yard door and was greeted by mother who was busy washing the kitchen windows. She paused as I drew breath to begin my usual out-pouring of all that had happened when a shadow suddenly fell over the yard accompanied by a thunderous roar overhead. With hands over my ears I gazed up in horror at a German war plane that appeared to almost touch the chimney pots in its urgency to get to wherever. I clearly saw the swastika insignia on its tail and a black and white cross, with black outline, on its fuselage. Immediately behind it, and at the same low height, followed one of our fighter planes plainly showing its red, white and blue circular body emblem. Quickly it opened fire and scores of spent cartridge cases fell upon house roofs like hailstones. One landed in the yard and furiously spun like a berserk whipping top until finally coming to rest at my feet. Out of curiosity I picked it up only to quickly drop it because it was still quite hot and, with a sore finger in my mouth, we ran in as a second low flying British fighter took up the chase.

Later, as mother went to close the back passage door, I heard our elderly next door neighbour shout from her yard, “Mrs Cane – did you hear those noisy motorbikes going through the street?” Without a word mum turned and, shaking her head, walked in muttering that some moments were too full for words! Needless to add that this incident, together with a report about my burnt finger, went into the school scrapbook and teacher, with a wry grin, added my name under a special list headed ‘war wounded.’

Night raids on Hull continued through June to September with bombs causing only slight damage to houses in Chamberlain Road, Telford Street and Holderness Road with no fatalities. Our scrapbook was quick to proclaim that on July 1st 1940 Hull made history by suffering the first daylight bombing raid on a northern city. In this instance a lone enemy bomber arrived undetected and flew low over the city furiously shooting at barrage balloons whilst dropping leaflets urging us to seek peace before it was too late. It then dropped several bombs on the nearby Saltend oil terminal, set a petrol storage tank on fire, and promptly flew away over the North Sea to the belated sound of the Hull air raid alarm.

From data supplied in post war reports the Battle of Britain ended in mid-September 1940 when, after a huge air battle in the Home Counties, Hitler decided that enough was enough and postponed indefinitely his plans to invade Britain. Landing barges were scrapped and German troop presence was reduced to that of an army of occupation. Noticeable coastal activity was the erecting of a substantial defence line that was an on-going process up to the time of the second front. During the twelve week Battle of Britain the Luftwaffe lost almost 1800 planes compared with about 800 British fighters. Additionally the RAF was now regularly bombing German cities including night raids on Berlin. This was Hitler's first major defeat of the war and was a massive tribute to Britain and its then Empire that, alone, stood against seemingly overwhelming odds. At the centre of this victory over the Luftwaffe was, undoubtedly, our Royal Air Force which was immortalised through the following words of tribute given by Churchill in the House of Commons:

> "Never in the field of human conflict was so much owed by so many to so few."

This was followed by a prolonged standing ovation.

By then Herman Goering, the Commander-in Chief of the Luftwaffe and Hitler's long standing supporter was out of favour. At the start of the war he assured Hitler and the German nation that he would destroy the RAF, and that no nation would ever be in a position to bomb German cities. History proved him wrong in both claims and all that had grown in his favour was his waistline, in response to his high standard of living. His expanding midriff had not gone unnoticed by my peers who, with no small measure of contempt, referred to him as '*Fatty Goring*' through which he became a regular figure of ridicule in Courtney Street School playground. Accordingly it was not long before he was being repeatedly taunted through the words of this local composition:

"It's raining, it pouring,
It's all through Fatty *Goring*,
He went to bed with a bullet in his head,
And didn't get up in the morning."

Perhaps more attention was given to the need to rhyme rather than effectiveness of words but, at least, it has remained with me for over seventy years!

Yet all this did not mean an end to the bombing terror. Having won our first Home Front battle we were soon to be faced with a second one that had expanded its aims to include civilians and non-strategic targets. German tactics dramatically changed and the Luftwaffe's new commission was the indiscriminate heavy bombing of our cities with the sole objective of breaking public morale. Again history was to show that they did not get it all their own way and our proven air force, helped by radar, took a heavy toll on enemy bombers. Additionally we stepped-up our bombing attacks on German cities helped by air crews who had escaped from European occupied countries.

Our morale was lifted again when our excellent teacher, who had the knack of thinking-up stirring postscripts, ended a morning assembly with the rousing caption, "Hitler has found out that if you throw stones at a wasps nest you'll soon get badly stung!" After those inspiring words it was agreed that TM3 would immediately remove her name from our list of possible German spies.

LIFE ON THE HOME FRONT

"Are you sure that you're alright," mother asked for the umpteenth time as she expressed her concern that I was, and had been for some days, unusually quiet. I smiled, nodded reassuringly, and returned to inner conflicts that were beyond my childhood power of reasoning – or were they? It had occurred to me that the war had restricted our lifestyle in many ways but, for me very importantly, it had taken away our right to be 'kids'. What was it that made me believe that I and my peers were no longer children? Had the state reclassified us as under sized adults? Perhaps my new mind-set was born from an increasing number of disturbed nights, in which my allocated hours of natural sleep were so often stolen, and replaced, by a numbing uncertainty which flourished between the sounding and cancellation of many air raid alerts. I say this by way of offering a reason why the early light of adult maturity prematurely pushed aside my childhood, and made me grasp reality, despite being surrounded by the *unreality* of a vicious and life destroying war.

But in Courtney Street and elsewhere we were not on the front line amidst tanks, bombs and all the other paraphernalia of direct death. We became victims of its *ripple effect* because it had spilled over into the minds of many as a deliberate attack on our mental survival. Even as children we were all very much part of this conflict, which took many dramatic and unexpected forms. For example my mind was being conditioned to sudden outbursts in the terrace or street when a wife or mother received news that the person closest to her had been killed or posted missing. The awesome spectrum of their emotional reactions would leave me white faced and shocked yet, unless mother was there to bundle me back into the house, I would be held captive by the scene before me. By way of an example I will share one such mind shattering incident with you. The lady concerned rushed out of her house and whilst waving a piece of paper, she told everyone within ear shot that her son had been killed in the Egyptian desert campaign. Initially she was matter-of -fact about it because she was convinced a dreadful mistake had been made because her son was too young to die. By now several neighbours had gathered closer as she laboured on in an attempt to dismiss the message in her hand. Looking around her she tried to prove her point by emitting a sort of gasping laugh that all too soon crumbled into a moan of rising distress, culminating in screams of unbearable anguish. Having lost control of everything she began punching herself and, as she fell to the ground, she pulled a large piece of hair from her head whilst incessantly gibbering in a strange tongue born from the pit of despair. I felt myself trembling, and I wanted to be sick, as I was pushed aside by neighbours who held her until a nurse was brought from the next terrace. Throughout the war years I witnessed other similar scenes and, even after the passage of seventy years, I still find them too moving to dwell upon. Thus it is sufficient, for the moment, that I share with you the above account which faithfully symbolises, and portrays, the sense of loss and acute mental suffering, experienced by so many in the war, even up to the last moments before peace was signed with Japan, and WW2 ended, on the 2nd September 1945.

Following my comments on this topic it was not surprising that the street had lost a lot of its pre-war vivacity which effectively dealt with matters, on a day to day basis, as dictated by several terrace end policy making groups. The then common philosophy that tomorrow would take care of itself no longer applied because by tomorrow the street, and all in it, could become just another set of air raid statistics. In a short space of time our former street life, as hard as it was, had become a happy memory that was now challenged by an uncertain future. Regardless of age there were many who yearned to have the old days back – Means Test Inspector and all. For example it was not usual for a large group of children to agree upon a point but, as one, we were adamant that shrapnel hunting could never replace a game of good old fashioned marbles, which the advent of street shelters had curtailed, due to their encroachment on roadside gutters so vital to this noble game. Despite the prevailing gloom there was, from some adults, a growing optimism in a future beyond this war which, quite correctly, they argued could not go on for ever. This, as a basic philosophy in logic, would be difficult to challenge and, in consequence, was a good rallying cry for many in the street. But to be fair I never heard anyone ever express opinions other than that Britain would, ultimately, win the war and afterwards it would be a fairer and more humane nation in which to live.

A visiting street preacher, beneath his banner bearing the word HOPE, proclaimed that the war would be won by a classless society whose blood and rivulets of tears would flow from hovels and mansions alike – words which were delivered with such strength and passion that they were often reiterated in doorstep or air raid shelter discussions. Thus our previous honoured dogma of not allowing life to drift over the border between today and tomorrow had been bridged by *Hope*, courtesy of a wandering street evangelist.

Indeed Courtney Street hopes were further justified through such parliamentary visionaries as Sir William Beveridge, who had unveiled his post war plan for a welfare state that would care for all citizens from the cradle to the grave. In broad terms his plan would require every wage earner to pay a weekly national insurance contribution. This would then help to finance benefits for the sick, widowed, retired and unemployed. In addition there would be an allowance for families which, if accepted in its entirety, would mean that the dreaded Means Test Inspector would be declared redundant. In partnership with Beveridge there came a politician, who would become a post-war Government Minister, named Aneurin Bevan. In due course he proved to be the chief architect of the National Health Service, which would lift yet another burden from many households.

Now armed with a their new vision of an effective life, beyond the parameters of a single day, Courtney Street demonstrated, to my growing mind, how the area was changing and that former life styles were gone forever. Now it seemed that everyone was helping to win the war by working harder on the Home Front. Children saved pennies, collected scrap metal and food waste, and knitted woolly hats for soldiers and refugees. BBC radio's Children's Hour ran a scrap-collecting competition and I remember listening to the applause when a young teenager was awarded a prize for collecting eight tons of scrap metal. With so many men away in the armed services vast numbers of women were working in factories, trams, buses and trains, and in hospitals and schools. Many thousands of women throughout the country joined the Women's Land Army to work on farms or were employed in forests with the Timber Corps and, as the war evolved, more and more British women enrolled to serve in the Army, Navy and Air force. So, in a few words, the Home Front was determined that Britain would win this war or they would know the reason why!

As for me I now belong to the waning few who can still clearly remember and compare street life before, during and after the war years, which has left me with a galaxy of nostalgic memories and an objective to try and preserve them in this book.

A few words about the *Daily Worker*

It would be towards the end of 1940 when a newspaper called the *Daily Worker* finally fell out of favour with the Government. For those who do not remember this paper, which was well read in Courtney Street, it was the official newspaper of the British Communist Party (BCP) and dad regularly brought home his copy; I believe he obtained it from a Party worker at Tan Yard. As the War progressed so did regular criticism from the BCP, via the Daily Worker, in which contributors argued that Britain and its Empire were wrong in their decision to wage war against Germany. This attitude reflected the fact that the BCP were devoted to Russia who, at this stage of events, was allied with Germany. Hitler and Stalin had carved-up Poland between them and, as if to seal their insincerity, had signed yet another *dodgy* non-aggression pact that would soon be broken. No doubt Government inner echelons were alarmed at such outpouring of negativity from the BCP, at this stage of the war, when national patriotism should not be eroded in any way. Thus without further ado printing and publication of the *Daily Worker* was banned by the Home Secretary although, in a short space of time, an illicit 'under the counter' version was available. I can clearly remember these banned publications because again, courtesy of a Tan Yard contact, copies were building up in a drawer alongside our fireplace. However these did not survive for very long because of a lingering fear that Hitler's forces may still invade Britain. Obviously something so horrendous carried in its wake a veritable storehouse of possibilities based on the knowledge that, in reality, Hitler hated the Communist Party and, in particular, any publications that supported its causes. From these facts someone with a fertile imagination painted a mental picture of the Gestapo, marching into every house in Courtney Street, in order to rummage through fireside drawer units looking for copies of the *Daily Worker*. And woe-betide anyone found with such in their possession! So in the interests of street impartiality, whilst awaiting eventual liberation, copies of the *Daily Worker* and other references to Communism were carefully burned and the resultant paper ash judiciously reduced to dust. With minimum ceremony my father dealt with several of his illicit copies in this way after commenting that many of his mates had done the same. However in early June 1941 Germany's invasion of Russia resulted in the *Daily Worker* turning its' fury upon Hitler which redeemed it in Government eyes and, despite paper shortages, it regained a place on newspaper display stands.

THE BLITZKRIEG CAME UPON US

It was a notable feature, as 1940 drew to a close, that Hull had suffered repeated air attacks, both by day and night, and the momentum was increasing. Daylight attacks were mainly aimed at destroying barrage balloons and creating terror by low level machine gun attacks on built-up areas. However the Luftwaffe had to be wary because our fighter planes were close behind them and eager to add further *kill symbols* on the fuselage of their planes. Night raids were mainly incendiary attacks on dockland estates or, as happened in the majority of cases, where they chanced to fall. There were several fatalities and an increasing number of people were both injured and deprived of their homes.

Hull Guildhall under attack

Before leaving 1940 I will relate one Hull air raid that made the news albeit using our now familiar title of an 'East Coast Town.' It was in mid-December 1940 which I remember well because of deep freeze weather conditions, and that it was nearing what was to be an austere Christmas. Nevertheless mother had put our 'trimmings' up which did little to cheer us as once again we leapt out of a warm bed, rushed downstairs, and huddled under the stairs. Increasing gunfire and the sound of several nearby windows being broken by shrapnel was our incentive to take shelter beneath a number of blankets that had been left there just for this purpose. The fire had long since gone out and, when gun flashes lit up the uncovered kitchen window, frozen condensate could be clearly seen on the *inside* of each pane.

It was indeed a bitterly cold night and the plight of our firemen, in those near arctic conditions, was remembered and talked about long after the war was over. Overall this was a particularly busy night for them with forty to fifty fires raging throughout Hull. The subject of this account is one particular outbreak which engulfed a building close to the Guildhall. Sparks from the conflagration fell continuously upon the Guildhall and, carried by gusts of wind, some gained entry through a number of broken windows. The future of this major civic landmark was in jeopardy – to say the least. Accordingly many jets of water were directed at the heart of the nearby fire and, as a result, sheets of thickening ice rapidly formed across Alfred Gelder Street. This meant that each fireman had increasing difficulty remaining on his feet. In later years I recalled this scene and mentally added Waldteufel' music for the Skater's Waltz to give background effect! According to one report firemen were dragged, full length, along the frozen road as they fought to control high pressure water hoses. But they persevered and due to their great bravery and tenacity they overcame multiple problems and extinguished the fire so saving the nearby Guildhall. After the raid it was discovered that the firemen's hoses were frozen and could not be rolled up. Not to be beaten they were uncoupled and, like a forest of Scottish cabers, they were transported to various stations to be thawed out in readiness for the next operation.

Welcome to the year 1941

This would turn out to be a momentous year, in terms of German bombing raids on this city, which was met by the *new look* Courtney Street that no longer lived for the day, but for a new and better life that would, hopefully, soon appear on their horizon. Unfortunately, before the advent of that day they would have to listen to 820 air raid alerts and endure much horror from the sky which, according to my memory, appeared to further strengthen their resolve. I am not sure that my 'resolve' was strengthened despite experiencing every air raid upon Hull. Perhaps it was the chemistry of fear, working on my still developing ten year old mind, that gave me the capacity to remember every one of them; albeit some more vividly than others. I mention this because if I presented each of these events in tabular form I would produce another index orientated reference book, to add to excellent reference publications already on the market. For this reason, and in support of my aim to present a local and social history of the street of my birth, I have restricted my narrative to those air raids that affected Courtney Street and district.

School life in 1941

By the end of February 1941 Hull had endured eight air raids in the course of which 24 people were killed and many more injured or made homeless. Nevertheless our schools tried hard to remain open but their effectiveness was hindered by two factors:

1. The former evacuees who hastily departed in September 1939 and, because of the *phony war*, had returned home by the end of that year were now, together with several new applicants, fast returning to the safety of the countryside. Obviously many staff members went with them leaving our schools, including Courtney Street, as ghost establishments devoid of staff and pupils. The accelerated rate of air attacks meant that remaining children stayed at home the following day therefore adding further uncertainty to the education system.

2. Accordingly emergency measures were brought into force which meant that local schools would operate on a rota system thus offering a semblance of education that, without doubt, was better than nothing. Consequently remaining Courtney lads and lasses spent time at Chapman Street, Buckingham Street and other schools in the area which, as a bonus, helped us to widen our experience and gain new friends. But it was not too long before accelerating air attacks made this system untenable, meaning that all schools closed for long periods with only spasmodic openings. This unavoidable situation, which lasted throughout 1941 and

1942, had for most pupil age groups a catastrophic effect on their educational development. In my case this had to be corrected by post school night class courses at my own expense.

Who the hell will sharpen our knives now?

The expression, "March came in like a lion," was very apt both weather and war wise. Gale force winds blew many headwind Courtney Street walkers to a standstill and ripped several barrage balloons from their moorings. The awesome presence of cable trailing bags of gas, hurtling along in the wind, meant imminent disaster for electricity pylons, factory chimneys and property in general, but on the credit side it gave the Home Guard marksmen excellent rifle practice when ordered to shoot them down. Sadly the only force to withstand the wind were German day time raider planes that, seemingly at will, regularly flew in on low level fire and run forays before the buzzers could sound and our fighters respond. All the aforementioned incidents were incapable of deterring a man who, every Saturday morning, came around to sharpen our kitchen knives on his bicycle powered grinding wheel. Although he lived in James Reckitt Avenue he faithfully covered his round that included most of the streets off Dansom Lane. Saturday March 1st was no exception and he was busy at his usual end of Burleigh Grove pitch, oblivious to a queue of knife clutching women who had little to say as they leant against the force of the wind.

Much to the delight of our Air Raid Warden the wind gradually abated as the day moved towards evening, as if in deference to his earlier prediction that there would be a massive raid that night and on no account did he want a strong wind to spread the fires. It was around nine o'clock when mum and I were on our way home after visiting her mother who lived across the road in Burleigh Grove. This was a daily visit because Gran was lame, partially deaf and was adamant that she would never enter an air raid shelter; her sole objection being that she did not fancy the prospect of the reinforced concrete roof falling on her head. She was happy enough wrapped up in her single bed beneath the staircase and was blissfully unaware, nor did she care, of what was happening outside.

Suddenly the quickly rising howl of the dreaded air raid siren began and was immediately followed by the accustomed regular throbbing sound of German bomber engines that were so different from our own planes. Fortunately for us and for reasons I covered earlier, the much feared Stuka dive bomber was rarely used although its flying companions meant serious business at our expense. Urgent action on our part was needed and our signal to run came when several nearby anti-aircraft batteries simultaneously opened fire. Their noisy presence was very welcome mainly as a morale booster because in night raids, even if the target was locked in the glare of a search light, it was most unusual to score a direct hit.

Dad, carrying an armful of blankets, met us in the terrace and rushed us back to the street and into the public air raid shelter. When we had got our breath back, and became aware of the first downfall of shrapnel bouncing off house roofs, matched by the clatter of falling tiles, dad went on to explain why we were not under the stairs. Apparently he had heard a news flash, on Rediffusion radio, which warned all listeners that a large number of German bombers were heading in Hull's direction and a heavy raid seemed likely. Therefore everyone should immediately take cover in municipal air raid shelters. Having recovered my breath I looked around the shelter and viewed, in the flickering light of a few candles, a line of middle aged to elderly ladies. One lady sitting in front of me was lost in her knitting whilst quietly muttering what, to me, were several unfathomable expressions including *knit one, purl one.* Despite an assortment of explosions outside, which through the months I had become thoroughly acclimatised to, my attention was drawn to the antics of *Mrs. Knitting Woman* before me. It was a sort of *wigging-in* that was dear to my heart. Suddenly becoming aware that she had my attention she gave a mischievous smile and continued aloud with:

"You knit one and purl one,
Drop a loop and blame John!"

This immediately stirred up the hitherto silent line of ladies to respond with their own contributions and, whilst not strictly relevant, they added extensive details of the particular branch of their family tree they had plucked them from. Becoming bored with this my eyes rested on a woman, almost lost in the shadows, who appeared to be fiddling around with a string of beads. In what to me was a whisper I enquired of my mother, "Why is that woman playing with her necklace?" A nudge from her elbow added emphasis to mother's command to 'shush,' as she then whispered in my ear that she was saying her rosary because she was a Catholic. My supposed undertone question, "What's a rosary?" was met by mother's hand clamped over my mouth followed by the command, "Will you shut up and listen to the air raid!"

It was a tradition within most street air raid shelters that women and children did not move from the bench seats whereas most of the men would pack into shelter entrances, or just outside in the street, if the warden wasn't hanging around. Accordingly assembled they would keep up a distorted commentary of what was happening both in the air and on the ground, at the same time offering their opinions on the best way to deal with various aspects of enemy activity around them. It was not unknown for differing views to develop into serious arguments only to be quelled by a strident female voice from within bellowing, "Will you noisy lot out there *shurrup*!"

But this occasion was different because one of the male commentators refused point blank to be quiet. He was adamant that in the last flash of guns he saw a parachute, carrying what looked like a large metal tube, slowly descending on to Courtney Street. Instantly silence reigned as many pairs of eyes awaited the next salvo of guns which, literally in a flash, went on to confirm the claimed sighting. Further debate was cut short when the area warden ran towards the shelters ordering everyone to get inside, because 'a parachute land mine was drifting our way.' Since this terror weapon was a new addition to the Luftwaffe's armoury, which would be used on Hull and elsewhere many time in the next three years, it is worth a brief description as to its potential. As the observer noted it consisted of a long metal cylinder that contained over a ton of high explosives. Supported by a large parachute these destructive items drifted to the ground and, by design, they took their time about it. Some even landed and exploded after the bombers had gone at the expense of rescue workers who had thought it safe to begin digging out the wounded and dead. The blast from these devices was devastating. Within a radius of several hundreds of yards they could destroy vast numbers of homes and other buildings and inflict great carnage upon human beings. In post war German records the land mine was, in their words, 'dropped with the intention of wreaking terror and slaughter upon large numbers of civilians.' Few victims of that era would argue that it had failed to achieve its objective.

"It would be best if you leant forward and put your hands over your ears, "advised the ARP warden. Without exception everyone complied and my last sighting before mother pulled me face down on to her knee, and held me thus with the top half of her body, was that the woman's fingers were working even faster on her rosary. As an aside I had, even as a ten year old, mixed feelings about my mother's desire to save me without regard for her own welfare. Obviously her prime intention was of the highest order and far above criticism in whatever form, and would gain deserved praise in a post raid obituary notice. In my case it may then go on to say that her son was spared death by enemy action only to be suffocated within a '*mother sandwich*' – with that I rest my case!

The land mine in question was obviously intended for the Stoneferry industrial area which had taken the brunt of the attack. As it happened it was off course and had drifted low over Courtney Street, along Dansom Lane, and finally exploded in James Reckitt Avenue causing wide spread damage to housing and killing ten people in the process. It felt like a minor earthquake when the mine exploded and the shelter quivered as cement dust drifted down from the roof. But mother's first concern was for my brother Jim who was at his girlfriend's house in Endymion Street and, as it later transpired, he was safe in a nearby street shelter.

Soon after this the 'All Clear' sounded and we had the amazing yet tragic experience of viewing, from Danny Lane corner, over fifty fires blazing away in Stoneferry and nearby areas. One fire in particular, centred on a varnish factory in Sculcoates Lane, burned for two days despite all attempts to put it out. Additionally my father had to make a wide detour, when walking to and from Tan Yard, because a number of storage tanks had been ruptured and highly viscous oil had oozed out and swamped several of the narrow streets.

There was yet more distressing news to come. It would have been at least three days later when word filtered through to Courtney Street that one of the James Reckitt Avenue land mine casualties was the man who had sharpened our kitchen knives for many years. The stunned silence on hearing this sad news was broken by an emotion filled voice murmuring, "Who the hell will sharpen our knives now?"

When meeting in the street many adults now refused to use the traditional 'Good Morning' greeting which they described as an insult to all those killed, injured or made homeless the night before. Alternatively any who reverted to the traditional new day greeting would be glowered at and given the obvious reply of, "What's good about it?" The best they could muster was a shake of the head and, after a few moments of silence continue with, "When will all this end?"

Mobile anti-aircraft guns

Still trapped in their minds was the noise and terror of last night's bombs and guns complimented with diving planes and machine gun fire. As if this entire din was not enough a new ear-splitting noise had literally burst upon us in the form of mobile anti-aircraft guns. These would tour the streets to get in the best position to fire at enemy planes caught in the searchlights and, as if to announce their presence, it was only the previous night that one pulled up alongside our street shelter and immediately opened fire. The sudden and unexpected shock of several ear-splitting explosions, at the other side of the shelter wall, promoted a variety of ill events including screams, hysteria and fainting bouts together with two admitted cases of lost bowel control. Within our crowded shelter the latter mishap elevated an already fetid atmosphere into the realms of unbearable. Therefore it was no surprise that incoming clouds of highly sulphurous by-product smoke, from the mobile gun outside became, without exception, a fragrance to be encouraged and wafted around the shelter!

It never ceased to amaze me that even in the midst of a severe blitz Courtney Street never lost its capacity for innocent humour as embodied in a tale related by our Air Raid Warden. Apparently when the mobile gun in the street had discharged a salvo, and was busy reloading, the gun captain looked down and, to his surprise, saw an elderly lady standing in the roadway totally oblivious of enemy bombers aloft and shrapnel falling around her. With a smile she thanked them for their hard work and asked if they would like a cup of tea!

And then there was Patriotic Depression

No amount of attacks by Hitler's bombers ever took away my interest in *wigging-in* from which a large proportion of this book is constructed. Granted that terrace end debaters were now in the minority there were still pickings to be had by dedicated eavesdroppers. From one small group I overheard a lady, who had a wide vocabulary gained from cleaning in a solicitor's office, giving her opinion on the state of morale in Courtney Street. In her closing remarks she summarised Courtney Street as being in a state of *patriotic depression*. Not surprisingly her conclusion passed unchallenged by the blank faces around her although, some years later, I realised the truth of her expression. Without doubt incessant air raids, rationing and fear for loved ones on some distant battlefield did promote widespread depression, but this was offset by an unflinching determination that we would win this war and string Hitler up from the nearest lamp post. From this viewpoint many in Courtney Street were both patriotic and depressed, as recognised by our 1941 street orator, when she brilliantly created the expression *patriotic depression*.

I suppose that my peers and I were of similar minds. We had lost interest in collecting shrapnel because there was an abundance of it lying around the street and air raid shelters had put an end to playing marbles in the gutter. Also we were not allowed to stray far from street shelters in the event that Gerry planes may sweep in with machine guns blazing. Also the Air Raid Warden had stopped us from climbing on the shelter roof because it would make us easy targets, as had been the case in other towns when children at play had been gunned down.

Just walking as far as Tin Mission called for maximum attention to sounds, and even the sudden noise of a policeman's motor cycle would cause us to throw ourselves into a garden, passage or whatever haven was at hand. It seemed that birds had stopped singing and that nature had been replaced by the sound of glass and roof tile fragments breaking beneath our feet. Everything we touched was coated with soot aided and abetted by drifting smoke, of the worse possible kind, that was intent on injuring the health of everyone it could make contact with. By contrast there were wood burning stoves in the area that, on a clear and cold winter's morning, gave an aroma of delight to all who came within range.

But the smoke of war that literally hung in Courtney Street and district was a vile by-product derived from burnt oil fortified with a cocktail of industrial chemicals, toxic and otherwise, that had been brewed in recent Stoneferry air attacks. Its legacy to the area was an acrid stench that nullified our sense of taste in exchange for sore throats and watering eyes. Nostalgia was ever to the fore as we wandered aimlessly from terrace to terrace within quick reach of a street shelter. We longed to go back to school but it seemed to us that those days had gone forever. I still kept daily records for the classroom diary but, looking at charred beams through a large hole in the junior school roof, caused by a recent incendiary bomb, I wondered if the school would ever be used again. In common with the adults around us we knew that one day we would win this war. Chalked and subsequently mutilated caricatures of Hitler and *Fatty Goring* on shelter walls bore testimony to the corporate strength of *patriotic depression* which was ours to keep – and keep it we did!

Back under the Staircase

Mum and dad had taken a 'management' decision through which we gave up using the street shelter in favour of returning to our former sanctuary beneath the staircase. Major driving features behind this decision were a return to home comforts, being able to talk or keep quiet as we chose or return to bed if the severity of the raid died down. Some other Courtney Street residents were of the same opinion and, as far as I could assess, there was a rough 50:50 split between street shelters and 'under the stairs'. Several neighbours held a rigid belief that if a bomb had your name on it then it would find you wherever you were. This was front line fatalism which was scorned by others but, in my assessment at the time, it did help many to over-ride natural fear which, at the height of the Blitz, was no bad thing.

Considering that almost every day we spent part of our lives underneath the stairs, it was right that we set out the area accordingly. Mother had her special bag which, on entering, she hid beneath a loose floor board near the meter. It contained life insurance policies, rent book, her purse and a small bottle of brandy in case things got really bad. Lest I forget I must draw attention to a special piece of paper within that purse, upon which was written serial numbers of one pound or ten shillings notes it may contain. This practice was followed by several women in Courtney Street following a dreadful incident when a shopper paid for her groceries with a one pound note, and was given change for ten shillings. Obviously a request for the shopkeeper to check serial numbers of bank notes in the till, against the list held by the shopper, would quickly resolve tense situations of this nature. Father made certain that his pipe and pouch of Erinmore flake tobacco remained with him and I settled for my small torch, a piece of plasticine and a recent copy of the Dandy comic. As mother once remarked, "If it wasn't for that Hitler then it would be quite comfy under here."

This was almost prophetic when, on four consecutive nights starting on March 13th 1941 Hull was battered by large numbers of German bombers meaning that we virtually lived beneath the stairs. One of the cries from the street was, "Why Hull – what the hell have we done." Sadly even on a cursory level of examination the answer was obvious. Our city was a perfect target for Luftwaffe bombing because of its importance as a port and industrial centre. Being on the east coast, at the meeting of two rivers and with readily identifiable docks in the city centre, it was also a relatively easy target. Even when raids had eased off in other parts of the country Hull remained under constant attack because the Germans, who invaded Russia in June 1941, knew that the bulk of convoys to Russia began in Hull.

The 13th March attack began with a delayed alert that had us running down the stairs as the first of the bombs came whistling down. "Another full night of it," dad grumbled as he noticed it was 10pm. For him, and all other workers in the street, it would mean eventually getting to their workplace and, in the case of dad, spending valuable piece work time clearing up broken glass and other damage from the night before; after which the scheduled work could begin. Sadly for many they arrived at their place of work to find it a smouldering ruin.

For my part I felt very tired so, according to my new tradition, I cocooned myself in a blanket, snuggled down on my cushion and viewed the world through a small gap left for that purpose. This arrangement minimized the sound of outside explosions and, on this particular night, it gave me a stunning view of the full moon shining through the kitchen window. I became mesmerised by its peaceful image and, as my thoughts wandered, I realised that it shared its calming beauty with Germans and British alike. Attempts by palls of smoke from mobile anti-aircraft guns to draw a curtain over its radiance failed abysmally, and it continued to shine upon all who would give it a glance. Was there a man in the moon I asked myself? If so what would he think to the behaviour of us human beings whose one aim was to kill and maim others whilst destroying their homes? I liked this question so I decided to write it down later so that I could add it to the school diary – if ever the day came when we could go back to school.

In common with many other families in Courtney Street our way of life had become programmed to accept this constant flow of air raids; and we paid little regard to the fact that our death may be within the next bomb to shriek its way to earth. Also hiding beneath the stairs meant that we could sleep better than in the street shelter in which we had to endure several chatty ladies going on at length about their ailments, and those of some distant relative. Occasionally a bomb exploding nearby would briefly wake us up and dad would mutter, "That was close," followed by estimates of where it may have landed. Through our growing experience of air raids we had learned that the close proximity of an exploding bomb could not always be related to a very loud explosion which, at times, could sound deceptively near due to wind direction. More importantly was the vibration of the ground on which we sat. When the house seemed to sway and cause the pans to topple off pantry shelves accompanied by the sound of breaking windows and tiles sliding off the roof then, without doubt – that was close to home. Eventually the 'All Clear' sounded at 3am and, according to later reports from the warden, eighty German bombers had taken part and the main target was the docks and factory areas. In the process many fires had been started so that, for the first time, Hull had to call for back-up from nearby towns and cities. As ever many residential areas were hit and over forty people were killed.

Robins or Airlie Birds?

In the mid 1860s two Rugby League clubs were formed in Hull and are still known as Hull FC, whose ground was in Airlie Street off the Boulevard and Hull Kingston Rovers who played at Craven Park on Holderness Road. Both teams had their staunch supporters, as they still have today, and the fact that the River Hull separated the two grounds meant the City was split into two camps; mainly identified by the team strip colours. Thus the Red and Whites, or the Robins, gained their support in east Hull and west Hull was the home of the Black and Whites also known as the Airlie Birds. Some of my earliest recollections were male visitors to the house singing the praises of the 'Robins' using words and terms that totally baffled me. As far as I can remember there was one Kingston Rover's player whose name frequently cropped up for acclamation which, to my distant memory, sounded like George Sanderson or it could have been 'Saddington.'

Following the end of World War One in 1918 the numerous manufacturing sites that had sprung-up in east Hull attracted many, including my own family, away from west Hull and its fishing fraternity to the relative safety of land based jobs. Nevertheless many of them still supported the Airlie Birds and, on match days, journeyed back to The Boulevard to cheer their team on until the start of World War Two caused all team fixtures to be suspended. Before then rival supporters were not slow to press home the merits of their chosen team, without reference to the Marquis of Queensbury rules, when passions boiled over during Saturday night sports – which is a topic I touched upon earlier in my narrative.

The reason I have raised this subject was by way of a lead into the air raid we had the following night which may well have broken more hearts in the whole of Hull than any other raid so far. The raid lasted until the early hours of the 15th and was again centred on the docks and Stoneferry factories. However a particularly powerful land mine slowly drifted down, probably off course because it missed the nearby docks, and landed in the centre of Bean Street which, in those days, ran from Anlaby Road through to Hessle Road. Like Courtney Street it was densely populated and consisted of a line of front houses, on both sides of the road, interspersed with side terraces leading off. This street was home to many families of fishermen and dock workers. It would be two days later that I walked with dad to view Bean Street on the way to visit my grandmother who lived off Selby Street. The damage was catastrophic. I looked in stunned silence at a waste of discoloured bricks from which protruded broken pieces of timber, roof tiles and items of furniture. Then, at irregular intervals, there emerged a few house dividing walls which by explosive chance had withstood the blast and, seemingly as an act of forlorn defiance, still supported their chimney stacks and pots. Here and there I saw tearful pet owners desperately scraping through the debris of their once house, whilst calling out the name of a cat or dog, in the hope that it was still alive and trapped in an air pocket. Further down the street many houses could be seen with windows no more than shards of glass from which fragments of net curtain fluttered in the breeze; and others that resembled a dolls house with its front removed thus displaying room furniture undamaged by the blast. I later learned that the mine killed twenty five people and seriously injured a further thirty. I feel certain that it was consolation for them to learn that many in Courtney Street, at the other side of the river, shared their grief because of family and friendship connections with the area. Also from my wigging-in to adult conversations I found that many mourners from Courtney Street attended the Bean Street communal funeral and a few men, wearing black and white scarves, were consoled by their team rivals, wearing red and white scarves, as they walked together in mutual grief.

Like mice in a hole

As mum and I left our house on the morning after the Bean Street bombing a little lady from the bottom of the terrace scurried past us muttering, "We're just like mice rushing out of our hole to find food and get back again before the trouble starts." That neighbour, who was aptly named Minnie, really summed up the feelings of those in Courtney Street with whom we had contact, and little did we know that it would remain a valid description at least until the end of 1943. For me shopping was once an enjoyable outing which had been wrecked by food rationing and predatory Messerschmitts that swept in firing at barrage balloons only to be shot at, in turn, by our fighter planes.

The close landing bomb that dad referred to last night had made a crater in the road at the top of Burleigh Street having just missed the railway bridge but, not to be thwarted, had demolished the tram lines. There was enough room for smaller vehicles to squeeze by on the opposite pavement but all trams were, for the moment, obliged to remain in the depot. Notices of changed services had, in desperation, been chalked on the pavement alongside the bus stops; and I remember thinking that I hoped it didn't rain. Maypole and adjacent shops had lost their windows meaning they were closed until the over worked glaziers could replace them. Mother managed to stock up on some essential food and, as a bonus, was able to get a supply of soap. Everyone was filthy because of the presence of soot in the air, and our eyes and throats were sore because of the previously mentioned acrid smoke and other vile pollutants that lingered in the atmosphere. Suddenly our ears were once more blasted by an air raid alarm that prompted mother to grab my arm and, as we ran down Courtney Street, she urged me along with, “Come on – Minnie was right. Let’s get back into our mouse hole!”

First of the big air raids

As part of my lifelong interest in local history, fortified by boyhood recollections and fond memories, I have studied post war German records of airborne raids upon Britain and particularly those on Hull; more so because I was an eye witness to each of the onslaughts. A notable feature of the many bombing sorties upon Hull was, according to later discovered German records, four super- blitzkriegs involving large numbers of aircraft which, according to them, had completely destroyed Hull as a port and industrial area. The first of these gigantic raids was on the 18th March 1941 when, according to German statistics, 420 aircraft took off and 378 arrived over Hull. Pre-target losses by the Luftwaffe were almost certainly due to the efficiency of our radar system and the effectiveness of fighter command.

“There’s nowt on the wireless,” dad muttered as he moved the Rediffusion wall switch to the centre off position. Looking around the room he grinned at me and nodded towards Jim who, with head back and mouth wide open, was hard asleep in the fireside chair. After an interim job elsewhere he had finally been taken on by Reckitt and Colman in their box making shop hence the need for sleep. Mother was sitting at the table ‘resting her eyes’ so, to use dad’s favourite expression, “It was time for us all to get ‘up the dancers’ to bed.” No one was concerned that the buzzers had sounded all of twenty minutes ago because, after 18 months of war, they were just a noisy interruption that meant another false alarm or many hours of intense bombing and gunfire; and we were hardened to both options. Jim, on hands and knees, was already making slow progress up the stairs and dad was busy poking ashes through into the grate when mother held up her hands and whispered, “Shush everybody.” Mum had excellent hearing and we strained hard to listen for whatever it was. “Surely you can all hear it,” she said in desperation.

"Hear what?" asked dad. "That rumbling sound in the distance – it's like a herd of elephants coming down the street." Suddenly I was aware that the floor was shaking and water in the goldfish bowl was seemingly coming to the boil; as was our neighbour's curiosity by the sound of alarmed yet excited voices up and down the terrace.

Having made certain that the house light was off we joined a dozen or so people, in our now strangely illuminated terrace, who were gazing at a sight above them. And what a picturesque sight it was! Seemingly hundreds of Chinese lanterns were slowly falling from the sky; their glowing descent brushed aside elements of darkness leaving Hull basking in artificial daylight. There were one or two gasps of amazement but, for the rest of us, the deep throated and pulsating vibrations, which came from darkness above the lanterns, was becoming unbearable to our ears. Suddenly searchlights were actively sweeping the sky and, as in all raids so far, it would take a finite time for one of them to catch a bomber in its beam. Now almost at once they could pick out planes with ease. The reason for this was that there were hundreds of German bombers above us and the Chinese lanterns were, in fact, our first experience of Chandelier Flares which had been released in order to illuminate target areas. Suddenly the rumbling thunder from the sky was challenged by an enraged barrage of fire from several ground and mobile gun batteries which rarely did anything other than uphold public morale. However on this occasion, probably because the sky was awash with hostile aircraft, a bomber directly above us was hit and its cargo of explosives immediately exploded. We stared in fear and amazement at the awesome yet, for the moment, silent display of destructive chemistry that had been initiated. The entire plane was enveloped in a vivid flash that quickly, in reverse order, displayed all colours of the spectrum as whirling pieces of aircraft and human remains were hurled in all directions. Then the moment came when the sound waves reached our ears in the form of a thunderous explosion that had us all running for house safety, and my last sighting was of a second plane rapidly losing height with flames spreading from one of its engines.

This terrifying display of seething hatred between attacking bombers and our guns and fighter planes went on until 4 o'clock the following morning when the breaking dawn, seemingly out of compassion, shed tears of rain on a city which, in spite of mourning its dead and fighting countless raging fires, never once contemplated defeat. There had been nothing selective in this attack, and the one objective had been a vain attempt to break our united spirit. Factories together with 700 houses had been destroyed and as many again could not be lived in, Beverley Road hospital had been hit and many wards evacuated, the centre of Hull now bore telling scars and, as an encore, the gas works had been badly damaged meaning that we were without gas for almost a week. The final casualty figure for this raid was 98 killed and over 70 seriously injured and once again surrounding towns and cities had given welcome back-up in terms of fire appliances and ambulances.

The morning after

Later in the day, after a good wash in the kitchen sink, I quickly lost my Fairy soap sheen when I stepped outside into the usual post raid atmosphere of soot, smoke and dust. For some time now the street had been awash with a range of solid hazards, and our once level pavement, that had been ideal for running and skipping on, was now an obstacle course of broken bricks, concrete, glass and other jetsam; courtesy of exploding mines and bombs in the area. A group of neighbours were excitedly pointing at a street roof upon which was a buckled bicycle part wrapped around a chimney stack. "Whatever next, now we have low flying bikes to contend with!" muttered a waggish onlooker. Women clutching shopping bags slowly and carefully picked their way to Holderness Road shops assuming they had something to sell or, more to the point, if they were still standing after last night's horror. Household routine was important to many Courtney housewives and they had a fixed day for every major chore in the house. So it came as no surprise to me to see a woman washing the only two panes of glass left intact in her bay window after last night's efforts, because this was window washing day and it would take more than Hitler to stop her! Heartened by this I walked on only to come down to earth when I reached my school to discover it had suffered a direct hit and was now a windowless shell filled with bricks, fallen timber and memories.

For a while I stood there in a state of total shock. Slowly I began to remember the junior school as it was, and the teachers who had helped build my confidence, and especially my favourite teacher who told us that we must never give up hope. How right she was I muttered to myself only to realise that I was not alone and that someone was gently gripping my arm. I turned in surprise and we looked at one another in a few moments of silence and then, through smoke tarnished vocal chords I croaked, "Hello Annie," whilst noticing that her face, like mine, bore a film of soot and general grime. But there was a noticeable difference. Her face also displayed tell-tale signs of tears that had run their course and left soot free streaks to prove their passage. Sensing that I had noticed her grief she immediately tried to recover her former cheerful nature which, in part, she lost whilst explaining that her grand-dad was '*badly*' again, so she was on her way to get some medicine for him. I offered to walk with her but she assured me that she was OK. Looking at the wreckage she gave an uncertain laugh and told me not to worry because they would soon build a new school for us, and then life would be as it was. Annie was about to say something more but her voice slowly trailed away as she gazed in silence at rubble around our feet. Could it be that emotion had caused her to pause, or had she run out of words? I saw her lip begin to tremble before she hurriedly reached down and picked up a fragment of brick. Briefly she looked at it then suddenly, in her now tightly clenched hand, she held it close to her chest and bowed her head as if in prayer. Quickly she recovered and, with a semblance of a smile, declared she would keep it in memory of school and our friendship. I searched for words as tears ran down her face and, as if a reply was not expected, she gave me a tear stained smile, uttered a quick 'tar rah for now,' and quickly ran towards Holderness Road.

Concerned for her I gazed after Annie until she had turned the corner then I slowly walked home and, in my reverie, I failed to register the fact that the former beer-off shop was also a burned out ruin.

How did the blitz affect those in Courtney Street and district?

Although I must restrict my comments to the area where I lived, and the people I lived with, I am certain that Hull and the entire country would unite with much that was proclaimed in Courtney houses, shops and street shelters. First of all a new thirst for news had entered most homes and radio bulletins were avidly anticipated and listened to. Through thin house walls cheers could be heard when news of British bombing raids over Hamburg and Berlin were announced. People loved to shout their views across the street using such expressions as, "Serves the buggers right – now they can taste their own medicine!" and many others in much stronger terms. Newsagent placards were enthusiastically read and commented on. They were overjoyed that Hitler, who had swept through Europe with consummate ease, had now found someone who could hit him back.

It is interesting to recall that in the early months of the war the Government policy was to be careful where the RAF dropped their bombs in Germany – and on no account must civilians be put in danger. Now the policy was to aim for strategic targets and if civilians got in the way then so be it. Then as the war progressed more and more civilians became the prime target for daytime machine gun attacks, and night time blitzkriegs, which intensified a growing sense of hatred, throughout the street, for Hitler and his supporters. Although only ten years old I could clearly remember when Courtney Street, in general, lived to a code of tolerance from which the maxim 'live and let live' was often quoted. Sadly unmitigated accounts of disasters, at home and abroad, quickly consigned this motto to their dustbin of failed intentions.

In my post-war studies I did note that German bomber crews, when their plane was damaged during a raid, would only as a last resort bail out over a blazing city. They feared that a successful landing would not guarantee their safety when faced with hostile and beleaguered citizens who, under the circumstances, may well have ignored both large and small print within the Geneva Convention. They would make every effort to crash land in the Humber or North Sea and frequently died in the attempt. I remember *wigging-in* on our air raid warden when he was talking to a group of adults, in the street, on the topic of attitudes towards captured bomber crews. He quoted a situation he knew about when a German plane crash landed and only one crew member survived although badly injured. In broken English he appealed for help to the leader of an armed group who saw the crash and ran to the scene. The same group leader later boasted that he agreed to help him enter the next world as a matter of urgency. With that he promptly shot him dead; and his colleagues supported his claim that the German had first tried to shoot him. With that the group of adults roared with laughter and I, feeling a little sick, slowly walked away feeling lost in this strange new world of unrestrained hatred. From my now regular night time position cocooned in our staircase shelter I would, in my odd way, become quite emotional at the thought of my German counterpart huddled beneath his staircase, as our bombs came screaming down upon him. Whereas all we both wanted to do was live in peace and play with a lump of plasticine – assuming that it was available in Germany.

But peace was as far away as ever and throughout 1941 the rate and severity of air attacks, involving hundreds of German bombers, eventually drove us back into the street shelter. For me it had some advantages because, by then, I was addicted to *wigging-in* and a public air raid shelter offered a rich harvest of material for my memory files; without which there would have been notable gaps in this book. For example I 'heard' that Courtney and most other streets ran a rota system of fire watchmen who, throughout the night, would patrol designated areas in the event that freshly dropped or delayed action incendiary bombs had started a fire. One night the head street warden could not find a particular fire watcher, so he went to knock him up only to be told by his wife that he was not there. However the said wife had her ideas where he was. Within minutes she was dressed and quickly led the warden to a certain residence occupied by a woman of an adventurous disposition. Immediately she charged into the house and there, on the carpet before the fire, was her husband and the lady of the house who, to say the least, were somewhat shocked and surprised at this sudden confrontation. His stammered excuse that it was a cold night and he had just popped in to warm his hands was, perhaps, not the brightest answer to give under the circumstances. I will leave the outcome to your imagination!

Also there were several accounts of possible war related fatalities. High on the list was the unexplained death of a night warden in his ARP post, a few streets away, where his body lay until discovered the following morning by his son. Then there was an intriguing story from a night watchman who claimed he saw and heard, whilst on his way home after his shift, a number of coins fall from the sky and land on the pavement before him. On inspection he found they were German coins which, so he argued, had been dropped by a benevolent Luftwaffe pilot before he left our skies for home. His claim and the authenticity of the said coins were not accepted by the majority of those he spoke to and his desire to sell his coins, at a handsome profit, ensured that his remarkable experience remained under dispute long after the war ended.

But it was a fact that public air raid shelters did allow people to ignore the constant barrage of explosions outside and lose themselves in banter, argument and even laughter which, sadly, did not last for long.

Life in the street Brickie Air Raid Shelter

In some ways public air raid shelters resembled pre-reformation churches in that victims of oppression, in this case courtesy of Hitler, ran for sanctuary within its walls. Like their middle-age counterparts they felt secure and untouched by unspeakable horrors raging outside and, to some extent, the smell of cordite and explosive flashes loosely approximated to the aroma of incense and the flicker of altar candles. Without doubt security was to be found within a *brickie shelter* and, as a ten year old, even I could feel a deep sense of trust in the reinforced concrete and bricks around me, regardless of a thunderous uproar from mobile guns and falling bombs. At the height of an air raid most shelter talk was of brief delivery and expressed thoughts to the fore of the speakers mind. I can clearly recall a recurring message that, in a séance pitched voice from a gloomy corner of the shelter, advised us that "We are all here waiting to die." Other less dramatic utterances I heard included, "I can't remember if I covered the canary cage" and "It's our Mary's birthday tomorrow," which were courteously ignored by those within hearing range; not that the speaker expected an answer.

Most adults in the shelter were concentrating on sounds of the raid and the response from their men-folk gathered in the shelter entrance. To me as an apprentice to Courtney Street conversational styles I learned much from life in the shelter where, for example, an excited male voice bellowing from without that 'the sky was full of Gerry planes' would, with the same degree of urgency, be matched by a female within asking for the 'lend of a cig, and a match to go with it.' In quiet moments I would muse on what I was listening to, which was so different from the way of Courtney Street life I was born into. Even in my developing years I was increasingly aware that life was changing and that the old days had gone for ever, that is if we managed to survive the increasing dangers of everyday existence. School was something that belonged in the past and much of our time was spent on quick shopping forages before the time came to return to the street shelter. Gone were the sounds of Hurdy-Gurdy players which had been replaced by an overhead rumble of disgruntled barrage balloons, as they incessantly flapped in strong winds induced by a ring of fire that, at the height of repeated air raids, burned night and day. Such scenes caused many to wonder, with justification, if there was anything left in Hull for the Gerry's to set fire to. Happily we could not foresee the future otherwise the thought of enduring this life or death situation, until mid-1943, may have been too much for the strongest in our midst. Even so we had to wait until long after the war was over to discover that Hull was the most bombed city outside of London, an achievement we could well have done without.

When I began this book I could see no purpose in cataloguing all of the air raids I lived through for they followed a style similar to the examples I have given. However in the interests of historical records I would fail badly if I did not stress the ever rising number of civilians killed and property destroyed; combined with a large number of homeless people who found temporary respite in church halls and other centres within villages local to Hull. Also those who remained in the beleaguered Hull of that period continued to snarl their defiance against their attackers, using words I would not care to reproduce. The subject of their hatred was, as one person aptly stated, 'against those hordes from hell above our heads.'

However I would like to share with you a small number of blitz-related events that were highly relevant to me and, in my view, complimentary to the objectives of this book.

A brief overview of Hull in 1940 – 1943

There were repeated air raids often involving hundreds of German bombers that, despite their constant heavy losses, continued their relentless bombardment of Hull which I both witnessed first-hand and gained from *wigged-in* reports, which will remain in my mind forever. The horror always began with incendiary and oil bombs that started hundreds of small fires. But that was just the beginning. The next wave of planes would drop endless numbers of high explosive bombs and land mines into these fires thus spreading an inferno of burning death carried in a man-made gale of unnatural fury. Whole streets were blocked with debris and people were trapped in buildings and had to be rescued by mobile fire escapes, if their operators could fight a way through the inferno. I heard reports that windows would glow red and then become molten yet the firemen fought on and were often met with intense fires on both sides of a street. The angry flames and billowing sparks, eager to find new sources of kindling, met in an infernal embrace to form an arch of fire across a street, which emergency services continued to pass under as just another hazard in their work of mercy.

Countless fires raged, some in the centre of the city were immense and numerous buildings were destroyed including the Prudential Building at the junction of King Edward and Paragon Streets and many of the shops and department stores. Additional problems were that the

Hull Royal Infirmary and Paragon Station were damaged and closed for a while and we were again without gas supplies, this time for six weeks, following severe damage to the Gasworks – and so it went on. Even to give an effective summary of damage caused to lives and property would take many pages although, as one of the deeper ironies of life, I would struggle to fill a quarter of a page with areas in Hull that were untouched by the repeated storms of aerial death that fell upon us.

Time for a quick walk?

It may be beneficial for us to take a short break from the war and explore together a long disappeared part of Holderness Road that, in order to proceed with my later narrative, I must restore for you and superimpose on what is now an area dominated with garages and commercial units.

Let us begin our walk along Courtney Street, say in the mid-1930s, and at its junction with Holderness Road turn right and concentrate on what is the north side of Holderness Road which is also on our right. With a cursory glance at Lipton's, and then Tripe Shop, we proceed over the railway crossing and briefly stop at the end of Beeton Street. I mention this, as an aside, because just along Beeton Street was a former Mission Hall that was being used as a Poor Persons Dispensary, at which my grandmother and many others were regular customers. Then without breaking step we cross over the entrances into Kent Street and Studley Street, and then pause and gaze into an open plan terrace with houses on both sides and a line of houses at the bottom to form a cul-de-sac. When we turn around and look across the road we can see the Ritz cinema which was a popular venue in its day together with the Co-op at the corner of Franklin Street. Adjacent to the shop is East Hull Baths and James Reckitt Library which recovered from war damage and remained in use for many years afterwards.

But let us turn back and look again down the open plan terrace in front of us, known as Ellis's Terrace, which rarely featured in Courtney Street conversations. However in the infants school I was friendly with a lad who lived in Ellis's Terrace but he was evacuated in 1939 and I never saw him again. Like the rest of the area this terrace was densely populated and, at the beginning of the war, a public shelter was built in the space between the rows of houses. As we continue our walk we soon meet up with Bright Street and an imposing Methodist Chapel on its town side corner. It was a substantial square shaped building with its main worship area sandwiched between basement and overhead rooms. What clearly remains in my mind were its ornate metal boundary railings that were soon to be cut down and presumably left to rust – as earlier discussed. Entrance to the Chapel was up a flight of stone steps with the choice of three arched entrance doors. A few yards further along we arrive at Wilton Street and the end of our brief historical tour which, hopefully, has set the stage for our tragic return to this area.

Hot days and nights

Many of the more senior members of Courtney Street declared that they had never met such high temperatures so early in the year; and the radio weather men hinted that it was the hottest May on record. It was on such a night that we sweated in the street shelter as opening salvos of incendiary bombs began to fall and one of the first, by shear chance, bounced along the roof of our shelter until it was retained within an old commercial tyre someone had thrown there. Immediately, the bomb burst into flames and was tackled by several fire watchers armed with stirrup pumps and sand bags. The now hot shelter roof raised the temperature inside even further and, throughout the rest of the war, it had a large scorch mark on its roof. One lady vowed she would never again use it because German pilots would see the burn mark and use it as a target for further bombs.

But German activity on this night in May 1941 was far hotter than the prevailing weather conditions. Although most of us were hardened to relentless bombing raids many of us felt the intensity had increased and, if terror could be measured in definable units, then new records were being set by the hour. The once routine monotone message from a dark corner of the shelter had suddenly changed to, “We’re all going to die" and was made all the more poignant when delivered with her newly acquired hysterical fervour.

"Come on you men I want you all inside the shelter where you'll stand a better chance of staying alive," came the order from a burly police sergeant as he and a PC pushed their way into the entrance. The continual *ping-ping* of shrapnel hitting the shelter roof confirmed his observation that it was coming down like 'bloody hailstones.' In between the whistle of falling bombs and the thunder of explosions he explained that the Reckitt's works in Dansom Lane had been hit and was well ablaze, meaning that the Huns would throw everything they had at that blaze. So far their aim had not been very good. Here the sergeant stopped when overtaken by a violent coughing bout which, he wheezed, was due to all the smoke outside and that his lungs were as tattered as his Long Johns! Following his nod to continue the PC went on to explain that things would no doubt get worse so it was essential that everyone remained inside the shelter and not stand in the entrance. He explained that at least four houses were on fire in our street and that property had been hit in Montrose and Upton Street whereas Mulgrave Street, off Cleveland Street close to Reckitt's factory had been badly damaged by a land mine and many people were dead and missing (it was later reported that 35 people had been killed, 130 injured and more than 800 made homeless). Here he paused and gave preference to the overhead shriek of a fast approaching bomb that, to everyone in the shelter, had the distinct intention of ending our lives without further ado. Immediately I was entombed within a previously described '*mother sandwich*' which did little to muffle an ear splitting explosion, accompanied by a crash of breaking glass, followed by a steady downpour of falling bricks and tiles made airborne by the nearby explosive force. Eventually I emerged breathless from my mother's lap and joined everyone else in a wide range of coughing styles, as we responded to an atmosphere of dust and smoke, made worse by the almost unbearable high temperature in the shelter.

"I think Ada has left us," murmured a voice to my left. Both mum and I looked at what was Ada, who lived at the bottom of the next terrace. She was in a half sitting and half slumped position on the bench seat.

Her eyes and mouth were partly open and she had died with a fixed expression of surprise on her face, which had managed to shine through all the dust and grime that covered her and everyone else in the shelter. Most people knew that Ada had a heart problem and, as soon as there was a lull, a District Nurse was called in from the next shelter. Her death was quickly confirmed, and the next stage of the process would have to wait until the raid was over. With due reverence a space was cleared on the bench and Ada's body, covered with her coat, was laid out and her friend's knee became a pillow for her head. Not to be upstaged the voice from corner shadows intoned, "Ada was first and we'll be next with *sluffed* hearts."

Perhaps I was tired or just overcome with all that was happening around me because I must have slipped into a half sleep, despite the noise of guns and bombs that filled my world outside. There was not a lot of room left on our bench and I was aware that Ada's feet were pressing on my leg. Dead bodies did not worry me because, as I mentioned earlier, I was accustomed to seeing them lying in state, in Courtney houses, when I called on my mates. But the sudden death of Ada did cause me to ponder what life was really all about, and I got myself into mental confusion when I envisaged that if I had been born as the daughter my parents had hoped for, then I would not have been me; hence I would not have been in this shelter waiting for my turn to die on the bench seat.

I returned to reality when mother nudged me and asked if I had heard what she said? My blank expression answered the question for her. "The warden has been in to tell us that the last bomb just missed us and blew-up two houses in Crystal Terrace, and some people have been killed" (this was four terraces from ours and opposite the sawmill).

I think the raid began at 9pm and involved repeated waves of German bombers but, all of a sudden, a noticeable lull set in around 1am. This led us to anticipate the *all clear* at any moment. Some of the men had slipped out and came back to confirm that rescue services were still working in Crystal Terrace and two bodies had been recovered. The ferocity of the explosion had, so they reported, blown the body of a third victim onto the roof of a house in the next terrace; and efforts were being made to recover it.

Then without warning the thunder of anti-aircraft guns began all over again. The familiar drone of German bombers once more became the background sound for bombs although, on this occasion, increased machine gun fire suggested that the RAF were staging their own blitz with German planes as their target (it was later claimed that over fifty enemy planes had been shot down and several more where so badly damaged that they would not make it back). "Will somebody tell those bloody Gerry's to clear off home cos their mothers is looking for 'em," was a verbal cheer-up that most of us needed and, as if they had taken heed, anti-aircraft guns ceased and machine gun fire faded into the distance as our fighters chased after them.

Holding his hand towards me dad came over from the entrance and said that I should come outside and see a sight I must never forget. Mother quickly approved and, as I later learned, she was not happy that I'd been forced to spend the last two hours squashed between her and a dead woman's feet. There were a lot of men outside so, to help me see better, dad lifted me up to witness a spectacle that is still before my eyes. Fire surrounded us. Flames and sparks danced out of two neighbouring terraces and far beyond our street the view merged into a matrix of pulsating fire and smoke. In wide eyed horror I felt that we were encircled, and hence imprisoned, by an unyielding wall of burning hatred straight from hell. In later reports I was not surprised to learn that those who lived in nearby villages, with a higher ground advantage, had concluded that every building and factory in Hull was on fire. Perhaps they were closer to the truth than they imagined. All eyes were held by the almost hypnotic sight before us until the spell was broken, by the hoarse voice of the police sergeant, bellowing at us to get back into the shelter – quickly!

We must have not moved fast enough and he urged us to 'look above our heads if we didn't believe him.' And there, some three or four hundred feet above Courtney Street, was a slowly descending parachute from which dangled a large glistening metal cylinder that, as if by a warning, reflected at us flashes of light originating from surrounding background fires. Several voices in unison confirmed the obvious as they gasped out, "Bloody hell it's a land mine coming straight at us!" It was Luftwaffe policy to drop land mines, just before they left, knowing that their slow descent would enable the bombers to clear the area long before they exploded. As I mentioned earlier this enemy ploy often took its toll on emergency services that, believing the raid was over, would be active in recovering the injured. But there was no doubt this diabolical weapon of death was relentlessly drifting down on to our street and there was nothing we could do to stop it – or so we thought. As if by divine intervention a sudden very strong updraft of hot air and sparks, caused by the collapse of a burning house roof in a nearby terrace, briefly lifted the parachute and its deadly load upwards and away from Courtney Street, only for it to resume its slow descent a little further along Holderness Road.

With that the spell was broken and we quickly disappeared into the shelter, closely followed by the police sergeant, and from an untidy heap on the floor we heard and felt the gigantic explosion as yet another land mine had achieved its purpose. The closeness and ferocity of the impact was evident in the amount of debris that was still falling some minutes after the blast, and one particular metallic clatter landing on the shelter roof turned out to be part of a washing mangle from someone's backyard.

Reckitt's ablaze

"Come on and we'll have a quick look at Reckitts from the street end," was not a regular invitation given to me at three o'clock in the morning. More so when it was from my own father who was faced with setting off for Tan Yard in two hours' time – assuming it was still standing. The *all clear* had barely faded away as a group of us picked our way through roof slates, glass and every kind of debris that events of the night had thrown our way until we were standing in Dansom Lane, at the railway crossing, with our eyes fixed upon the overwhelming spectacle before us. The centre of the blaze was the main office building, some four or five storeys high, which stood between the Francis Reckitt Institute and Starch House Lane. To report that it was well alight would be a serious understatement. Flames roared through the entire shell of the large building and reached heights I could not see. The fire was in total command of the situation and, at its pleasure, tore through former door and window spaces or leapt, with random joy, through what had once been the roof of the building. Company commerce in the form of thousands of burning paper documents pirouetted high into the sky, only to fall as crumbling flakes of black snow over most of East Hull. Fire engines were nearby but, as I later discovered, were helpless due to the destruction of water mains and static water tanks. One hose was reported to be at work drawing water from nearby Sutton Drain.

Another new feature for me to digest was the noise made by a fire of such proportions. The chemistry of combustion generated a chimney effect of less dense burning gasses, which rose with great energy, only for cooler ground level air to be drawn in to both fuel and continue the cycle. This rotational effect produced the sound and sensation of a gale force wind which, over one hundred yards away, felt as if I would be blown off my feet and drawn into the inferno that was once a landmark office block. Suddenly our attention was drawn to a group of firemen who were fast running towards us and, as they turned quickly into Chapman Street, one of them bellowed in a loud voice, "Get the hell out of it!" The reason for their alarm was soon evident when, even from our distance, we could see that one of the high main walls was swaying and in imminent danger of collapse. The fact that none of us had ever seen anything as awesome as this before held us spellbound and, despite the warning given, dad, as he later admitted, decided to watch for just a few more seconds.

Soon the crippled wall ceded to the inevitable and, seemingly in slow motion, collapsed inwards into the core of the conflagration. The noise from this massive weight of falling masonry was deafening and, for a few moments, it appeared to have extinguished the fire. But this was not the case. The internal pressure of the entombed hellhole could not, for the moment, travel upwards so it burst through any ground level gaps it could find and, with a *whoosh* to be remembered, thundered along Dansom Lane with all the malevolent intent of a dragon's breath.

Instantly dad realised why we had been advised to leave and swept me off my feet and began to run. Not caring to remain in the open we crouched in the cycle shop doorway, facing Tin Mission, as a brief blast of sparks and hot air roared past us. Fortunately for us this pressure surge quickly subsided when the main core of fire broke through fallen masonry and regained its preferred upward motion. Initially I thought the road was on fire until I realised it was smoke from overheated tar holding the road blocks in place; such was the high temperature it had been subjected to. Forgetting the danger around us I then became fascinated at the sight of a wooden signal box that controlled the level crossing, which had been in the path of the hot blast, and had been left scorched and smouldering. I was about to ask dad if it would catch fire when, without ceremony, he yanked me to my feet and we, and other spectators, ran quickly to the safety of our homes.

The morning after

I do not imagine I was alone in my recognition of the intrusive way that air raids could destabilise our balance of reality. Few of us are strangers to unreal and sometimes disturbing dreams that vaporise when we take our place in the dawn of a new day. Yet as the dreadful war progressed this line of demarcation, between fanciful and factual mind-sets, was less defined and often I would wake up and yearn to return to vague dreams, rather than face reality in the form of yet another day of survival-style living and destruction from the skies.

Such thoughts were in my mind as, according to plan, we carefully picked our way along Courtney Street that was awash with mementos from last night's explosions. Two houses in Crystal Terrace had been totally destroyed and several others were without roofs and windows. As ever there was an abundance of glass, wood and general debris covering most parts of the street and, intertwined in this rubble, were small household items that looked so pathetic and out of place in their new surroundings. It would not be too long before my curiosity would cause me to pause, crouch down, and examine personal items that had been violently wrenched from a once loving owner. For example a family wedding photograph stirred in the breeze as if striving to return to its sideboard home, and a child's teddy bear lay forlorn with wide open arms yearning for the warmth of its lost cot mate.

As ever parental prompting would lift me from my rubble of memories, and we continued to carefully pick our way to the end of Courtney Street. When achieved we were met with a sight which brought us to an immediate halt, and condemned us to a period of wordless shock. Whichever way we looked the once busy road was now devoid of traffic and played host to small craters, piles of debris and telegraph posts that had been blown into the road or through shop windows.

In due course we decided to turn to our right and quickly saw that the level crossing gates had parted with their broken hinges and lay face down on the road, as if still hiding from last night's horrors, whilst a stray dog scampered away with something snatched from a windowless shop. Aghast, we briefly stopped and stared at a number of smouldering houses down Beeton Street and, a few steps later, we found that Kent Street properties were little better since many were without roof tiles and chimney stacks.

Here we paused, turned and the view across the road caused us to catch our breath; for our once cherished Ritz Cinema had been reduced to a few standing remains. Of its once ornate frontage there was no sign and, in its place, was a wide bomb crater that extended into the centre of Holderness Road. There was a large amount of water in it, probably from burst water mains, but an unexpected sight were several seagulls drifting on its surface, thoroughly at ease, and seemingly enjoying their spring morning swim.

We looked away only to find that many houses in Studley Street had been razed to the ground and, a little further on, we carefully picked our way through increasing piles of rubble until we stood at the entrance to what was Ellis's Terrace. A number of men were still digging through masses of rubble surrounding a large crater that marked the site of the terrace air raid shelter, and a number of ambulances were parked wherever they could find a spot amidst wreckage that was once Bright Street. A solitary flag, flapping in the morning breeze, reminded all onlookers that people were still buried beneath that morass of destruction which, according to later reports, had taken the lives of forty men, women and children with a similar number hospitalised with severe injuries. Perhaps the culprit was last night's mine that had been diverted from above Courtney Street but, to this day, I care not to think too deeply about that floating lottery of death.

Together with other people we stood in silent vigil aghast that an entire terrace, and surrounding streets, had been wiped out by this dreadful weapon of destruction. For many years afterwards there was an account that a woman had survived the blast because, in a lull, she had left the shelter and returned home for milk for her baby. When the mine exploded she was buried in the house and, although badly injured, she was rescued and fully recovered in body, but not in mind. The reason being that her husband and baby were killed in that fateful shelter which was literally blown into fragments.

No one had noticed that alongside us, on the badly damaged frontage of Bright Street Methodist Church, a small group of Salvation Army musicians had silently gathered and, in subdued tones, began playing the hymn 'Nearer my God to Thee...' With heads bowed those who knew the words silently whispered them whilst small groups of people, totally overwhelmed by the grief around them, simply held the nearest hand as tears rolled and fell in tribute to those so cruelly snatched from this life. There is nothing more I can say other than suggest that we now leave Ellis's Terrace, and it's tragic memories, to those special pages of history upon which the tears of memory will never dry.

As the raids and carnage continued there were frequent communal funerals for human remains that could not be formally identified and, for reasons I never knew, I attended one with my mum and dad. I can remember seeing military personnel stop their work, line up at the pavement edge, and salute as the funeral procession went by. The presence and help given by our soldiers was greatly appreciated. They were involved in demolishing dangerous buildings, recovering the living and dead from bombed buildings, directing traffic and even driving public transport vehicles. Another branch of the military were Italian prisoners of war who, to be fair, never wanted to fight and were glad to be out for the duration. They could be recognised by a large yellow circle on the back of their tunic and they willingly helped clear bomb sites, sweep the streets and do general labouring work. Elsewhere they gave valuable service to the farming community.

And then we received a letter

Despite all that had happened I did have a brief moment of hope. This happened a few days after the severe raid involving the destruction of Ellis's Terrace, when mother called me in and said she had received a note from school. With eyes agog I elatedly asked if school was opening again and jumped up and down in anticipation of a positive answer. Mum sadly shook her head, and my joy faded as she said, "There's to be a funeral of one of your school friends who died in an air raid and the teachers would like as many children as possible to line the pavement, outside Courtney Senior School, to pay their respects as the funeral passes by." I felt the colour drain from my face as I slowly asked who it was who had died. "Do you remember a few nights ago when two houses in Crystal Terrace were bombed?" I nodded impatiently yet, deep within, I wanted the interview to stop – and then disappear as if it was a random memory of no consequence. Mother could see that I was in a state of shock, but she continued in a voice that carried with it a level of compassion so obvious in her face.

"When that bomb exploded three were killed and one of them was a child from your class, in fact you both began school at around the same time. Her name was Annie – do you know who I mean?" Immediately I turned and ran into the yard and, with clenched fists, stood motionless staring at the closed back door. I felt myself wondering how much more savagery, pain and grief this dreadful war would throw at me; whilst mentally screaming at Hitler that not being happy with stealing my childhood he had now killed my friend. I remember blurting out words that meant, "Is life all about waiting for the next bomb to land and end it all?" Suddenly my turmoil was stilled when mother's hand gently gripped my shoulder and I felt the tension slowly leave me. She said not a word nor did she need to. The warmth of her hand upon me was, as ever, enough for my needs.

Annie's Funeral

Through the years I collected various war time statistics from which I learned that air raids on Hull killed about 1200 people of which, despite evacuation, 240 of these were children. Hence it was inevitable that some of my school friends would die and, as I later found, this day would be the first of several such tragic events.

There were not many of the original junior classes left because quite a number had moved away in the second drive to evacuate children when the raids began. Also many had been bombed-out and were living in church halls, outside Hull, waiting to be rehoused. However there were enough of us left to form two rows at the pavement edge and, as usual, I managed to get prime position on the front row. Behind us were some of our teachers who, like us, were frustrated that schools were still unable to open in the face of repeated raids both day and night. On the opposite side of the road, standing just in the roadway, were a line of men including our two air-raid wardens, the area policeman and a number of soldiers who were helping to clear bomb sites. Behind them on the pavement, and stretching along Courtney Street were many neighbours, friends and others who were strangers to the street, but not to the bond of grief, which they had come to share.

"All stand up straight," was a sudden command from behind us as the funeral procession, which had briefly paused at Crystal Terrace, continued its slow progress towards the school. In front of the cortege was the Chief Undertaker walking in a measured step derived from years of experience. He looked every inch an imposing figure in his black top hat and tails, and his major-domo role was complimented by the symbolic swing of his ceremonial walking cane as his motorcade of sorrow slowly advanced towards us. Strangely I felt excited because, for me, this was a new school experience and, without thinking, I looked around wondering if Annie was standing with us – because she also enjoyed something different – and her, "I love new adventures," could have been her motto; as stupidity could have been mine when I suddenly remembered why I was standing there. As the hearse drew closer there was a sudden verbal command, and the line of men snapped to attention and saluted the funeral party. This was the signal for the Chief Undertaker to raise his cane and the entire cortege came to a halt and, as chance would have it, the hearse bearing Annie's coffin stopped a few feet in front of me.

"Hello Annie," I silently whispered to that small polished box within its glass cage. Her reply was a flow of happy memories including the time her wave of support gave me strength to hum the *Caliph of Baghdad* at an early primary class concert. Then there was the sight of her enjoyment when she ravenously ate one of my jam sandwiches, which I had willingly given to her, and never once did I regret doing it. With my eyes fixed upon the coffin before me past joys came and went until I became aware of tears running down my face. Like most young boys I was no stranger to tears which invariably were born from frustration, rage or simply not being able to get my own way. That type of tear simply served to lubricate and thus increase the flow of anger and potential violence towards whatever had thwarted me.

But the tears now flowing were so very different. They warmed, soothed and encouraged an inner peace like I had never known before. In fact they caused me to smile and whisper "Thank you Annie," as the cane of office was raised and the cortege moved slowly towards Holderness Road. As Annie slipped into history I suddenly felt that I had grown up; because I now knew how to weep, smile and give thanks all at the same time.

Our war time flit to Upton Street

My brother Jim was in love and that was an indisputable fact. If adults were to reason with him on this matter they would be dismissed as unheard or, in my situation as his younger brother, with whom he held nothing in common, threats of violence were options I could not afford to ignore. Nevertheless his behaviour both intrigued me and led me to believe that I was faced with my first lesson, as a spectator, into the antics of adolescents in love.

There were times when his inner turmoil of passions caused me to believe that Jim had become a *someone else*, whose wide range of mood changes both baffled and alarmed me. There can be no denying that he played with his food as he gazed, with an almost imbecilic look on his face, at a distant object that, as far as I knew, may well have been a golden frame set around the image of his loved one. My mother was witness to the fact that he once set off for work without anything on his feet and, despite his denials, there were witnesses to lovelorn Jim walking into a lamp post after bidding a tender farewell to his intended. He defended the reason for this collision, and his ensuing cut forehead, on the black-out and that he had forgotten his torch. Sadly all this came to nought when it was revealed that the incident happened in the mid-afternoon of a sunny June day!

Following this introduction it will not come as a surprise that Jim continually nattered at his mother to rent another house with a separate front parlour off an entry passage, which would afford privacy to him and his Doris, away from my prying eyes and irritating presence. With that he looked over at me and, by way of return, I conjured up what I thought to be a truly angelic picture of facial innocence. Mother glanced my way and told me to stop pulling faces at my brother or go out and play in the street! Realising that I must not lose the opportunity to *wig-in* and harvest to the full all this conversation offered, I picked up an old edition of the Dandy comic, currently suspended because of the air attacks, and in a pretend *huff* retired to the kitchen taking care not to fully close the door – through which I became privy to all that was going to happen.

Jim's argument was that, in the next draft, his turn to join the armed forces would almost certainly come and (using modern terms) he wanted quality time with his future wife. Thus a house with a private front room, rather than our present sham-four which was designed for communal living throughout, would answer his problems. Mother's dilemma was that she loved 13, Leonards Avenue and would have been happy to spend her remaining years in that house. Her often stated view was that it had a 'happy feel to it' and, for reasons she could not explain, she felt ill luck would follow her family if we moved elsewhere.

Faced with this impasse I, soon after, *overheard* mum and dad talking about it, and they decided they would move house both for Jim's sake and their own. They knew he would soon be conscripted into the army and, if anything was to happen to him, then they would never forgive themselves for not letting him and Doris have a room, where they could close the door, and be together until the war effort pulled them apart. I listened intently and found that mother had found such a house, through her present landlord, and it was in Upton Street which was separated from Courtney Street by Tin Mission, a Dental Mechanic Laboratory, two houses, the Sunkist Fruit Store, a Fish and Chip shop, a further two houses and Ethel's grocery shop which was on the corner of Upton Street. Already I had decided to spend my free time in Courtney Street because I knew no one in Upton Street and, to be fair, I preferred the street of my birth above all others. Of course my dearest wish was that I would soon return to Courtney Street School but, with almost daily air raid alerts, I did not see that happening in the near future.

Meet Mr Barnes the Courtney piano mover

When the day came to flit most of the items were carried by hand, with help from some of our neighbours, and larger items were transported on a cart that Jim borrowed from Reckitts. But our piano, which was a specialized item, relied upon expert hands to oversee its transfer. Fortunately there lived in Courtney Street such a person who was a veritable master of the art of piano moving. Undeniably an upright piano was considered to be the focal point of many households fortunate enough to own one and, when it came to flitting, its transfer was never, within my memory, ever begun without the presence of the street expert namely Mr Barnes.

On this one occasion I have used the real name of a street character, lest a non-de-plume should obscure the memory of such a man. Without doubt he was a true craftsman when it came to moving pianos and he may even have been in that trade before he retired. He loved the kudos that, to him, went with the job and he would arrive at the house pretty much like a surgeon, of proven renown, walking into the operating theatre. Indeed he had presence, born from his ability to inspire confidence. His tools were a low level trolley upon which, with due care, the piano would be placed. Then there was the matter of a wooden ramp which fitted between the raised doorstep and house front. His third, and no less important aide, was a simple tape measure that was at the hub of his entire operation.

Silence fell as he stood, with his hand on his chin, and assessed the task before him. A twitch of his bushy moustache was the signal that he was ready, and his first move was to crouch down with his trolley ready to slide underneath the piano. When he was satisfied with all he saw he gave one nod of his head as the signal for his two helpers to slowly lift the end of the piano closest to him, allowing Mr Barnes to slide the trolley into the exact position he wanted. When this preliminary manoeuvre was completed the removal stage began. Mr Barnes stood just outside the front door as two men, at either end of the piano, slowly moved the instrument into the doorway. A third person had been instructed to hold the door back to avoid its interference with the process.

"Stop," bellowed Mr Barnes as he moved forward and, with his tape measure, noted the distance that existed between the piano and the doorframe. "We have just two inches on either side so take it slowly," he ordered as the piano began to gently pass through the door frame. With eyes as intent as those of a lion about to leap on its prey, and every muscle tensed accordingly, Mr Barnes watched the progress until another "Stop" was immediately obeyed. Following repeated measurements he gravely advised, "We have no more than a quarter of an inch on your right side so slowly does it...edge to the left...no....back a bit ...no ....stop ...forward very... very slowly ...steady now .....mind your fingers in the gap ... now once again....steady....steady...watch your foot.....good lads ... you're through the door!" With a smile of satisfaction at a job well done he turned, in the manner of a latter day Moses, as he led his piano moving team towards Upton Street which, according to my brother Jim, was our promised land.

What can we do to remember this great man of undoubted piano moving ability? The Courtney Street of 2012 is totally devoid of houses and pianos yet, to me, it is very much alive with memories. Thus I have this vision of a simple plaque, set in a central place, accordingly inscribed and dedicated to, "Mr Barnes, Piano Mover Extraordinaire, who was ever in tune with our needs."

Life as an exile in Upton Street

Whatever Jim claimed to the contrary there was no denying that the floor and yard area of 4, Upton Street was the same as that of Courtney houses which meant, in terms of living space, that the front room was smaller having sacrificed space to accommodate a narrow corridor leading from the front door into the back kitchen. The piano, couch and a plant stand almost filled the front room whereas the back kitchen had to double-up as a living room and dining area courtesy of a Yorkist range.

Leading from the back kitchen was a small brick addition, designed for single occupation only and contained the pantry, sink and a brick copper. This extension, in competition with the toilet and coal house, effectively reduced available yard space that caused chaos on wash days and frustration when searching for storage space. For my part it was of no consequence because I spent my social time back in Courtney Street, either visiting my grandmother who knew of my liking for bread and jam, or playing with my mates; whilst having to live down such jocular jibes as, "You don't live down this street Caney!"

But all these matters were surface issues that made no impact on the almost daily pattern of air raids upon Hull. Flames from houses, factories, shops and public buildings continued to light up the night sky. Aeroplanes, guns and bombs remained locked in a deadly duel of explosive hatred from which the public death toll grew by the day. There were no brick and concrete shelters down Upton Street although extended Anderson style shelters had been erected, in long side gardens, at the entrance to each terrace. Not knowing many people we chose to keep our own company and remain indoors when the buzzers sounded which, by now, was no new experience for us. We returned to the traditional sanctuary found beneath the staircase which, in this house, included a small meter cupboard. Immediately this became my personal shelter and, much to my relief, I was finally liberated from the dreaded grip of a *mother sandwich* when air-raids became really rough.

Looting from bombed properties

Without doubt looting was the most detestable crime that could be committed against already distraught victims of conflict from the skies. Emergency legislation meant that the death penalty could be imposed on any adult convicted of stealing from bombed properties. Looters could, in fact, have been shot on sight, although I've never found any records of this happening, or indeed of the death penalty being imposed for this crime. Sentences of five years imprisonment were the norm and, in those days, it must be remembered that five years in prison meant just that; and prison conditions were considerably harsher than those of today.

This loathsome crime against humanity was, from reports I have read, widespread in most major cities with London heading the list. Sometimes it was random theft of belongings found lying outside bombed property or, according to reports, there were organised gangs stealing to order. There appeared to be no limit to what was taken. At the lower end gas and electricity meters in bomb damaged houses were relieved of their coins and, at the pinnacle of human wickedness, there were those nefarious creatures of the night who would surge into freshly bombed nightclubs, regardless of the sound of approaching emergency vehicles, and hastily kick aside the rubble in order to rip jewellery from dead and dying victims. Invariably they escaped but not always. In fact there were complaints in the press, from anonymous criminals, who claimed the police took matters into their own hands and dispensed beatings on any caught red handed. I am not aware these complaints were ever acted upon.

However I was aware that looting did occur in the area where I lived because of an incident I witnessed when walking from Upton to Courtney Street. As I approached Tin Mission a noisy group of people turned out of Courtney Street and headed towards the ARP post alongside the mission. They were mainly women closely following in the wake of our ARP warden who held, by the scruff of his neck, a filthy and dishevelled youth with blood running from cuts to his forehead and face.

Most of the women were waving sticks and screaming abuse at the arrested youth as two assistant wardens, none too gently, kept them at bay. "The police and Black Maria are on the way so let them deal with him, we'll have no lamp post hangings in Courtney Street, "one of them said. During his frog-march the youth protested, between snorts and sniffles, that it was not his fault because his father had made him pinch stuff from bombed houses. This was fuel to the fire of retribution that burned within those ladies. If left to their intent they would happily have lynched father and son then celebrated the event over a communal jug of beer. But this was not to be and, as they waited for the police to arrive, they unloaded their emotions on a gathering crowd – which I happily mingled with in my quest to *wig-in*.

During the previous night's raid a large number of bombs fell nearby and four exploded, in line formation, from the end of Upton Street, with two in the wood yard, and the fourth in front of a house at the top end of Courtney Street. All its windows and doors were blown-in and the elderly occupant had been taken to hospital. Consequently neighbours were guarding the property and, during the morning, it was not too long before they realised that someone was rummaging about inside the house. Having previously armed themselves for this duty they rushed in and gave him a good *braying* (their words) with their sticks. Howling with fear he had taken refuge in the coal house, and was furiously holding his attackers at bay by throwing lumps of coal at them.

It was at this stage that the passing ARP warden, alerted by the uproar, intervened and stopped the conflict. He then placed the youth under arrest and frog-marched him to the ARP post, followed by his accusers. Quickly the police arrived, the crowd dispersed, and the accused was taken away for questioning. I later *overheard* that police raided his house and found large amounts of stolen property, which father and son had collected from the beginning of the raids. For these criminal deeds the father was sentenced to six years in prison and his son four years. The lady of the house, who believed they had started a legal second hand business, was given a caution but not charged. Conversely street opinion thought differently meaning that she was ostracised to the extent that she soon left the area.

Some memories of my visits to Courtney Street

"Hello love, we don't half miss you all; number thirteen seems like a different house," exclaimed a lady standing at the street end of Leonards Avenue, "Have you settled down in Upton Street?" I frowned and shook my head which, no doubt, would be taken to mean my entire family were unsettled; whereas I was merely expressing *my* feelings towards her question. I got on well with this particular ex neighbour because of her interest in my piano playing which, on one memorable day, led to me playing the '*Blue Danube waltz*' on her piano because, to her express regret, 'no one ever played it these days.' Her applause had sounded genuine as was the shilling piece (five pence) she slipped into my hand after the recital. She lived at number one which, in the view of many, fitted her status because her husband worked in the City Council office.

Although we were half way through 1942 I still spent most of my time in Courtney Street, more so when we were able to return to school for two or three days a week. Using a modern expression I never did *bond* with my peers in Upton Street because I seized every opportunity to return to my place of birth. With the hindsight of age I can now see that Courtney Street had, and in a strange way still does, an attraction for me that is hard to resist as they, in turn, were drawn to me. I say this because as soon as I appeared in the street I was immediately drawn into whatever was topical at that moment and, after a few minutes it felt that I had never left Leonards Avenue; especially when the time came for me to go home when I would automatically turn into our old back passage! Also it was a regular feature for Courtney Street adults to ask how we Upton Street exiles were and, as we parted company, most of them would quietly add, 'See you tomorrow luv, Lord willing,' which was another sign of changing attitudes in times of uncertainty. The verbal bounce had gone out of all adult conversations I now *wigged into*. For example pre-war street exchanges invariably ended with joyously expressive terms such as, "Tar- rah and see yer tomorrow luv, and don't you do owt I wouldn't do!"

I will not try to disguise the fact that the cold blast of war had blown those happy memories away only to admit the dark spectre of reality which haunted us daily. It tormented us in many forms not least of which were food shortages, air raids and the ever present stench of burning buildings that seemed to mock its victims as they wept over heaps of rubble that were once their homes. It goes without saying that all who lived through the last war will be fortunate if they emerged unscathed, by a previously unthinkable level of toxic hatred, that was liberally spread by air, sea and land by attackers and defenders alike. For me, even after all these decades, its memory is still alive in occasional flashbacks to the sound of air raid sirens or being a witness to scenes of intense grief. There was one such example that I will share with you although it has similarities to one I have already mentioned. I have included it because it remains with me as a heart touching incident wherein the motherly care of a terrace lady helped restore the sanity of a grief stricken woman.

On one of my visits I arrived at the end of Blanche Grove as a newly widowed wife began pacing up and down the terrace oblivious to neighbours watching from their doorsteps. In her hand was a crumpled

War Office Telegram confirming that her husband had been killed, but she, in a panic-stricken voice, was repeatedly shouting that her husband was not dead and that he would be home soon. Her mental state was fast collapsing until a motherly figure appeared, as indeed every terrace had one, and quickly gathered the grieving wife into her arms as an experienced mother would comfort her heartbroken daughter. Immediately the floodgates of tears opened and the young woman was inconsolable yet appreciated the arms of compassion that held her and the shoulder she wept on. After a while she calmed down and her comforter whispered to her, "Come home with me luv, the kettles singing and a cup of tea is on the way." A terrace of tears stared after them in silence as the house door slowly closed yet, for me, that memory will ever live on.

How different it all was to pre-war times when the street was confident that we had a future awaiting us, so we should just live for the day and patiently await the birth of better times. But the Grim Reaper had swept away that simple hope forever. Every time the air-raid alert sounded we, of all ages, were aware that this air raid may well be the last one as far as we were concerned. There was the time when I thought that death came along strictly in age order, but not anymore. That once traditional childhood thought had, without mercy, been snatched out of my developing mind when several of my peers, including Annie, had died beneath Hitler's bombs. As I look back upon those days in Courtney Street, I can clearly see that, at my then age of eleven years, I had accepted imminent death as inevitable and was learning to live accordingly.

The night we were bombed out

Nevertheless we did survive the many air-raids of 1941 and now in the autumn of 1942, despite continuing air attacks, we were still here. As a bonus I even managed to attend school although it was in any one-from-four establishments not too far from Upton Street.

It was becoming noticeable that the Luftwaffe was not as accurate as in their original attacks, mainly because they had lost many experienced pilots in their invasion of Russia in June 1941. Nevertheless the conflict was intensified in December 1941 when Hitler decided to declare war on America following Japan's attack upon Pearl Harbour. This act left the contestants clearly identified as Germany, Italy and Japan taking on the entire world, in a war that would end only when one side was brought to their knees and millions of lives had been lost.

Air attacks on the UK had diminished principally because Germany had other demands on their resources, but their bombers continued to batter away at Hull because convoys of supplies to Russia sailed from our docks. At this stage of the war the German nation's confidence, generated by earlier successes, began to wane due to an increasing shortage of food and the growing ferocity of assaults by British and American bombers on their cities and industrial areas. Furthermore, as the Russian forces were initially driven back by the weight of the German onslaught, they consistently used what became known as a 'scorched earth policy' meaning that all sources of food were destroyed and the Germans had to advance over what was a desolate and smoking ruin. This meant that essential supplies depended entirely on lengthening lines of communication, impeded by air attacks and the severe Russian winter. As time went by their plight eventually became untenable, but many more would have to die long before this nightmare ended for both sides.

Whether we were becoming hardened or indifferent to war, assuming that such a way of life was really possible, it is hard to say. Nonetheless more and more we remained in bed and ignored the war above us which, to be fair, most other people, in many other streets, did exactly the same. The well-used saying, "If the bomb has got your name on it then it will find you either in bed or the shelter,' had almost become the eleventh Commandment in lives that had learned to accept violent death as inescapable.

However there had to be exceptions and one was a night in late October 1942 when, as later reported, around eighty German aircraft were unloading their bombs on everything other than the docks they were supposedly aiming for. From a continuous rattle of machine gun fire it was obvious that our now increased numbers of fighter planes were giving them a hard time, and many German pilots played the philosophy of dropping their bombs anywhere over the city or even outside it, then speeding away before they were shot out of the sky.

As yet another bomb screamed down and exploded close by father decreed that the time had arrived for us to get under the stairs. In no time I was tucked-up in a blanket in the meter cupboard, and the rest of my family were, following a well-rehearsed tradition, huddled on the floor waiting for the night to end. From my position in the meter cupboard I had a clear view down the entrance passage, and became alarmed at the large number of vivid bomb and gun flashes I could see through two vertical strips of glass in the front door. It just felt as if I was repeatedly opening and shutting my eyes when facing a strong multi-coloured light source which was there to alarm rather than entertain. Also from my position I had a clear view down Clovelly Avenue at the bottom of which was a wood yard, stacked high with timber, and I could see at least one pile was already alight. Beyond this was a commercial garage with several large vehicles parked in its compound. I have mentioned this stage-set because of the important part it was about to play in, perhaps, saving many lives including ours. I glanced at my mother who was visibly more afraid than I had seen her in many an raid and, with her eyes closed, she was murmuring over and over again, "Please God – please God."

Suddenly our minds were on full alert when two near explosions blew our front door wide open with such vigour that it slammed violently against the passage wall, and shattered its glass panels in the process. I will add that father always left the front door unlocked, during a raid, for easy access to rescuers should we become trapped. Jim, being the nearest, ran to close it but first peered into the street to see what was happening. Now I must stress that my brother was noted for his calm approach to life and his aversion to urgency, in its many forms, irritated me beyond words. But he had never before faced what he saw through that open door on that fateful night. In a voice I hardly recognised he gasped out that a land mine was just touching down in the wood yard. Dad immediately shouted at him to get back under the stairs but, instead, he closed and tried to bolt the door, as if to keep the land mine out of the house!

What happened next would be measured in micro-seconds but, to me, there was a detectable portion of time between each incident. Initially, I did not hear an explosion, confirming the many claims that if you are very close to a bomb then you never hear it detonate. My first real sensation was that of an enormous build-up in pressure that, seemingly, threatened to crush my ear drums. Then I was aware of a deep purple light filling the room with its unearthly glow followed by a harsh splintering crash as every window in the house, and indeed the street, were blown simultaneously to smithereens. The front door, with Jim safely underneath it, was blown down the passage followed by house tiles and debris that flew around in abundance. The floor beneath me gave way and I found myself looking up at the electricity meter from a large hole. Fortunately I was wrapped in a blanket that had cushioned me against cuts and bruises – but soot was everywhere and, for days afterwards, whatever I ate seemed to be flavoured with residual soot that had lined my intake system. It felt as if the exploding mine had generated a hurricane force wind that roared down the street and through houses now devoid of windows, doors and roofs. As mother was helping me out from beneath the floor she suddenly threw herself over me as, with a mighty crash, ceiling plaster, laths and bricks crashed down about us.

It was quickly decided that we could no longer remain in a house that had been weakened to the extent that, at any moment, it may collapse upon us. So a quick dash across the road to the Clovelly Avenue air raid shelter became our sole objective. As I indicated earlier it was fortunate for all of us that the mine exploded in a commercial lorry compound which was hemmed in by a railway embankment on one side, and a wood yard piled high with timber stacks on the other. Lorries and lumber heaps absorbed much of the blast that otherwise would have created total carnage within our densely populated area. In its rage the exploding mine had showered Upton Street, and surrounding zones, with fragments of road vehicles and large sections of timber – much of which was on fire.

"Come on mother," yelled Jim as, holding her hand, he carefully led her across Upton Street, taking care to avoid all types of debris littering the street, some of which was glowing red hot. Despite falling shrapnel it had to be taken slowly and, in order to see clearly, they paused to await sudden bursts of light from guns, bombs and surrounding fires. Dad and I held our breath as they made slow progress until they reached the safety of the terrace shelter. Whilst we were waiting I looked in horror at great clouds of black smoke, surrounding a large deep red core of burning oil, which billowed up from the lorry yard and, as if in competition, many fires raging in the wood yard in turn spread to the roofs of houses at the bottom of adjoining terraces. The howling inferno-induced gale, reminiscent of the time Reckitts was on fire, further tormented us by scooping thick black smoke from above and hurling it back into the eyes and lungs of many that huddled in that already beleaguered street. Blasts of hatred from passing anti-aircraft gun carriers, and the continuous rattle of machine gun fire from above, confirmed that death was still very active both overhead and around us.

My inner panic increased as a cluster of incendiary bombs bounced along part of the street and, as a show of their malevolent anger, began whizzing around whilst discharging phosphorus flame at anything within range. Dad gripped my arm when he realised that my nerve had completely failed me. I was literally paralysed with fear and there was no way I could move off that doorstep because to do so was, in my then mind, a sure way to die in the numerous hazards between us and the shelter. There can be few people who, when looking back at their lives, cannot identify moments that will stay with them forever; and such an instant was born for me at the height of that blitz. I was shaking badly and dad knelt alongside me and looked me full in the face. For the first time I noticed that he was bleeding from a cut on the bridge of his nose which added to my rising fear. Looking very serious he said that he wanted to share a secret with me before it was too late to do so. Coming out of the smoke as it did I listened attentively as he told me that he too was scared, in fact he was 'bloody terrified' at the thought of crossing that road, and he was trusting in me to get him across and into the safety of the shelter.

His psychology was fantastic! In an instant I had become a man, and more to the point a man that my dad needed to help him cross that road. Holding hands we crossed Upton Street in record time and, before I knew it, I was in the hands of those waiting within that pitch black shelter. The shelter felt as if it was full but no one spoke, which was understandable bearing in mind all that was happening outside. I seemed to slide down into a corner furthest from the entrance and found myself pressed up against what I thought to be a fur coat. It was in fact someone's dog that was trembling and glad of company. Immediately my arm went around the dog and, as it snuffled my face, we trembled together and, as companions in fear, we both calmed each other to sleep. I awoke in the first light of dawn to the sound of the 'all clear' blowing; but my companion had gone. My immediate question was, "Where's my dog?" People, including my parents, looked amazed and someone from the terrace replied, "You must have had a vivid dream luv, there wasn't a dog in here last night, cos no one in the terrace owns one." Yet I could still feel him trembling, and hear him whimpering, as all hell raged outside. I once read that guardian angels can take many forms ....

The morning after

The first sight that caught our attention, as we struggled out of the shelter, was a large plume of black smoke dominating the skyline above the lorry compound that had been host to the land mine. Firemen at the top of a ladder with hosepipes stretched from the fire-engine were directing water into the heart of the blaze which was still resisting attempts to extinguish it. With that we turned round and, as a family group, walked in silent awe towards the wreck that was once our house. All the windows plus frames had gone and practically all of the roof tiles, plus chimney stack, were nowhere to be seen. Flying glass fragments had etched and scratched their presence all over the front of the piano and, what appeared to be part of a lorry axle had, in javelin style, buried itself in the wall between the now sagging ceiling and the top of the piano. Then my mind suddenly became re-focused as I cried out, "But what about Percy – where is he?" I dashed into the back room kicking aside glass and stirring-up clouds of soot. But nothing much mattered to me other than rescuing Percy the goldfish – that's if he was still alive. Eventually I found, lying on its side, a small bevelled part of the goldfish bowl just where the base began its upward curve. Water had been retained within that curved section and I shouted with joy at the sight of Percy, barely able to move, yet opening and closing its mouth, as goldfish do, whilst seemingly saying, "OK – now you've had your little joke so where's my ants eggs – cos I'm famished!"

Some years later I read several expert views on when the tide of war turned against Hitler and began to flow in our favour. Debate ranged from losing the Battle of Britain, declaring war on America, invading Russia or Stalin's victory in the 1,800 tank battle at Kursk. I believe they were all wrong. It was this glorious act of defiance shown by Percy the goldfish who had withstood the might of the Luftwaffe, had the house blown apart around him yet lived on as if in total contempt of all that Hitler stood for. I will never be shaken from my belief that Percy's boldness marked the moment when Hitler began to lose the war, and I am more than happy to be quoted on that issue!

Certainly our plight was not ignored by groups dedicated to our welfare. For example, and as if from nowhere, mobile food vans, staffed by volunteers, suddenly appeared in the street and began serving hot meals on temporary tables set up in wind shield canopies – this was to give some protection against dust filled gusts of strong wind. Also a small team of nurses were tending many superficial wounds and, fortunately, only a handful of people had to be taken to hospital. Also representatives from the Hull City Mission wandered around talking and listening to people who wanted to unburden themselves. Finally, and prompted by a forecast of heavy rain to come, soldiers arrived and covered gaping holes in house roofs with blue waterproof sheeting which they firmly lashed down. Dad and Jim agreed to remain in the house to protect our belongings against looters, whilst mother and I were to temporarily live with my grandmother in Burleigh Grove, Courtney Street. Additionally the onus was on my mother to find us somewhere to live which, because of her good reputation for never missing with the rent, would not turn out to be a problem; in fact she had a special idea all of her own which, for the moment, she decided to keep quiet about.

A matter of compensation

At the time of writing this narrative there were increasing concerns throughout the Nation that we, in the 21st century, are fast becoming a compensation age fired by regular publicity drives encouraging people to consider their eligibility. To me this was nothing new because throughout WW2, and for many years afterwards, it was a flourishing campaign. Obviously there were many genuine claims ranging from minor damage of furniture to total loss of house contents, which was met by appropriate Government departments. I cannot comment about damage to houses because everyone I knew in those days rented their property through the services of a landlord.

Mother and father lodged their claim for content damage and were initially visited by an assessor, who examined and reported on scratched and damaged furniture, including the piano, and duly sifted through a pile of torn curtains, bedding and clothing. The entire claim was approved and, considering the times, was dealt with quickly. As ever I was interested in listening to other people talk about their compensation claims and, within my earshot, the majority appeared to have claimed only for what they had lost; mainly because they did not want to get into trouble with the police. Notwithstanding there were those in terraces, and the open street, who happily boasted that they had claimed for the loss of household items they had never possessed. "I got my old man four new shirts and, for myself, I claimed a lovely coat and dress on top of what was really damaged," and this was but one of many inflated war damage claims that fell within my *wigging-in* range.

I also heard that a man in east Hull regularly submitted damage claims for having been bombed out no less that twelve times in eight months. Eventually his luck ran out and he went to prison for two years. The national press were quick to claim that theft and cheating had reached epidemic proportions and, according to radio news reports towards the end of the war, the crime rate had increased by 70% since 1939 and that the underworld of 'spivs' was a flourishing organisation.

Then the time arrived for us to leave Upton Street

Shortly after the raid three houses, for safety reasons, had to be demolished immediately and, within a few days, Upton Street had become a sad looking area comprised of boarded-up houses with tarpaulin sheets acting as roofs. Basic front doors had been fitted that were no match against early November icy blasts that found delight in racing through unheated houses. Despite a mass exodus of mice and 'black clocks', in favour of warmer buildings, Dad and Jim stuck faithfully to their task as guardians of the property. They even disturbed and chased after a man they caught in the yard of a nearby temporarily abandoned house. He was helping himself to the contents of the coalhouse and, in his haste to escape he left behind his bag and shovel which Dad confiscated. "We will need these when our turn comes to flit," he muttered and Jim readily agreed with him.

I had happily settled down in my new base which was my grandmother's back bedroom. I had a mattress on the floor, some plasticine in my pocket and bread and jam downstairs, as far as rationing would permit. No one bothered me because mother was rarely in the house and I assumed that she was busy trying to find a new house for us to rent. Consequently I was free to meet up with my friends for grand tours of exploration in which damaged houses to be investigated were seen in abundance; so much so that it was becoming hard to find any type of property that had escaped the ravages of air attacks – more so since the advent of the mine that bombed us out. Additionally I was given several opportunities to relate my experiences on the topic of being 'bombed out,' both to adults and my mates, until I began to feel like a local celebrity!

Then the day came for us to flit away from Upton Street and, as before, Jim borrowed a cart from Reckitts and the indispensable Mr Barnes was at hand to supervise the transfer of our war-torn piano. By now you may be wondering where we were moving to? Well, mother had played the same guessing game with Jim and me and, following much coaxing and promises to wash up and tidy our bedroom, she finally announced that we were moving back to Courtney Street and, more to the point, we were returning to Leonards Avenue having rented house number 4! That was the 'special idea' she had in mind when the search began for another house.

Our former neighbours were delighted and several of them helped carry our belongings 'back home' as they termed it. Several times they told us that we should never have left Courtney Street because we belonged there; which made me feel proud because I was the only one in the family who had been both *born and bred* in that street. Jim took the loss of his courting front room philosophically because, just after Christmas, he had to report to the Army reception barracks at Beverley. He also remarked that after his experiences with the Upton Street land mine he thought life would be safer in the armed forces!

When we were finally installed at number 4 Leonards Avenue dad returned to our battered Upton Street house just to make certain we had not left anything behind before handing-in the key. His only observation was centred on our former coalhouse which he and Jim had cleared of every piece of coal. When we left someone had climbed over the wall and opened the back passage door. They had then entered the yard and swept up all traces of coal dust from the coalhouse floor such that, to quote dad, "it was clean enough to eat off!" Times were hard and days were getting cold.

On the day I returned to Courtney Street I felt much like the Prodigal Son, who featured directly and indirectly in several Sunday school stories, which always ended with eating a *fatted calf*. Although my official return to Courtney Street fell far short of this delicacy I was, much to my delight, given a bite of Jimmy Watson's Spam sandwich followed by a pre-licked finger end of fizzy Sherbet direct from John Hobson's pocket lining.

It was my original intent to close this section at this stage but, on reflection, I felt the urge to tell you about a school playground song that had become all the rage. As air attacks upon Hull began to ease off Courtney school was almost back to normal. After the summer holiday my class year was elevated to the senior school, under the headship of the locally well-known Mr Percival Gillgrass, aided by the equally popular Mr Stan Adams – who was also the sports teacher. However our class was taken by a Mr Myers who made school time a joy if you behaved yourself, and a physical pain to those who chose otherwise. I believe it was a member of the latter group who composed a song about the said Mr Myers, who was noted for riding to school on his bicycle, as will become apparent in the following lyrics:

Old Pop Myers he rides on tyres,
and goes the church on Sundays.
He prays to God to give him strength,
To bray the kids on Mondays.

These words were sung with great gusto far away from teacher's ears!

PART SEVEN

1943 – 1945

D DAY TO THE END OF THE WAR

It was a consolation to us that air raids tended to be more spasmodic during 1943 and, numerically, they sharply decreased in 1944 and 1945. The final UK air raid of the Second World War also fell on Hull, in March 1945, when much damage was caused in Morrill and Holland Street areas during which fourteen people were killed. Sadly this was yet another record that Hull could well have done without. However this decline in the rate of air attacks meant that time could be given to clearing bomb sites, repairing rail and road networks and other essential services.

Whilst morale lifting in their own rights such acts of rehabilitation did little to disperse a cloud of gloom that, to my mind, hung heavily over Courtney Street despite outbursts of joviality. There had to be a reason for an apparent sharp increase in drunken behaviour both in the pubs, on the street and at home. Some argued that it was premature celebration because, as we moved into 1944, it was obvious that the west were going to win the war. An interesting counter opinion, that was rife in the street at that time, was that people sought escapism in alcohol not because they were afraid of the war, which they were hardened to but, rather, of the peace that would soon be upon them. War in the view of many I listened to had united the street, and indeed the entire country, into a team that was dedicated to defeating Hitler. They had a pronounced unity of purpose which they feared would end when peace came along and many, due to the promise of growing prosperity, would revert to becoming 'individuals in isolation' with their own aims as paramount.

But before then, on the 6th June 1944, the largest sea invasion in history occurred when combined allied forces, in what became known as D-Day, stormed the Normandy beaches and began their liberation of occupied Europe. In fairness it must be said that the German army put up stubborn resistance, against great odds, but it was not too long before Hitler's situation became indefensible because Russian forces, in 1945, were closing-in on Berlin. Trapped in the depths of his Berlin bunker Hitler committed suicide after which Germany surrendered on the 8th May 1945. Japan carried on fighting until the arrival of the atomic bomb wiped out two of their cities, with appalling loss of life, after which they agreed to surrender on the 2nd September 1945. This left a stunned, tired and shattered world with the task of rebuilding itself within the darkening shadow of a divided Europe, and rising tension, between the two super-powers America and Russia.

LIGHTS ON FOR STREET PARTY TIME

When one of our neighbours was asked how she celebrated the surrender of Germany she replied that as soon as darkness fell she turned on every house light and opened all the curtains and doors. Then with outstretched arms, amidst a swarm of dazzled moths, she stood outside enjoying once illegal illuminations. Everyone delighted in the rare treat of restored street lights after six years of stumbling about in total blackout. The lights were particularly appreciated when the pubs, which were filled to capacity, churned out their more than tipsy patrons.

Towards the end of the war a song of hope entitled, 'When the lights go on again all over the world," composed by Benjamin, Marcus and Seiler, was very popular and decidedly apt when it's much sung theme became a reality. There were street and terrace end parties and I can remember crowds of civilians and service personnel singing and dancing together, more so to the popular 'Conga' dance, as its long line of revellers swayed and side-kicked their way along Courtney Street. After all it was a glorious opportunity to rid themselves of six years' worth of war that had set new records in areas of death and destruction. Indeed there was much to celebrate; not least that the Fascist movement, together with all the evil it stood for had, hopefully, been destroyed for all time.

Naturally the press gave much publicity to what they called, 'A Nation in Celebration,' but from my view, as a 14 year old boy, who had survived the war but was still a victim of its memories, I saw a different picture. The atmosphere was not entirely *electric* as reported in the national newspapers who, in their excitement, failed to notice those who remained at home or sat quietly in the background – and there were many of them. Since I have never been a party-goer I tended to mingle with these people, and listened to them express their feelings now that the war was over.

Recollections from Granville Terrace

The invitation, "Cum and sit down with us luv, you look lonely standing there," broke into my reverie as I stood on the kerb edge watching many party antics along the length of the street. In fact I was rather hoping that the Galloping Major would make a special appearance in honour of the occasion! However it was not often that I was invited to *wig-in* so I gratefully joined a group at the end of Granville Terrace, who had set-up a communal cluster of tables and chairs. "I bet your mam and dad are in the pub aren't they?" added Joan, my friendly hostess, as she handed me a cup of lemonade. My nod of agreement was received accordingly because it was a fact that relatives had called and, as a group, they had retired to the Full Measure pub in Cleveland Street; on the understanding that they would not be away for long. This meant that a victory day celebration, in the form of a house 'do' was on the agenda, but minus a pianist because Jim was away in his Churchill Tank, somewhere in Germany.

Looking around I realised that I was in a group of around fifteen men and women of mid to later years who, like me, had lived through every air raid on Hull. They were keen to talk and even answer the occasional question which was a delight to my curious nature. Additionally my experience took a leap forward when an orator, perhaps overcome with emotion, lapsed into what I later called a *period of expressive silence* when, locked in this state, he successfully completed his non-verbal story with facial and body movements. Looking back I was able to recall similar methods of effective communication in air raid shelters when the blitz was at its height. Again in later years this experience helped me to better appreciate the works of the Victorian writer Thomas Carlyle when he stressed that 'Silence is more eloquent than words' although, in fairness, he was born far too early to apply his philosophy to a Courtney Street air raid shelter!

"Come on Jack, don't fall asleep on us," said my hostess Joan to a man who appeared detached from the group. "Tek no notice of me," he muttered as he stared silently as his glass of beer. "I was thinking of all those who will never come home to dance up and down the street. I wish somebody would tell me how the drunken antics of well-meaning people could ever be a substitute for their loved ones, vast numbers of whom are in foreign graves or entombed within rusting ships on the sea bed."

His words seemed to hang around our ears as if seeking agreement or consolation from mouths unable to find the right reply. Then suddenly fate intervened and broke the silence when, seemingly from nowhere, a couple of men dressed up as Kentucky Minstrels danced over to our group whilst singing a well-known song from the twenties, 'O Dem Golden Slippers.' Their banjo playing and singing was superb and soon they had several heads nodding and hands clapping by way of accompaniment. Despite our pleas for an encore they waved goodbye and, with a heavy schedule ahead, they danced on to the next terrace. Old Jack, now free from his forlorn memories, smiled, waved and then drained his glass of beer. Wiping his mouth with the back of his hand he declared that it had done him a power of good; which left me wondering if he meant the variety turn or the beer?

"You look thoughtful our Gladys," was a comment cum question from the now alert Jack. Immediately all eyes turned towards the said Gladys who, I had earlier learned, had cause to remember this day for another reason, because it was the first anniversary of the death of her husband after 45 years of marriage. Following a generous mouthful of stout she put her glass down and, with a wide smile said, "My dear Ernie would have loved to have been with us and, without any persuasion, he would have spent the entire evening entertaining us on his mouth organ." The group's response to her prophetic declaration was a mixture of throaty half-words, of varying pitch and intensity, which tactfully disguised the fact that truth had been sacrificed on the altar of respect! However Gladys was delighted when a male voice added, "I can see Ernie now perched on a cloud and playing his mouth organ to foot tapping angels!"

A feature that made this terrace end celebration stick in my mind was just how quickly the mood could change from hilarity to despair which, in pre-war days, was rarely seen except when the conversation suddenly focused on the Means Test Inspector. For example there was a lady named Edna who, from time to time, had been watching the terrace end party from her front window and, despite friendly come-and join-us gestures, she remained indoors. In due course she suddenly appeared and happily sat with her neighbours. Her greeting of, "You can't beat being with friends," was well received and a cup of beer, from a communal jug, was pushed in front of her. Soon happiness reigned and Edna, who could reliably hold a tune, led the group in a rousing version of 'Bless em All.'

It went very well, and a number of passing people stopped to watch and listen; that was until Edna suddenly sat down and stared at the table in silence. As the singing faded away a worried voice broke in with, "What's the matter luv – aren't you feeling well,"

With that she began so speak slowly and firmly, and her clenched hands betrayed the tension within, as she announced that she could take no more of it. "Is there anything we can do to help you Edna?" asked a kindly voice. "Thank you but no," Edna replied. "It is because beer and singing stick in my throat when I suddenly remember all those mornings after an air-raid, and the many large mounds of smoking rubble containing bodies waiting to be dug out." With that she slowly walked back to her house and the silence was finally broken by the sound of her door closing. Those remaining tried to recoup a little of the original party spirit but memories of the blitz, so graphically left by Edna, was really the end of the Granville Terrace event. Some decided to walk around and see other celebrations whilst the rest, justified by symbolic yawns, simply went home leaving the terrace end to Jack and Joan whilst I hung on wondering what else would happen.

Normally at a stage such as this I would have closed the literary curtain on Granville Terrace and moved on but, had I done so, posterity would have lost Jack's excellent storybook comparison of the status of Courtney Street both before and after the war. It began with him asking the question, "Have you ever on a glorious summer's day walked on a beach of golden sand?" Without waiting for an answer he quickly added, "Well that, to me, was life in Courtney Street before the war. Then a ferocious and lengthy storm called World War Two broke and tremendous waves, rain and gales beat incessantly upon the coastline." At this stage Jack paused to allow yet another line of noisy Conga dancers to side kick their way towards Dansom Lane. "But," he then continued," The people of the coastline did not worry because they believed that when the storm ended, and the water receded, the same golden beach would still be there awaiting their pleasure. They were correct because the storm did end and the water fell back only to reveal a beach of hard black rock for them to walk on, because the storm had washed away every grain of their beloved sand." He looked hard at us and we nodded our agreement when he concluded with, "and after this war Courtney Street, like that depressing beach, will never be the same again."

Tar- rah for now

Not long afterwards I, with thanks to my hosts, wandered towards Holderness Road only to pause and slowly enter Crystal Terrace which, by comparison with the rest of the street, was very quiet as if in mourning. Perhaps it was restored terrace lights that now illuminated an ominous gap marking the site of houses destroyed in one of the raids I described. Behind me the drunken tempo of carnival style jubilation gained momentum, yet I felt this injured terrace preferred to be left alone with its memories as I, in turn, felt part of them. Kneeling before the bomb site I placed my hands on the cold soil that once supported three houses and whispered, "I will not forget you Annie." As I relived those happy school days a little bit of me, in the form of a falling tear, fell upon and remained with that site. At the terrace end I paused and turned to the mental echo of "Tar-rah for now" which were Annie's last words to me.

Deep in thought I slowly walked home and went straight to bed. In fact I was hard asleep long before the 'do' began downstairs.

The beginning of Post War Courtney Street

But from my viewpoint I found day to day living to be so very different after the war, and it was becoming hard to remember life in Courtney Street before all this began. I often thought back to those prophetic words from Gypsy Boswell, and more recently restated by Jack of Granville Terrace, that post-war life would never again be the same for Courtney Street or, indeed, anyone else in this nation.

In many ways it was a good thing because there was now plenty of work available rebuilding both the structure and economy of this nation. Also more and more women, due to their wartime contributions, were now keen to retain employment and rely upon household labour saving devices that were becoming the vogue. Consequently family incomes increased and so did standards of living. On the downside there were many labour disputes leading to strikes and general unrest which was not helped by food and commodity rationing that drifted on until 1954 when meat, the last rationed item, became freely available again.

Recite your alphabet Caney

I left school at the age of 14 and began work as a labourer in Reckitt's sawmill during which my resolve to improve and advance myself was born from one brief moment of reflection. This happened as the music 'Calling All Workers' (written by Eric Coates and also known as Music While You Work) was blasting out above the noise of machinery when, for no apparent reason, I mentally challenged myself to recite the alphabet. To my horror I found that I could not do this because, like so many others, I was paying the penalty of wartime closed schools and spasmodic education.

Immediately I resolved to put matters right so, to begin with, I took stock of my finances. My wage was nineteen shillings (95p) per week which I gave to mother who returned ten shillings (50p) of it to me for pocket money. From this I financed myself at night school on English and Mathematic courses after which, when I was promoted to the laboratory as 'lab boy,' I paid my National Certificate in Chemistry course fees at the Hull Technical College from which I eventually progressed, through the years, to professional qualifications. The long hours spent at work during the day and studying at night meant I had little time for a teenage social life but it was well worth it, and the outcome is now my history.

It goes without saying that none of this would have happened but for the lessons I learned, and the hard work I lived with, during those formative years in my beloved Courtney Street.

EPITAPH

I have thoroughly enjoyed this opportunity to share with you my memories of Courtney Street and district that will ever have a special place in the best parlour of my mind. Be assured that these memories are not dormant and a small spark of coincidence does awaken and restore them to centre stage. For example during my business life, or on holiday, I have travelled to many places far removed from East Hull yet circumstances have caused me to remember Tin Mission when viewing an ornate church in San Francisco. Then I found myself comparing Leonards Avenue with residential areas in St. Petersburg not forgetting the leisurely pace of Courtney Street traffic when caught in immense traffic jams in Hyderabad, India.

When in East Hull I still enjoy wandering the length of Courtney Street and, in the time it has taken me to write this book, the former Midland Bank cum social club, situated on its corner with Holderness Road has, together with some derelict shops, been demolished for reasons I am unsure about. This decision now means Tin Mission, at the Dansom Lane end of the street, is the only remaining building from the Courtney Street into which I was born; and long may it survive!

It is true that happy memories are ours to keep, and are a joy to relate as we pass through this life. I believe it is our duty to offer them to other interested readers so, like living dreams, they may be added to from their memory banks of distant times. Such memories, although deprived of modern technology and fast life styles, can still be inspirational to souls in need.

As a restless octogenarian, who is ever striving to address the many inequalities of this life, I know that I reside in the *departure lounge of life* awaiting my call to the leaving gate. When that time arrives I will pass through it all the happier knowing I have left this book behind, as a way of keeping alive the memory of many long departed friends in Courtney Street who, knowing them as I do, will be delighted to find they have not been entirely forgotten.

Every blessing,

Charles. June 2013.

REFERENCES

1. Hull Rope Works in 1838 taken from the SDUK Penny Cyclopaedia (internet).

2. Fowler, M. *Holderness Road (history of)*

3. Markham, John, *Streets of Hull: a History of their Names* (Highgate of Beverley, 1998)

4. ' Education'- A History of the County of York East Riding. (Volume 1: The City of Kingston upon Hull 1969).

5. In 1911 the National Insurance Act was passed. All employers and employees made contributions to a fund. If a worker was ill he was entitled to free treatment by a doctor. (Normally you had to pay and it was expensive). If he could not work because of illness the worker was given a small amount of money to live on. However his family was *not* entitled to free medical treatment. (England in the 20th Century by Tim Lambert).

6. Old ropes and cables that were once used on ships were cut up and then finely picked into fibres to make oakum. In the 17th and 18th centuries oakum was mixed with tar and used to fill in gaps between planks in wooden ships. Following the advent of ocean going iron ships the oakum-tar amalgam was still used to seal deck planking and other items that needed to be water-proofed. (Copied from Wikipedia Internet Encyclopaedia).

ABOUT THE AUTHOR

Courtney Street and its school was central to Charles Cane's formative years ranging from his birth in 1931 through to 1945 when he began work in Reckitt's sawmill. Within this period he amassed a wealth of social and local history through his own observations fortified by listening-in to adult conversations. Many of the anecdotes in this book came via this latter process, which was locally known as 'wigging-in,' that developed into a skill much loved by the author. In later years Charles recognised the need, through his book, to keep alive the social and local history of Courtney Street through the poverty stricken 1930's, followed by the horrors of World War Two, and how it appeared in post-war Britain.

Fortunately Charles was employed by a caring and progressive company that ran day continuation classes for boys of his age which led to his transfer from the sawmill to the laboratory. He immediately formed a deep attachment to chemistry such that, at his own expense, he attended a local Technical College and studied chemistry, physics and mathematics together with improving his knowledge of spoken and written English. His studies were interrupted by National Service in the RAMC in which he served as Unit Accountant, at Company Headquarters, and achieved the rank of sergeant.

Returning to civilian life Charles was employed as a senior laboratory assistant in a major international company and, through study and research, was eventually admitted as a Member of the Royal Society of Chemistry (MRSC) entitled to use the designation Chartered Chemist (CCHEM). Following his promotion to the position of Production and Research Laboratory Manager his career took him to conference rooms and laboratories in France, Germany, Denmark, Poland and the USA. After his official retirement he spent a further three years as a working research consultant in the same company.

When he finally left his beloved laboratory career he embarked upon a 15 year period as a part time chaplain in a local prison together with the role of a fully trained volunteer in the national charity Victim Support. He is still totally involved in the latter role having completed 19 years of service which, a few years ago, was recognised by receiving a service certificate from HRH The Princess Royal. In parallel Charles has studied for and has been accredited as a Local Preacher within the Methodist Church.

Yet throughout his life he has never lost sight of his beginnings in Courtney Street and the debt he owes to those hard working folk who inspired him to achieve all that he has. There is little doubt that this book is born from his gratitude to them.

ALSO BY THE SAME AUTHOR

MY EVER BEST FRIEND

Ever since the early Church's widespread belief in, and understanding of, reincarnation was formally suppressed at the Council of Constantinople of 553AD, a great deal of brainwashing has been carried out by clergy and by others in positions of power. And so it takes a brave man to defy his upbringing by proclaiming what he knows from personal experience to be the truth. Charles Cane is one such, and I strongly recommend this book to historians and to the spiritually minded alike. His story is riveting, his style compelling, and I sincerely hope that it will awaken many people to some of the long lost knowledge and wisdom that we all hold deep in our subconscious.

Ann Merivale,
Woolger-trained Deep Memory Process therapist and author

Available from www.ypdbooks.com
ISBN 978-0-9567201-0-8
Price £9.95